One Man's Traitor is Another's Patriot

George Washington and Robert Rogers

Book title is from the words of
George William Curtis (1824-1892)
American Writer and Public Speaker

Cover is from a painting of George Washington by Charles Willson Peale, 1772
Courtesy of the Library of Congress

by Michael A Eggleston

Published by CreateSpace Copyright © 2017 Michael A. Eggleston
All rights reserved.
ISBN-10: 1546302204
ISBN-13: 978-1546302209

Other Books

by

Michael A. Eggleston

10th Minnesota Volunteers, McFarland & Company Publishers, 2012.

The White Man's Fight, Author House, 2012.

President Lincoln's Recruiter, General Lorenzo Thomas and the United States Colored Troops in the Civil War, McFarland & Company Publishers, 2013.

Exiting Vietnam, The Era of Vietnamization and American Withdrawal Revealed in First-Person Accounts, McFarland & Company Publishers, 2014.

The 5th Marine Devil Dogs in World War I, McFarland & Company Publishers 2016.

Dak To and the Border Battles of Vietnam, McFarland & Company Publishers 2017.

Table of Contents

Preface *9*
Introduction *15*
1.   War in the New World *23*
Celoron's Expedition *34*
Battle of Jumonville Glen – 28 May 1754 .... *36*
To Counterfeit is Death *43*
Braddock's Defeat – July 1755 .... *46*
Battle of Lake George – 8 September 1755 .... *51*
Ambush – 21 January 1757 .... *54*
British Defeat at Fort William Henry – August 1757 .... *64*
Mutiny on Rogers' Island – 6 December 1757 .... *68*
The Battle on Snowshoes – 13 March 1758 .... *70*
British Assault on Carillon Repulsed – 8 July 1758 .... *75*
Battle of Fort Anne – 8 August 1758 .... *82*
The Atrocities *85*
2.   The Saint Francis Raid *89*
3.   On to Montreal *131*
4.   Closing In *145*
Fort Detroit Surrenders to Robert Rogers – 29 November 1760 .... *145*
The Cherokee War *151*
5.   The Uneasy Peace *163*
Legacy of the War *163*
Pontiac's War Begins – 7 May 1763 .... *163*
The Carver Expedition Begins – 3 September 1766 .... *182*
6.   War of Independence and After *201*
Battle of Long Island, 27 August 1776 .... *232*

Battle of White Plains, 28 October 1776 .... *249*
Battle of Trenton, 26 December 1776 .... *255*
Epilogue.. *269*
Biographical Sketches.. *283*
Appendix A, Names, Acronyms and Terms *303*
Appendix B, Chronology... *311*
Appendix C, Rogers' Ranging Rules.. *317*
Appendix D, The Ranger Roster *323*
Bibliography... *341*
Chapter Notes... *365*
Index... *386*

Acknowledgments

I would like to thank my wife Margaret Rogers Eggleston for her endless patience and efforts to comment on and edit this book. I would also like to express my gratitude to John Eggleston, Irvin "Bugs" Moran and Frances Rogers who contributed to this book.

Preface

George Washington and Robert Rogers were both born in America and were of about the same age (born in 1731/2). They both fought in the French and Indian War as well as the War of Independence. Both achieved notoriety in the French and Indian War and were frequently mentioned in the press. The power of the press then and now shaped public opinion and was used by some to their own advantage. Period newspaper articles are used to elaborate on events throughout this book. These provide information not found elsewhere and also identify the mood of the citizens and in some cases their opinion of individuals.

Rogers achieved greater fame than Washington during the French and Indian War and his activities were carefully followed by the press.[1] Washington's reaction to his first exposure to war was similar to Rogers. Washington wrote in 1754. "I heard the bullets whistle, and, believe me, there is something charming in the sound."[2] Rogers only reference to his youthful experience was more general.

> Between the years 1743 and 1753, I was led to a general acquaintance both with British and French settlements in North America, and especially with the uncultivated desert, the mountains, valleys, rivers, lakes, and several passes that lay between and contiguous to the said settlements. Nor did I content myself with the accounts I received from the Indians, but travelled over large tracts of country myself, which tended, not more to gratify my curiosity than to inure me to hardship, and to quality me for my later services.[3]
> ***Robert Rogers***

Both Rogers and Washington were Freemasons. Both were inspiring leaders who rallied their troops; however, their differences were vast. Washington was born into wealth and advantage while the Rogers family was dirt poor. Robert

Rogers was a New Englander born in Massachusetts while Washington was a Virginian. Washington became father of his country while Rogers is remembered by few. Many paintings were created of Washington, but only one of Rogers which is more of a cartoon than a portrait and is merely an artist's conception of what he might have looked like. A description provided by an acquaintance (Caleb Stark) is one of few that survive.

> He was six feet in stature, well proportioned, and one of the most athletic men of his time – well known in all the trials of strength or activity among the young men of his vicinity, and for several miles around. He was endowed with great presence of mind, intrepidity, perseverance, and possessed a plausible address.[4]
>
> ***Caleb Stark***

The London press also provided a description ". . . a handsome giant with red hair and blue eyes."[5]

The title of this book tells a part of the story. To the British, Washington was a traitor, but to the Americans, he was a Patriot, perhaps our greatest. Rogers seemed to wander between the two terms. Even when he betrayed one of our most famous patriots and was clearly a traitor to the American cause, he was still considered a Patriot to a few, even to this day. Readers will need to come to their own conclusion after reading this book, which tells the story of Robert Rogers and why his best intentions led him into conflict with Washington and his fall from grace.

In a 60 Minutes interview on 4 November 2012, Historian David McCullough provided his insight.

> The only way to teach history, to write history, to bring people into the magic of transforming yourself into other times is through the vehicle of the story. ***It isn't just the chronology, it's about people. History is human.*** Jefferson said "when in the course of human events . . . " human is the operative word here.

This book tells the human story of George Washington, Robert Rogers and his rangers with emphasis on the ranger Saint Francis Raid in 1759 against the Abenaki tribe of Native Americans in what is now Canada. The ranger leader, Robert Rogers is considered by many to be the father of the U. S. Army Special Forces and rangers. His Rules for Ranging are still quoted today. Many books have been written about Robert Rogers and the best is Gary Stephen Zaboly's *A True Ranger: The Life and Many Wars of Major Robert Rogers*. Zaboly's book shows an amazing level of detail and reveals a vast number of contemporary documents that are frequently quoted. Robert Rogers was a puzzle to his contemporaries and to those who study his life today. Conflicting opinions exist about Rogers.

> He is wild, vain, of little understanding, and of as little Principle, but withal has a share of Cunning, No Modesty or veracity and sticks at Nothing.[6]
> **General Sir Thomas Gage, 9 January 1766**

> The late Duke of Newcastle scrupled not to acknowledge Colonel Washington and Major Rogers "two of the bravest and most experienced Officers in the King's Service" – The Colonel is now in his own Service; and if he could fight so courageously for his King, there is no Doubt of his displaying a redoubled valour for himself.[7]
> **New Hampshire Gazette, 15 August 1775**

Many books about Rogers including Zaboly's tend to be sympathetic in their treatment of him. The reader will decide if he deserves sympathy after reading this book. A common thread in the history of Robert Rogers is the financial mess of his life. He seemed to be constantly seeking a quick financial payoff, from counterfeiting to an endless stream of financial claims submitted to the Crown. On the other hand, he was always in debt and sometimes sued for debts. Many of his money problems stemmed from his expenditures to buy equipment for his rangers and a stingy government reimbursement that never matched his cost.

The reader will find oral traditions of the Abenaki tribe that were recorded and published over the last century as well as documentation of the French. I took advantage of today's on-line search engines to find answers to specific questions something not available to earlier historians. The Internet provides quick access to documents that took months to locate in past research efforts.[8] From these I found surprises related in the account that follows. I hope that researchers and genealogists will find documents identified herein useful to their efforts.

This history provides background about the war before the raid as well as what happened to rangers after the raid including the War of Independence. It explains the French and Indian War by following the parallel paths of two soldiers: George Washington who fought in the west and Robert Rogers in the north. The paths of the two would cross during the War of Independence with unhappy results. Although both were Freemasons, things did not go well between them.

I've incorporated several conventions to provide clarity. I have used state names such as New York and Vermont rather than their colonial names. Indeed, Vermont did not even exist as a colony, but was part of others. Using current state names makes it easier to place the location in this story. Colonial documents presented in this history have many spelling errors and these have not been corrected but are presented as written. I have not cluttered the documents with "sic" notations commonly used to identify errors in a text. Some locations changed names such as Carillon the French fort that became Fort Ticonderoga when it was captured by the British. I initially call it Carillon and then change it to Fort Ticonderoga. In all cases the names are cross-referenced in Appendix A; Names, Acronyms and Terms. Other appendices provide background information: Appendix B, Chronology; Appendix C, Rogers' Ranging Rules; and Appendix D, The Ranger Roster which may be of interest to genealogists. Biographical Sketches provide information about key individuals in this history. Battle casualty numbers reported in battles varied a great deal. The numbers depended upon who was stating them (commanders tended to downplay their losses) and when in the battle they were defined. I used those that I found that were reasonable, but none are exact. Ranks of individuals are provided. When several are shown for the same individual, I have quoted the highest rank held.

My interest concerning this raid piqued when I discovered that one of my ancestors, Daniel Barnes was a ranger on the Saint Francis Raid. Barnes later fought in the War of Independence.[9] He outlived most of his ranger comrades dying in 1813.

Michael A. Eggleston, Nokesville, Virginia, 2017

Introduction

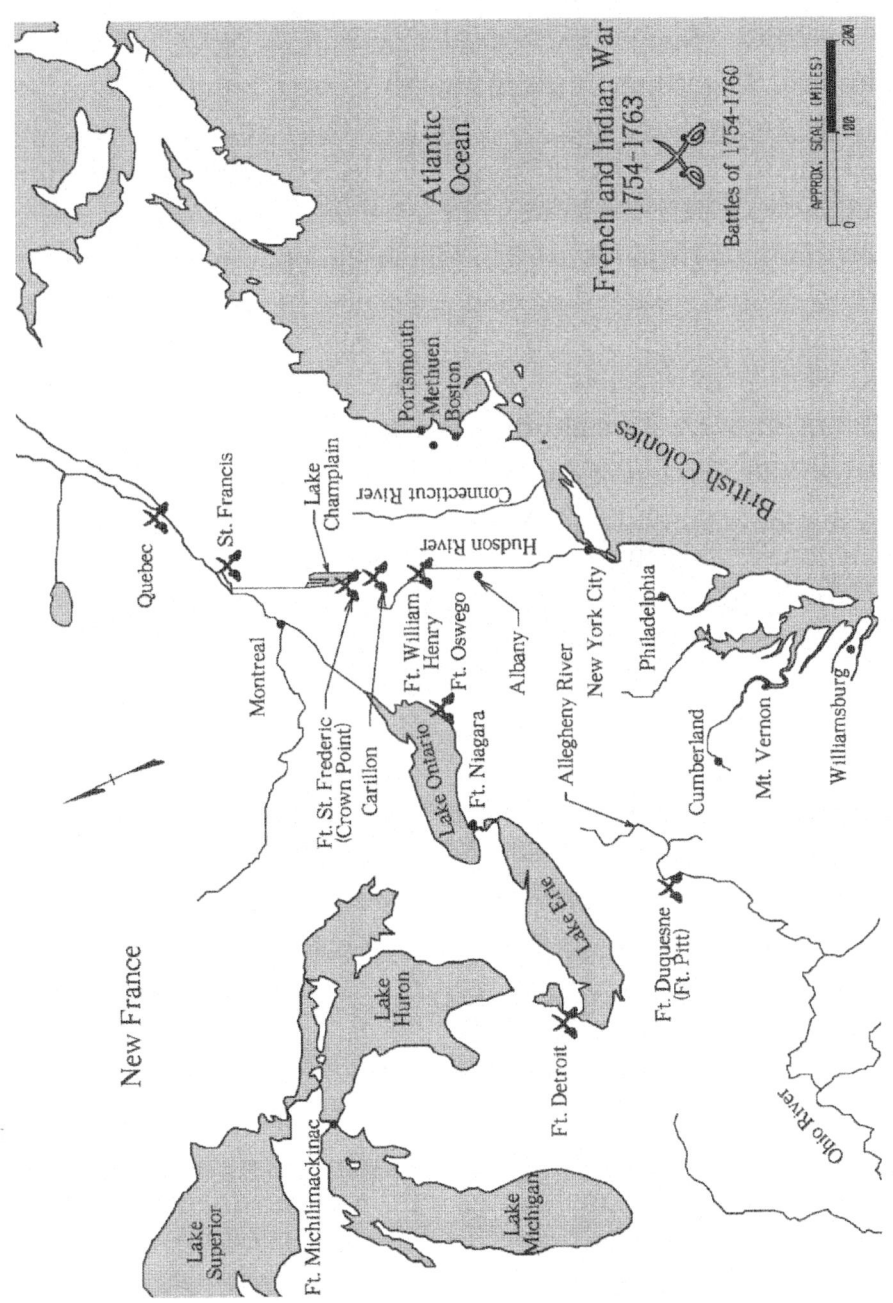

New France and the British Colonies (Connor Eggleston)

While Spain had discovered the New World and colonized it starting in the fifteenth Century, France and Great Britain started later and by 1700, British settlements occupied the east coast of what is now the United States while France lightly populated what was then called New France, an area encompassing what is now Canada and parts of the northern United States. Spain retained colonies in South and Central America. The French government had difficulty persuading their people to populate New France and by 1700, the French settlements were focused on trading with the Indians with forts built around the Great Lakes, strategic positions in Illinois, and along the Mississippi River. France pushed colonization south along the Mississippi to its mouth and New Orleans was born (1718). French traders ventured deep into the wilderness often following waterways and brought back furs which provided a handsome reward but game was becoming scarce.[10]

Britain dominated the Atlantic seaboard with settlements running from New Hampshire south to Georgia. The British population flourished in spite of high death rates from disease and Indian attacks. English philosopher Thomas Hobbs summarized: life tended to be "nasty, brutish and short."[11] Small pox was a common cause of death and had devastating effects on Indian tribes that had no built-in immunity enjoyed by the whites. In spite of the high death rate, the British population continued to rise. The lore of the land brought more colonists from Britain to the New World. The French occupation continued to focus on traders rather than settlers. The French did not encourage farming and manufacturing in New France. Indeed, it was discouraged. French mercantilists viewed manufacturing in New France as unwanted competition.[12] By 1750, the British population approached two million while French population numbered only sixty thousand.[13] The Spanish empire in the New World continued to decline due to military defeats in Europe and rebellions against their rule in South America. The fact remained that the New World colonies were pawns in wars launched by the major powers in Europe. These wars accomplished little other than some minor changes in land ownership between Britain and France, but a greater more widespread conflict was brewing.[14] Historian William M. Fowler summarized.

> From the very first days of permanent settlement in North America the French and English had been at each other's throats. Competition for trade, uncertain boundaries, and a rambunctious population of frontier men kindled violence on both sides. Men in Paris and London knew full well that there was an absence of peace in North America, but minor skirmishes, a raid here and there, a few homes burned, were petty events hardly worthy of notice when compared to the pageants of Europe. Indeed, on those several occasions in the seventeenth and eighteenth centuries when wars between the great powers came to North America, they arrived as imports from Europe.
>
> In 1689 the War of the League of Augsburg began in Europe. By the time it reached America it was known as King William's War. In 1702 the War of Spanish Succession erupted, to be titled Queen Anne's War when the shooting began in America. The War of the Austrian Succession swept Europe in 1744 and crossed the Atlantic the next year as King George's War. The last and greatest of these struggles, however, followed a very different pattern. The French and Indian War reversed the traditional course of events; beginning in America, it was exported to Europe.[15]

War would be fought between the colonies of Great Britain and France along the borders between New France and the British colonies with help from the mother countries. Boundaries between colonies were along natural barriers such as mountain ranges and waterways rather than many state borders seen today. For this reason Virginia would send troops far to the west as seen later in George Washington's encounter near Pittsburgh. Borders were sometimes contested among British colonies. As an example, both New Hampshire and New York claimed the land known today as

Vermont. Massachusetts and New York fought over their border. Indian allies would align with one side or the other. The coming war would be fought mainly on the frontiers and the French viewed the waterways as a natural defensive barrier for New France.[16] Any conflict between the French and British might well be decided by their Indian allies. Native American tribes were being courted by both sides.

The Tribes

Sir William Johnson (1715-1774) (Library of Congress)

William Johnson was born in County Meath, Ireland, circa 1715. His uncle, Peter Warren, purchased a large tract of land along the Mohawk River in the province of New York. Warren convinced Johnson to move to New York and establish a settlement along the Mohawk to be named Warrensburgh and Johnson accepted, arriving in the Mohawk River Valley in 1738. Johnson befriended members of the Mohawk tribe located there. The Mohawks were one of the Six Nations of the Iroquois League. The Mohawks thought that an alliance with Johnson would advance their interests in the British Empire and in 1742 they adopted him as an honorary chief. In 1744 when the War of the Austrian Succession arrived in the New World, Johnson was appointed as the "Colonel of the Warriors of the Six Nations." He was ordered to recruit warriors and colonists to fight the French. He did this and sent raiding parties to attack the French with some success. He would later achieve greater success during the French and Indian War. His influence with the Iroquois League increased and in the campaigns of the French and Indian War he would field as many as a thousand Iroquois warriors. The British promoted him to the rank of major general although he had no military experience and his successes were largely a result of his influence with the tribes. His negotiations to recruit Indian allies of the French were also successful.

On the other side, the French could count on the Seven Nations of Canada. These included the Abenaki, Huron, Onondaga and others. Potawatomi's, Ojibwas, Ottawa's, and other Indian groups also fought for France. Many of the Indians were converted to Catholicism by the French. These "domesticated" Indians were perceived as the most reliable, as they could be counted on to remain after a battle and hold newly won territory rather than immediately embark on the long trip home. In the Ohio Valley, the Delaware's and Shawnees became France's most important allies. Until they reached a separate peace with England in 1758, Ohio Indians conducted devastating raids on frontier settlements in Virginia, Maryland, and Pennsylvania.

The reader will find that this book summarizes the actions of Robert Rogers and George Washington in the events of the French and Indian War and the War of Independence. The roles that they played and how they emerged from each conflict is described to compare how they achieved their place in history.

1. War in the New World

The total war concept did not exist as it does today. In other words an 18th century war would be fought, land or money given by the loser, and governments returned to business as usual. Governments did not topple. Royalty returned to eating, drinking, and whoring as usual while the armies recruited and retrained. Eightieth century wars were usually named for monarchs such as King George's War, but since small wars were frequent, more interesting names often appeared and were used such as the "War of Jenkins' Ear." Robert Jenkins, a captain of a British merchant ship and acknowledged smuggler was stopped by the Spanish and had his ear severed.[1] This was delivered to Parliament as a warning. Britain was upset and a war followed.

The French and Indian War (1754-1763) was part of a larger global conflict between France and Great Britain that became known as the Seven Years' War which involved most countries on the planet. The principal alliances were France and Austria opposed by Great Britain and Prussia. The conflict was caused by disputes over possessions.

Weapons of War & Tactics

The military weapons used globally during the mid-eightieth century were flintlock smooth bore muskets and pistols. The muskets used a powder charge and round ball rammed home with a rod from the muzzle. The lead ball was large, nearly three quarters of an inch in diameter and, thanks to gravity, would fall to the ground shortly after leaving the barrel perhaps in as little as one hundred meters. The most common musket used during the period was the British Army musket commonly called the "Brown Bess." This may have been a reference to Queen Elizabeth I and the brown color of the stock and barrel. The weapon weighed 10.2 pounds and was 58.5 inches long plus bayonet (another eighteen inches).

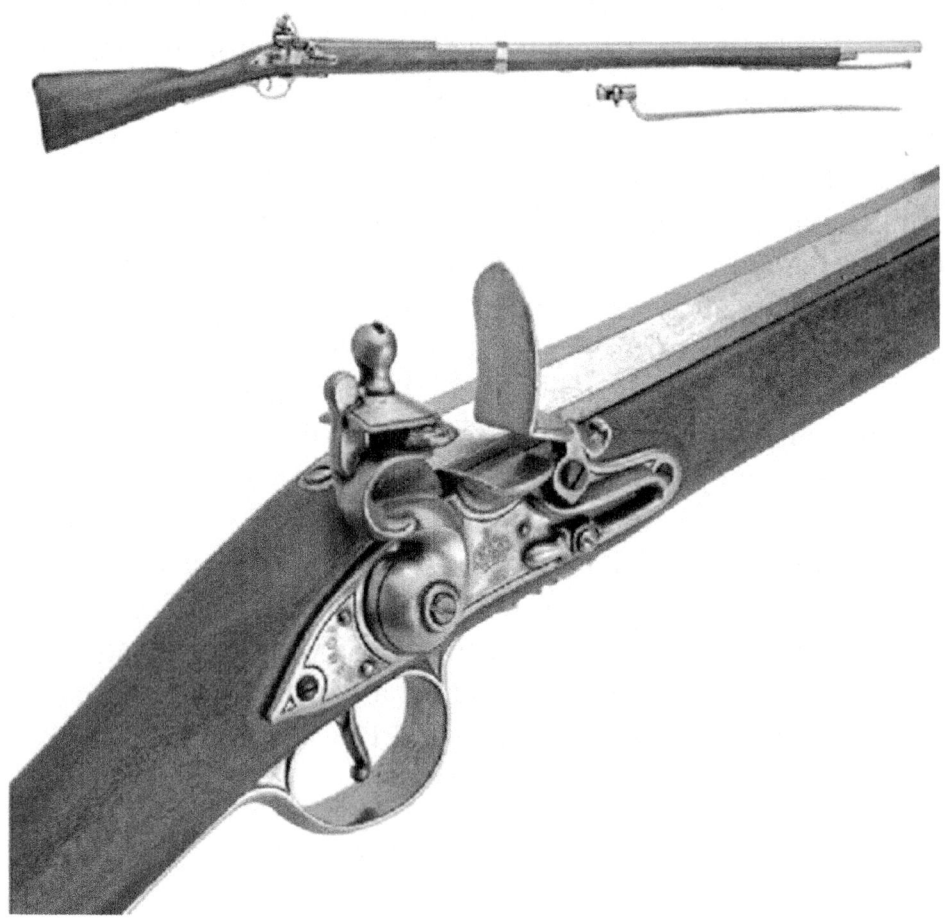

The Brown Bess (Wikipedia)

In an era when soldiers averaged five and a half feet tall, handling the weapon was a challenge. Firing was difficult. Squeezing the trigger did not produce an instant ignition. Instead, the hammer holding a piece of flint would fall striking a piece of metal called a frizzen and this would produce sparks that would fall on a small bed of gunpowder below called a flash pan. This would ignite the powder that would burn through a small hole in the rear of the barrel and the gunpowder in the barrel would explode sending the bullet on its way. The entire arrangement produced inaccuracy and the best that could happen was that the bullet headed in the general direction of the enemy. Misfires were a way of life and rain stopped all firing since the powder became wet. Tactics evolved to counter the inadequacies of the weapons: soldiers lined up shoulder to shoulder firing volleys at close range until in the words of one observer "Things became rather bloody." One side or the other would withdraw and hope for a better day. There were other weapons such as bayonets, hatchets, knives, and bows. These became keys to survival since the troops had one-shot weapons that took time to reload. The rangers were clothed and equipped differently from the regular troops and colonials.

> Their green uniforms, chosen for camouflage in the woods, at once distinguished them from the red-coated regulars. Over a buckskin shirt they wore two layers: a kind of sleeved waistcoat and an outer body-warming short sleeveless jacket; both these garments were lined with green serge. Over their trousers they sometimes wore an imitation kilt or philibeg and always thigh-length brown leggings with moccasins on their feet. On parade they wore tricorne hats, but once in the bush they switched to flat Scots bonnets. They carried regulation-issue muskets, and a leather sling on the left side, hanging from a belt that ran over the right shoulder, held a bayonet and tomahawk, while at the waist was a sheathed scalping knife; they also had a cartridge box and (under the right arm) a powder horn suspended from a belt looped over the left shoulder. Blankets were carried in rolls except when worn for extra warmth on the march, and their knapsacks contained the iron rations on which they would eke out a living in the wilderness. The officers carried a small compass fixed in the bottom of their powder horns. It was Loudoun who had first agreed to uniforms for the Rangers, though Rogers's enemies constantly groused that the cost of supplying this special apparel and the general costs of the Rangers — some £35,000 a year — could have been better diverted to providing another two regiments of regulars for the same price.[2]

The Indians did not follow the European tactics of the day, but would instead use terrain for cover and concealment preferring to pick off the enemy and then lunge forward for the kill if numbers and situation favored them. If not, withdraw to fight another day. It was guerrilla warfare. Father Roubaud, the French Catholic Pastor at Saint Francis described the Abenaki warriors.

> Imagine a great assembly of savages adorned with every ornament most suited to disfigure them in European eyes, painted with vermilion, white, green, yellow and black made of soot and the scrapings of pots. A single savage face combines all these different colours, methodically laid on with the help of a little tallow, which serves for pomatum. The head is shaved except at the top, where there is a small tuft, to which are fastened feathers, a few beads of wampum, or some such trinket. Every part of the head has its ornament. Pendants hang from the nose and also from the ears, which are split in infancy and drawn down by weights till they flap at last against the shoulders. The rest of the equipment answers to this fantastic decoration: a shirt bedaubed with vermilion, wampum collars, silver bracelets, a large knife hanging on the breast, moose-skin moccasins, and a belt of various colours always absurdly combined. The sachems and war-chiefs are distinguished from the rest: the latter by a gorget, and the former by a medal, with the King's portrait on one side, and on the other Mars and Bellona joining hands, with the device, Virtus et Honor . . . They proceed to nominate the chiefs who were to take command. As soon as one was named he rose and took the head of some animal that had been butchered for the feast. He raised it aloft so that all the company could see it and cried: 'Behold the head of the enemy!' Applause and cries of joy from all parts of the assembly. The chief, with the head in his hands, passed down between the lines, singing his war-song, bragging of his exploits, taunting and defying the enemy, and glorifying himself beyond all measure. To hear his self-laudation in these moments of martial transport one would think him a conquering hero ready to sweep everything before him. As he passed in front of the other savages, they would respond by dull broken cries jerked up from the depths of their stomachs, and accompanied by movements of their bodies so odd

that one must be well used to them to keep countenance. In the course of this song the chief would utter from time to time some grotesque witticism; then he would stop, as if pleased with himself, or rather to listen to the thousand confused cries of applause that g r e e t e d his ears. He kept up his martial promenade as long as he liked the sport; and when he had enough, ended by flinging down the head of the animal to show that his warlike appetite craved meat of another sort.[3]

Pere Pierre-Joseph Roubaud

The Rangers

Barnes must have been exhausted. The rangers had been on the trail for several days with little food, a heavy load, and no sleep. The Abenaki were gaining on them. The attack on the village had gone well with few casualties and Saint Francis was wrapped in flames as they left. Now things were going against them and they were starting to lose people from exhaustion and occasional accidents. It was then that Barnes saw it and let the rest of the rangers go past. He later wrote down a record that would survive more than 250 years. His purpose must have been to find his way back to this point later. Vermont historian Abby Hemenway told his story a century after the event.

> A man by the name of Barnes lived in Barnet a short time, at an early period, who belonged to Rogers's party, and said that the silver image [later called the silver Madonna] weighing ten pounds, which they took from the chapel of Saint Francis, was hid on the way in a crevice of a rock, and covered with leaves. He said also that they took from the chapel two gold candlesticks, which they hid in the woods, under the root of a tree, near the Canada line, and that he went back after some years and searched for them, but could not find where he hid them. It is said that this part of his story was confirmed by a report in the newspaper, about 1816, that two gold candlesticks worth $1,000, were found in the woods in Hatley, C. E., which lay in Rogers's way.[4]

There is nothing new about rangers. They have been employed by military forces since the Romans. Rangers as we know them today emerged centuries ago.

> The word *ranger* had emerged in the written record in the thirteenth-century England as applied to a far-traveling forester or borderer. By the late sixteenth century border rangers, units of irregular militia patrolled the violent frontier between England and Scotland. Northern immigrants to the New World brought these procedures along with them. By the late seventeenth century, as a series of Indian wars erupted, the colonists could not look for support to a regular/army, and their ranger forces had to develop both offensive and defensive capabilities.[5]

Two and a half centuries ago other concepts were relevant that better describe the rangers of the period: the ability to fight enemy guerillas (the tribes) on their own ground with their own weapons and tactics.

Robert Rogers

Barnes and the other rangers were led by a most remarkable man, Robert Rogers. Robert Rogers was born to James and Mary McFatridge Rogers on 7 November 1731 in Methuen, a small town in northeastern Massachusetts. James and Mary Rogers were immigrants from Ireland and as Catholics they were outsiders known as "Black Papists" and shunned by their Puritan neighbors.[6] The family had obtained new land and had moved north across the New Hampshire border near Concord when Robert was age eight. This was a primitive frontier with land carved out of earth that had never seen a plow before. There were frequent attacks by the Indians, especially the Abenaki tribe that came down from New France. Led by the French on raids that extended as far south as Massachusetts. Farms were sometimes abandoned as the settlers withdrew into nearby population centers. For defense, the colonists organized a cooperative system. Some colonists would work the abandoned farms while other colonists stood guard. Robert Rogers early in his youth learned the forest skills that would later bring him fame on his campaigns.[7] Biographer John Ross explained.

> . . . . the boy had mastered basic lessons: he learned to "eye," or sweep his gaze to pick up unexpected patches of color, movement, or texture standing out against the forest tint; to sit quietly for hours on end to become invisible to forest creatures; and to identify the scat and prints of game animals.
>
> Young Rogers became immersed in the rhythms and lore of the flora and fauna-the passage of migrating birds, the spawning of fish, the days when the sap ran richly from the sugar maples, and those when deer became more reckless and easier to hunt during the rutting season. He learned that an ideal time to kill a moose came when it stuck its head into a bog or pond to eat water-lily roots, and that its nose made particularly good eating. Out of plain necessity Rogers came to understand how plants manage their energy, storing it according to the seasons in their roots, leaves, and seeds. The season-related behaviors of both plants and animals became waypoints around which to orient oneself in the woods and in life; in much the same way the Eastern Woodlands Indians might agree, at the end of the moon of the deer mating season, to leave on a scout.[8]

In 1744, France declared war on Great Britain and the news spread throughout the colonies. As expected in the years that followed, the barbaric Indian attacks from New France increased along the frontier with men, women and children hacked to death. Some were taken captives back to Indian settlements such as Saint Francis. John Stark, who later served as a ranger captain under Rogers, and his friend, Amos Eastman, were surprised by the Abenaki and taken prisoner. They were taken back to Saint Francis.

> The women, girls, boys, and older men gathered sticks, clubs, and rocks and formed two long parallel lines along the shore.

The prisoners were to be compelled to run the gauntlet, the ritual induction of captives. The warriors stood aside and watched. The canoes grounded on the sandy riverbank. If the raiders followed tradition, they had stopped earlier in the day, and now both captives, stark naked, bore stripes of vermilion and bear grease. The Indians pushed Eastman out of the boat; he had no choice but run under the drumming clubs up the embankment toward the village. Someone had thrust an eight-foot pole mounted with an animal skin into his hands. As he stumbled on, shielding his head with his arms, he loudly chanted an Algonquin phrase taught him by Titigaw, *Nen nuttattagkompish wameug nunkompeog* – "*I'll beat all your young men*" – which inflamed the already-excited villagers to hammer him even harder as he staggered by. He crested the bluff and collapsed. . . . An Indian shoved a coonskin-adorned pole into Stark's hands and pushed him between the rows of fierce, excited faces. Unaware of its meaning, he sang, *Nutchipwuttoonapish wameug nonokkishquog,* or "I'll kiss all your young women." The first few blows brought his Scots-Irish blood to a boil, and he poled several Indians into the dirt-to howls of admiring laughter from his other captors; he completed the gauntlet untouched, then tended to the bruised and terrified Eastman.[9]

Stark and Eastman escaped and returned home. Stark would not forget his treatment at Saint Francis.

John Stark (1728-1822) during the War of Independence (Wikipedia)

In the spring of 1745, a call for volunteers went out and at age 14, Robert Rogers answered the call. Rogers' company continued beating the bushes looking for the hostiles without success throughout the summer and in October the company was disbanded. This was Robert Rogers first experience as a soldier and he discovered that it was much more pleasing than tilling the soil and listening to screaming babies. He had been bitten by the excitement of being a soldier. He would get the excitement that he wanted. The French and Indian War would soon begin.

Robert Rogers (1731-1795) [10] *(Library of Congress)*

Celoron's Expedition

In June of 1747, the Governor-General of New France, the Marquis de la Galissoniere, became concerned about the increasing influence of British traders in the Ohio country. He ordered Pierre-Joseph Celoron to lead a military expedition through the area to confirm the French claim to the land. Celoron was an experienced veteran who had served as commandant of Crown Point and Detroit. More important, the expedition would impress the Indians with a show of force and assure their allegiance to France. The expedition would cover over 4800 kilometers between June and November 1749. Celoron would lead two hundred troops and thirty Indians. Celoron followed the shores of Lake Ontario and the southern shore of Lake Erie moving inland to the Allegheny River which he followed. If he met British traders, he told them to leave. He met with Indian tribes and passed on trinkets reminding them that this land belonged to France and they should not trade with the British. Celoron's comments were not well received and he was informed that the Indians owned the Ohio country and they would trade with whomever they pleased.

Along his route of travel, Celoron buried engraved lead plates stating the French claim to the Ohio country. He did not realize that it would be lead in a different form that would decide land ownership more than ten years later. While Celoron was busy burying lead plates, the British colonists were sending an increasing stream of settlers to the Ohio country. The Ohio Land Company was formed with a grant of 200,000 acres of land west of the Appalachians from Virginia.[11] A disappointed Celoron arrived back at Montreal in November, 1749. He wrote in his report "All I can say is that the Natives of these localities are very badly disposed toward the French and are entirely devoted to the English. I don't know in what way they could be brought back."[12]

The result of Celoron's trip and the British transgressions that followed was the construction of a series of French forts along the upper Ohio River in 1753 that would strengthen New France's frontier. The Indian tribes were starting to feel the pinch. An Iroquois chief told British Indian agent William Johnson "We don't know what you Christians, English and French, together, intend. We are so hemmed in by both that we have hardly a hunting place left. In a little while, if we find a bear in a tree, there will immediately appear an owner of the land to challenge the property, and hinder us from killing it, which is our livelihood."[13]

On 11 December 1753, a young man from Virginia unknown to the traders appeared in Ohio country. He was twenty-one-year old George Washington who held a major's colonial commission and a mission from the Virginia lieutenant governor, Robert Dinwiddie: proclaim to the French "our undoubted rights to such of the said river Ohio as are within the limits of our province of Virginia, or any other."[14] Washington was to deliver a letter to the French "requiring your peaceable departure."[15] If such entreaties were to fail, Dinwiddie was authorized to repel force with force and would build a string of forts to counter the French threat. Washington received a cordial reception from the French who promised nothing and sent the young major back to Williamsburg, Virginia (capitol of Virginia at that time) to render his report.

Battle of Jumonville Glen – 28 May 1754

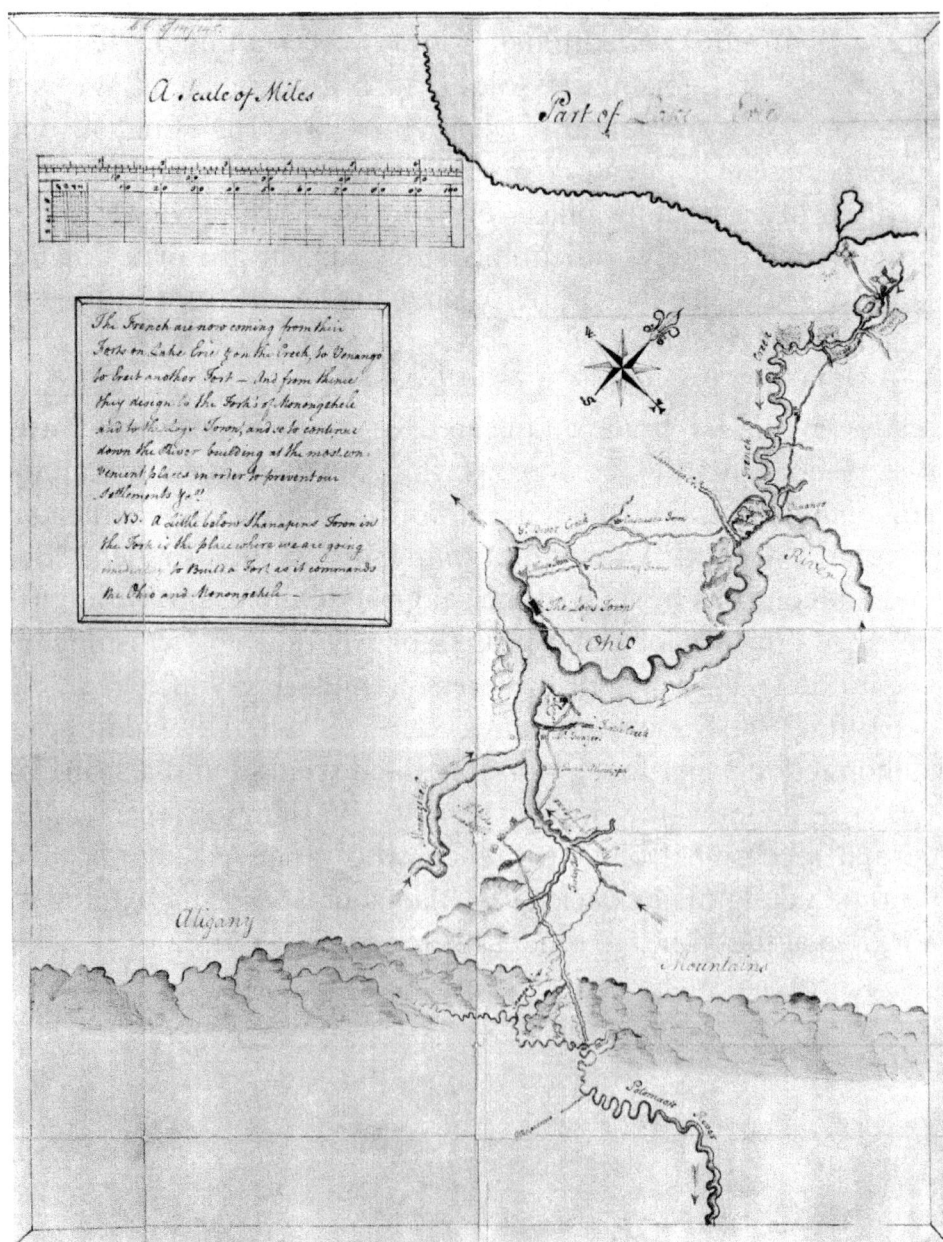

Washington's Map of the Ohio River showing the Forks (Library of Congress)

While Washington was on his month long journey back to Williamsburg, Dinwiddie dispatched a former fur trader, Captain William Trent to occupy the forks of the Ohio River and establish a fort. Dinwiddie knew that this would provoke a strong response from the French and the fort was a trip-wire on the banks of the Ohio. Trent had less than fifty men and the French would counter with a spring offensive of over six hundred men and supporting artillery. The French commander, Contrecour's, orders were clear: expel the British. They arrived at Presque Island on the shore of Lake Erie in March after a difficult journey in bad weather.

While Trent had arrived on the banks of the Ohio in mid-February he had made little progress in building the fort due to the bad weather that had also plagued Contrecour's trek to Lake Erie. The French arrived at the Forks on 16 April 1754. As they approached, Trent took off to seek help leaving his brother-in-law, Ensign Edward Ward in command. Ward immediately surrendered on the condition that he and his troops were allowed to return home to Virginia. The French agreed and offered rations for the homeward journey and what could best be described as a farewell dinner complete with good French wine and the best French cuisine. Ward wondered if the French were confused about which side he was on. As Ward left, Contrcour took over Ward's tools and materials and went to work building what he named Fort Duquesne where the Allegheny and Monongahela Rivers meet to form the Ohio River.[16] The site is, today, under the pavement of downtown Pittsburgh, Pennsylvania.

In the same month that Contrcour was moving south, Dinwiddie promoted Washington to Lieutenant Colonel and ordered him to raise an army and move west to the Ohio to complete the fort. It took weeks to recruit his army and Washington described his new command as ". . . loose, idle persons. . . many without shoes, others want stockings, some are without shirts, and not a few . . . have scarce a coat, or waistcoat to their backs."[17] On 2 April 1754, Washington assembled his small army (30 people) and headed west. Toward the end of May, Washington halted at a place called Great Meadows, about fifty miles from the Forks. Things were not going well. He had had desertions and the troops were exhausted. The open field was two miles long and offered good pasture for the animals, but it was soggy and marching feet turned it into a muddy mess.

The French knew a British force was advancing and Contrcour dispatched a thirty-man patrol under Ensign Joseph Coulon DeVillers de Jumonville to find the British and gather intelligence. Shortly after Washington arrived at Great Meadows, a local British trader and a friendly Indian chief, Silverheels, arrived to warn him of the French approach. Silverheels brought about a dozen warriors and these added to Washington's strength. Fearing the French would attack, Washington moved out to meet the threat. Early on the morning of 28 May 1754, Washington reached the French camp. They were asleep and had failed to post a guard. Washington ordered a volley. The French rushed to their muskets, but it was too late. The battle was over in fifteen minutes when the Indians swarmed in to scalp the dead and wounded. Washington lost one dead and three wounded. The French lost ten dead including Ensign Jumonville. Twenty-one of the French were taken prisoner. One escaped. This was Washington's first time under fire and he reported to Dinwiddie "I heard the bullets whistle, and, believe me, there is something charming in the sound."[18] A newspaper in Williamsburg, Virginia printed Captain Maccay's account of the battle.

> WILLIAMSBURG July 19. On Wednesday last arrived in Town Colonel Washington, and Captain Maccay, who gave the following Account to his Honour the Governor, of the Action

between them and the French, at the Great Meadows in the Western Part of the Dominion.

The third of this Instant July, about nine a Clock, we received Intelligence that the French having been reinforced with 700 Recruits, had left Monongahela, and were in full March with 900 Men to attack us. Upon this, our Numbers were so unequal (our Force net exceeding 300) we prepared for our Defence in the best Manner we could by throwing up a small Intrenchment, which we had no Time to perfect, before our Centinel gave Notice, about 11 o Clock of their Approach by firing his Piece, which he did at the Enemy, and as we learned afterwards, killed three of the Men, on which they began to fire upon us, at about 600 Yards Distance, but without any Effect: We immediately called all our Men to their Arms, and drew up in Order before Trenches; but as we looked upon this distant Fire of the Enemy only as an Artifice to intimidate, or draw our Fire from us, we waited their nearer approach before we returned their Salute.

They were advanced in a very irregular Manner to another Point of Woods, about 60 Yards off, and from thence made a second Discharge; upon which, finding they had no intention of Attacking us in the open Field, we returned into our Trenches, and still reserved our Fire, as we expected from their great Superiority of Numbers, that they would endeavour to force our Trenches; but finding they did nor seem to intend this neither, the Colonel gave Orders to Fire, which was done with great Alacrity and Undauntedness.

We continued the unequal Fight, with an Enemy sheltered behind the Trees, ourselves without Shelter in Trenches full of Water, in a settled Rain, and the Enemy galling us on all Sides incessantly from the Woods, till 8 a Clock at Night, when the French called to parley: From the great Improbability that such a vastly superior Force, and possessed of such an Advantage would offer a Parley first, we suspected a Deceit, and therefore refused to consent that they should come among us; on which, they desired us to send an Officer to them, and engaged their Parole for his Safety; we then sent Capt. Van Braam, and Mr. Peyronee to receive this Proposal, which they Did, and about Midnight we agreed that each Side should retire without Molestation, they back to their Fort, at Monongahela, and we to Will's Creek: That we should march away with all Honours of War, and with all the Stores, Effects and

Baggage. Accordingly the next Morning, with our Drums beating, and our Colours flying, we began our March in good Order with our Stores, &c. in Convoy; but we were interrupted by the Arrival of a Reinforcement of One Hundred Indians, among the French, who were hardly restrained from Attacking us, and did us considerable Damage, by the pilfering of our Baggage. We then proceeded, but soon found it necessary to leave our Baggage and Stores; the great scarcity of our Provisions obliged us to use the utmost Expedition, and having neither Waggons nor Horses to transport them, The Enemy had deprived us of all our Creatures, by killing, in the Beginning of the Engagement, our Horses, Cattle, and every living Thing they could; even to the very Dogs [Actually, Washington ordered his dogs killed because he was concerned that their barking would betray his position.]. The Number of the killed on our Side was 30, and 70 wounded; among the former was Lieutenant Mercier, of Captain Maccay's Independent Company; a Gentleman of true Military Worth, and whose Bravery would not permit him to retire, tho' dangerously wounded, 'till a second Shot disabled him, and a third put an End to his Life, as he was carrying to the Surgeon.

Our Men behaved with singular Intrepedity, and we determined not to ask for Quarters, but with our Bayonets screw's, to sell our Lives as deadly as possible we could. From the Number of the Enemy, and our Station we could not hope for Victory; and from the Character of those we had to encounter, we expected no Mercy, but on Terms that we positively resolved not to submit to. The Number killed and wounded of the Enemy is uncertain, but by the Information given by some of the Dutch in their Service to their Countrymen in ours, we learnt that it amounts to above 300; and we are induced to believe it must be very considerable, by their being busy all Night in burying their Dead, and yet many remained the next Day; and their wounded we know was considerable, by one of our Men, who had been made Prisoner by them after signing the Articles, and who, on his Return, told us, that he saw great Numbers much wounded and carried off upon Litters.

We were also told by some of the Indians after the Action, that the French had an Officer of distinguishable Rank killed [Ensign Jumonville], Some considerable blow they must have received, to induce them to call first Parley, knowing as they perfectly did the Circumstances we were in. Col. Washington, and Capt. Maccay, left Capt. Clarke at Winchester, on the 11th last, and his Men were not then arrived there. Thus have a few brave Men been exposed, to be butchered, by the Negligence of those, who in Obedience to their Sovereign's Command, ought to have been with them many Months before; and it is evident certain, that had the Companies from New York been in expedition as Capt. Maccay's from South Carolina, our Camp would have been secure from the Insults of the French and our brave Men still alive to serve their King and Country. Surely this will remove the Infatuation that seems to have prevailed too much among our Neighbours, and inforce a late ingenerous Emblem well worthy of their Attention and Consideration.[19]

Captain Maccay

As seen in wars since then, the facts were rearranged to meet political goals. This romantic version of the battle is at odds with the facts provided by historian Ron Chernow, below. The rationale for stretching the truth was the need to clearly show the French at fault.

Finger-pointing started immediately. The French claimed that Jumonville was on a peace mission, an "embassy." Washington had attacked a sleeping camp when both nations were at peace. Washington counterclaimed that the French were spies and the Indian chief claimed that the French were of "bad heart" and deserved their fate.[20]

Dinwiddie [Virginia's lieutenant governor] found Washington's explanation less than persuasive. In a politic move to evade responsibility, he told his London superiors: "This little skirmish was by the Half King [the British Indian ally] and the Indians. We were auxiliaries to them, as my orders to the commander of our forces was to be on the defensive." The lieutenant governor suspected that, in the words of Sir Horace Walpole, Washington may well have "set the world on fire."[21]

It did not matter. France and Britain were soon at war. Historian Ron Chernow summarized.

> On the morning of May 28, Washington and the Half King decided to pounce on the French intruders. Washington was convinced of their hostile intention: by the stealthy way they had moved about. As he afterward explained, the French "came secretly and sought after the most hidden retreats ... and remained hid for whole days together and that no more than five miles from us. From thence they sent spies to reconnoiter our camp." Washington's sense of the situation, however faulty, likely predisposed him to launch a preemptive attack.
>
> Early that morning the Half King led him to a "low obscure place" where thirty-five Frenchmen lay encamped in a secluded glen, surrounded by rocks. For Washington, this "skulking place" underscored the clandestine nature of the French mission. He marched bravely at the head of his column, placing himself in the most vulnerable position as they approached the sheltered hollow. With Washington's men in front of them and the Indians slipping behind them to block their escape, the French were encircled. According to Washington's version of events, the French soldiers, when they spied the British, instantly scurried for their arms and unleashed a brisk fire. Washington gave orders to fire in return, and his men ripped off two quick volleys. Trapped on low ground, the ambushed French soon threw down their arms and surrendered. The casualty count showed a lopsided contest in which ten French were killed and another twenty-one were captured, compared with only one dead and two or three wounded on Washington's side. Clearly, Washington and his men overpowered the French before they had a chance to respond, making it seem unlikely that the latter had fired first. The whole bloody affair was wrapped up in fifteen minutes.[22]

To Counterfeit is Death[23]

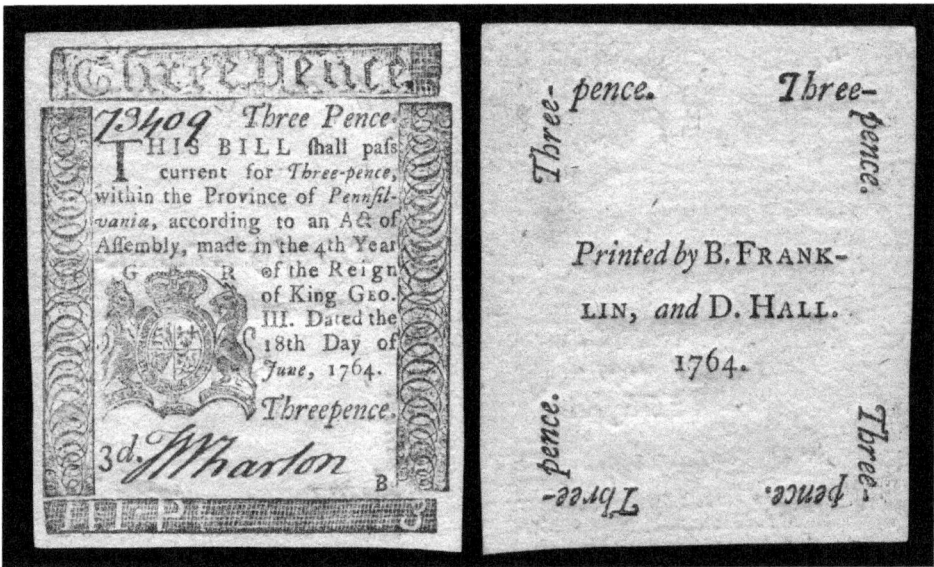

Signed Three Pence Note (Wikipedia)

While Washington was engaged in fighting the French on the western frontier, Robert Rogers had started his career as a counterfeiter. Much had changed since he first answered the call to arms at age fourteen. He had learned the customs and habits of Native Americans from Mohawk traders and he had hunted with them. He seemed to have an intense curiosity about wildlife and the Indians. Indian murders continued to occur and in the summer of 1754 the governor of New Hampshire called out the militia. At age 22, Rogers enlisted in Lieutenant John Goffee's company and spent about two months patrolling and tracking the Indians without success. He was discharged in September. He purchased his own land and at this time met Owen Sullivan, a specialist in engraving and passing counterfeit money. Owen Sullivan is considered by many to be the most successful moneymaker (to use the colonial term) in colonial America. While imprisoned in 1749, he cut a plate to manufacture New Hampshire notes and ran off money to pay for his release.[24] Acts curtailing legal tender caused people to claim counterfeiting was ". . . no sin, for it would make money plentiful among poor people."[25] Historian John Ross explained.

> Britain kept the colonies on a short leash, restricting their foreign trade by limiting the circulation of internationally accepted currency. Specie earned in export soon made its way back to the mother country. The lack of circulating money particularly hamstrung ordinary people. Counterfeiters, especially in the backcountry, often emerged as folk heroes who sometimes enlisted whole communities in their illegal business. Sullivan could count on many a loft and barn whenever he needed a place to hide.[26]

Sullivan paid Rogers (in counterfeit money) to pasture his cattle on the Rogers' land. Rogers in turn used Sullivan's money to buy things and realized how easy it was to pass counterfeit money. Rogers was a fast learner and with his brother, Richard, got into the counterfeiting business with Sullivan. The down side was that it was a hanging offense. There were; however, other less fatal penalties such as branding and ear cropping, but none of these were very attractive to the Rogers boys. The extent of counterfeiting and complaints of the rich caused the New Hampshire legislature to pass legislation calling for local constables to compile lists of moneymakers and arrest them. The Rogers brothers ended up on the local list and they were arrested. Robert Rogers was desperate and he penned a note to Carty Gilman, a merchant who was a co-conspirator. His style of writing seen later in his journals was to write phonetically. During the period, proper nouns and words that needed emphasis were frequently capitalized by writers.

> Mr. Gilman for gods sake do the work that you promised me that you would Do by No means fail or you Will Destroy me for Ever. Sir, my life lays att your providence now Ons [once] more I adjure you by your Maker, to Do it for whie [why] should such an onest [honest] Man be Killed.
> Sir, I am your souned [sound] friend.[27]
>
> **Robert Rogers**

Charges were dropped against Richard Rogers, but Robert Rogers was in jail pending trial in February, 1755 when fate intervened. War with France was making manpower demands on the colonies and a call for volunteers went out the day Robert Rogers' trial was to start. While he was a sorry counterfeiter, he was recognized as a top soldier. Rogers was released and started his career by enlisting twenty-four New Hampshire men to fight. These were paid an enlistment bonus of $30 each with money Rogers obtained from a Massachusetts recruiting officer. Rogers and his men would fight for New Hampshire with money paid initially by Massachusetts which caused consternation in Boston. Rogers was not overly concerned. He had been a citizen of New Hampshire since childhood and he would move north as a part of the New Hampshire forces. This may also have been pay-back in a small way for the "Black Papists" insults hurled at his family by his Massachusetts puritan neighbors when he was a child. By March he had rounded up fifty men and was made captain of a company in Colonel Joseph Blanchard's regiment. Blanchard was the justice that had heard Rogers' case two months earlier.

> For the moment the looming war trumped everything else-a very good thing for Rogers: luck finally seemed to have broken on his side. On April 24 Undersheriff John Light knocked on Carty Gilman's door in Exeter to serve a warrant; he found him stuffing a piece of paper into his mouth with one hand, while gripping two counterfeit six-shilling New Hampshire bills in the other. The sheriff wrestled him to the ground and pulled the cud out of his mouth and found the half-consumed remains of Rogers's hasty but mightily incriminating injunction to his hapless accomplice.[28]

Braddock's Defeat – July 1755

Edward Braddock (1695-1755) (Library of Congress)

  The conflict with France had evolved into a two front war. While Robert Rogers was moving north to the frontier, in the west, the French had reinforced their forces in the Great Lakes region and the Ohio Valley. Oddly, no formal declaration of war had been declared at this time and the British campaign was justified based on the statement that ". . . these movements were simply designed to expel the French from lands that legitimately belonged to England."[29] The British plan of operations for 1755 included an attack by Sir William Johnson (including Robert Rogers) to seize Fort St. Frederic (later called Crown Point) on Lake Champlain in the north and an attack against Fort Duquesne near Lake Erie. Other tasks were to fortify Fort Oswego and attack Fort Niagara. To this end, the British army assembled the largest force yet seen in the New World. The French saw the British force leave Great Britain and also sent reinforcements to the New World. This would become a race. General Braddock with Lieutenant Colonel Washington as his aide would lead an expedition of fifteen hundred British and colonial troops west.

The expedition kicked off from Cumberland, Maryland on 10 June 1755. Braddock would follow Washington's earlier trail and was determined to evict the French from Fort Duquesne. Due to squabbling in the colonies, Braddock had not included the British Indian allies. It was a disaster. As the column approached Fort Duquesne, the French and their Indian allies were waiting. Initially, it was more of a meeting engagement than an ambush (as is often claimed), but the British had failed to secure a nearby hill and the French poured divesting fire on the column from it. Among Braddock's other blunders was that he left the troops in column rather than assembling and forming up to stand firm. When a bullet finally found Braddock and he fell mortally wounded, the British troops fled in panic.

Death of General Braddock (Library of Congress)

    Washington later wrote "When we endeavored to rally them, it was with as much success as if we attempted to stop the wild bears of the mountains."[30] It was a massacre with nearly one thousand troops killed or wounded. Nearly 500 men in the British force had died. Years later their bones were so thick that one observer stated that they could be laid in a carpet a hundred yards wide and half a mile in length. William Shirley, Jr., the son of the Massachusetts governor was among the dead. He died shot through the head standing next to Braddock. French losses were twenty-eight killed and about the same number wounded. The Indians lost eleven killed and twenty-nine wounded.[31]

Washington and Lieutenant Colonel Thomas Gage finally rallied the survivors and made their way back to Cumberland. In a twist of fate, Washington and Gage would face each other as opposing commanders during the War of Independence.

It would become known as the Battle of the Monongahela or more commonly Braddock's Defeat.[32] On the battlefield the French found the plans for the entire British campaign including the attack on Crown Point. This was an unexpected bonus for the French. The Philadelphia press provided details of the engagement.

> Philadelphia, 31 July
> . . . Extract of a Letter from an Officer; dated at Fort Cumberland July 18, 1755.
> The 9th Inst. We passed and repassed the Monongahela, by advancing first a Party of 300 Men, which was immediately followed by another 200. The General, with his Columns of Artillery, Baggage, and the main Body of the Army, passed the River the last Time about one a Clock. As soon as the whole had gone on the Fort Side of the Monongahela, we heard a very heavy and quick Fire in our Front; and Immediately advanced in order to sustain them; but the Detachment of the 200 and 300 Men gave Way, and fell back upon us, which caused such Confusion, and struck so great a Panick among our Men, that afterwards no military Expedient could be made use of that had any Effect on them: The Men were so extremely deaf to the Exhortation of the General, and the Officers, that they fired away, in the most irregular Manner, all their Artillery fired and then run off, leaving the Enemy, the Artillery, Ammunition,

Provisions and Baggage; nor could they be persuaded to stop till they got so far as Geist's Plantation, nor their only in Part, many of them proceeding as far as Col. Dunbar's Party, who lay six Miles on this Side.

The Officers were absolutely sacrificed by the unparalleled good Behavour, advancing sometimes in Bodies, and sometimes separately, hoping by such Example to engage the Soldiers to follow them, but to no Purpose.

The General [Braddock] had five Horses killed under him, and at Last received a Wound through his Right Arm into his Lungs, of which he died the 13th Instant. Secretary Shirley [the governor's son] was shot thro' the Head; Capt. Morris wounded; Mr. Washington had two Horses shot under him and his Clothes shot thro' in several Places behaving the whole Time with the greatest Courage and Resolution. Sir Burton and Sir John St. Clair wounded; and enclosed I have sent a List of the Killed and Wounded, according to an exact Account as we are yet able to get.

Upon our proceeding with the whole Convoy to the little Meadow, it was found impracticable to advance with Twelve Hundred Men, with the necessary Artillery, Ammunition and Provisions, leaving the main Body of the Convoy under the Command of Col. Dunbar, with orders to join him as soon as possible.

In this Manner we proceeded with Safety and Expedition, 'til the fatal Day I just related; and happy it was, that this Disposition was made, otherwise the whole must either have starved, or fallen into the Hands of the Enemy, as Numbers would have been of no Service to us, and our Provisions all lost.

As our Number of Horses was so much reduced, and those extremely weak, and many Carriages being wanted for the Wounded Men, occasioned our destroying the Ammunition and superfluous Part of the Provisions left in Col. Dunbar's Convoy to prevent its falling into the Hands of the Enemy.

As the whole of the Artillery is lost, and the Troops are entirely weakened by Deaths, Wounds and Sickness, it was judged impossible to make any further Attempts; therefore Col. Dunbar is moving to Fort Cumberland, with every Thing he is able to bring up with him. By the particular Disposition of the French and Indians it was impossible to judge of the Numbers they had that Day in the Field.[33]

Battle of Lake George – 8 September 1755

While Washington was struggling back from Fort Duquesne, Robert Rogers had reached the southern edge of Lake George. This would become a depot to stockpile supplies and was named Fort Edward. Rogers had proceeded up the Hudson River from Albany as a part of Sir William Johnson's effort to seize Crown Point. Rogers watched as workers built bateau that Johnson would use to sail to the northern end of the lake to attack Crown Point. Fort Edward was hastily constructed. Here a flood of supplies from Albany were stockpiled for the attack on Crown Point. The French were not idle. They had the British plan recovered from Braddock's captured baggage at Fort Duquesne and now moved to attack Fort Edward. Baron Dieskau commanding three thousand French and Indian allies had left Montreal to attack Fort Edward. By the evening of 7 September 1755, he was within striking distance of the fort and planned a night attack. The French got lost in the woods, but eventually reached the shore of Lake George. Meanwhile Johnson learned of the French advance and sent a thousand troops under Colonel Ephrain Williams to reinforce Fort Edward. Chief Hendrick led two hundred Mohawk warriors with the Williams column. Both forces were on the move when two Mohawk scouts, one from each column, met in the center of the road and decided to discuss the situation to the horror of Williams and Dieskau. Both realized that the element of surprise had been lost. Hendrick called out to his cousins to leave the French and join him. A shot rang out and Hendrick fell dead. The battle was on. Williams was shot early in the battle and the British fell back. Johnson sent reinforcements and a barricade was set up. The French assault was broken by British artillery that stopped the

French regulars and scattered their Indian allies. The battle was a stalemate. Johnson was wounded and Dieskau was captured. Over the next few weeks, both sides laid plans to control Lake George. The French built Carillon while the British constructed Fort William Henry.[34]

Robert Rogers was escorting supply wagons as this fight occurred. With Chief Hendrick dead, the Mohawks deserted the British and that left Johnson without scouts. Johnson asked Colonel Blanchard to send a candidate to accomplish scouting. Blanchard sent Rogers as a candidate and Johnson liked what he saw. The fact that Johnson was also an Irishman and a Freemason may have helped Rogers get hired since Rogers was also Irish and a Freemason. Johnson laid out a demanding mission for Rogers. Rogers was to move out to reach Crown Point and determine if the French were building new facilities. Along the way Rogers was to determine if it was feasible to build an artillery-worthy road. Rogers picked two men and they were rowed across the lake to start their journey.[35] The small group of three was successful and returned to Johnson with their report. Robert Rogers had started to evolve from a colonial infantryman to a ranger. The rangers were born. Over the next three years Rogers expanded his rangers to twelve companies. The following year did not go well for the British and in August 1756 the French under General Louis-Joseph Montcalm captured the garrison of Fort Oswego and destroyed fortifications at the Battle of Oswego in New York.

Louis-Joseph de, Marquis de. Montcalm (1712-1759)
(Library of Congress)

Ambush – 21 January 1757

During the winter of 1756-1757, Rogers and several of his ranger companies were stationed at Fort William Henry at the southern tip of Lake George and at Fort Edward on the upper Hudson River. These forts formed the frontier between the British colonies and New France. The rangers were on a scouting expedition from Fort Edward and stopped at Fort William Henry to resupply and pick up snowshoes. Rogers left Fort William Henry with 86 men on 17 January heading down the frozen Lake George. Twelve men soon turned back due to injuries while the remainder moved on reaching Lake Champlain on 21 January. They spotted a sled moving on the lake and Rogers sent John Stark to investigate. As he closed, Stark spotted other sleds and he was seen by the French who turned back to Carillon. The rangers gave chase and managed to take seven prisoners but the others who escaped reached Carillon and alerted the French commander, Paul-Louis de. Lusignan, the fort commander. Rogers learned from the prisoners that a war party had recently arrived at Carillon and about a thousand French regulars were now located at Carillon (later called Fort Ticonderoga) and Crown Point. Lusignan immediately dispatched 90 regulars and 90 Canadians and Indians to find and capture the rangers.

Rogers knew his force would be hunted down and moved as quickly as possible to return on snowshoes to his last camp. In spite of their lack of snowshoes, the French managed to set up an ambush that caught the rangers. Rogers estimated the enemy force at 250. In the fight that followed, the French lost the advantage due to wet gunpowder that caused many misfires and their lack of snowshoes. John Stark formed a rear guard that enabled the rangers to escape. The French prisoners were killed in order to speed up the return. The rangers arrived at Fort William Henry on 23 January with 48 able-bodied men and six wounded. The French had taken several prisoners during the ranger retreat and from these they learned the British disposition of troops and supplies from Albany to Fort William Henry. This may have been the most significant result of the battle.[36]

Newspapers reported the battle and in Boston the following account was published.

> BOSTON Feb. 7. Friday last an Express came in from the Westward, and brought Advice, that toward the latter end of last Month, the Captains Rogers and Speakman, with 70 Men, marched out from Fort Edward, near Lake George, on the Discovery, and between Ticonderoga and an advanced Fort of the French, met with 6 sleds with Provisions, drove by eight Frenchmen, who our People made Prisoners, and were on their return home; but the French having got Intelligence of this Affair, sent out 200 Men after them, who attack'd our Party about nine o'Clock in the Morning, and the conflict continued very fierce till the Evening, when the French drew off and left our People the Field of Battle. 'Tis said the French lost 50 or 60 Men, at least, and on our Side Capt. Speakman and his Lieutenant (Kennedy) with 16 others were killed, and Capt. Rogers wounded in several Places, but not dangerously. After the Action, he got safe to Fort Edward, with his wounded Men, and, some say, with fifteen Scalps. This Account however imperfect, is the best we are able to obtain at present. 'Tis said the French were all Regulars.[37]

The British prisoners were turned over to the Indians as slaves and one, Thomas Brown, later provided a detailed account of his ordeal.

> I was born in Charlestown, near Boston, in New England, in 1740, and was apprenticed by my father to Mr. Mark White of Acton. In May, 1756, I enlisted in Major Rogers' Corps of Rangers, in the company commanded by Captain Spikeman. We marched to Albany, where we arrived the first of August, and from there to Fort Edward. I was out on several scouting patrols, on one of which I killed an Indian.

On the eighteenth of January, 1757, we marched on a patrol from Fort William Henry. Major Rogers himself headed us. All of us were volunteers. Coming to the road leading from Ticonderoga to Crown Point, we saw about fifty sleighs on Lake Champlain, which was frozen over. The major thought it proper to attack them and ordered us all-about sixty in number-to lie in ambush. When they were close enough we were ordered to pursue them.

I happened to be near the major when he took the first prisoner, a Frenchman. I singled one out, too, and followed him; some fled one way and some another, but I soon caught up with my man and took him prisoner. We captured seven in all-the rest escaped, some to Crown Point and some to Ticonderoga, where they had come from. When we had brought the prisoners to land, the major questioned them. They informed him that there were thirty-five Indians and five hundred regulars at Ticonderoga.

It was a rainy day, so we made a fire and dried our guns. The major thought it best to return to Fort William Henry by the same path we had come, as the snow was very deep. We marched in Indian file and kept the prisoners in the rear, in case we should be attacked.

We went on in this order about a mile and a half. As we were going up a hill, and the center of our line was at the top, a party of about four hundred French and thirty or forty Indians opened fire on us before we had even seen them. The major ordered us to advance. At the first volley from the enemy I received a wound through the body. When I was able, I went to the rear; to the prisoner I had taken on the lake. I knocked him on the head and killed him-we did not want him to give information to the enemy.

As I was going to take shelter behind a large rock, an Indian started up from the other side of it. I threw myself backward into the snow. It was very deep and I sank so low that I broke my snowshoes. In a moment I had pulled 'em off, but I was obliged to let my shoes go with them. One Indian threw his tomahawk at me, and another was just about to seize me, but I was lucky enough to escape and get to the center of our men.

Hiding behind a large pine, I loaded and fired at every opportunity. After I had discharged my gun six or seven times, a ball came and cut it off just at the lock. About half an hour later, I received a shot in my knee. I crawled to the rear again and, as I was turning about, received a shot in my shoulder.

The engagement lasted, as near as I could guess, five and one-half hours and, as I learned afterward, we killed more of the enemy than there were of us. By this time it had grown dark and the firing ceased on both sides. Taking advantage of the night, the major escaped with the well men without telling the wounded his plans, so they could not inform the enemy, who might pursue him before he was out of their reach.[38]

Captain Spikeman, a man named Baker, and myself, all very badly wounded, had made a small fire. After sitting about it for half an hour, we looked round and could not see any of our men. Captain Spikeman called to Major Rogers but received no answer, except from the enemy at some distance. We concluded our people had fled. All our hope of escape vanished now. We were so badly wounded that we could not travel; I could just barely walk, the others could scarcely move. We decided to surrender to the French.

Just as we came to this decision I saw an Indian coming towards us over a small stream that separated us from the enemy. I crawled away from the fire so that I could not be seen, though I could see what happened there. The Indian came to Captain Spikeman, who was not able to resist, and stripped him and scalped him alive. Baker, who was lying by the captain, pulled out his knife to stab himself. But the Indian prevented him and carried him away.

Seeing this frightful tragedy, I made up my mind to crawl into the woods if possible and die there of my wounds. But I was not far from Captain Spikeman and he saw me. "For God's sake," he begged me, "give me a tomahawk so I can put an end to my life!"

I refused him, and exhorted him as well as I could to pray, as he could not live many minutes in that deplorable condition on the frozen ground, covered with snow. He asked me to let his wife know if I lived to get home — the dreadful death he died.

I traveled on as well as I could. As I was creeping along, I found one of our people dead. I pulled off his stockings-he had no shoes- and put them on my own legs. By this time the enemy had made a fire and had a large number of sentries out on the Rangers' path. I was obliged to creep completely round them before I could get into the path again. Just before I came to it I saw a Frenchman behind a tree. He was within ten yards of me, but the fire was shining right on him and prevented him from seeing me. About every quarter of an hour they cried out in

French, "All is well!" While the man that was so near me was calling out, I took the opportunity to creep away, so that he did not hear me and I got back into our path.

I had no shoes, and the snow and cold put my feet into such pain that I soon could go on no longer. I sat down by a brook and wrapped my feet in my blanket. But my body became very cold from sitting still. I got up and crawled along in this miserable condition the rest of the night. The next day, about eleven o'clock, I heard the shouts of Indians behind me and I supposed they had seen me. Within a few minutes four of them came running towards me. I threw off my blanket, and fear and dread quickened my pace for a while. But I had lost so much blood from my wounds that my strength soon gave out.

When the Indians were within ten or fifteen yards they cocked their guns and called me to stop. I refused, hoping they would fire and kill me on the spot; I preferred this to the terrible death Captain Spikeman had died.

The savages soon came up with me, but instead of scalping me they took me by the neck and kissed me. On searching my pockets they found some money. They were so fond of it that they almost killed me in trying to see who could get the most. Then they took some dry leaves and put them into my wounds, and turned about and ordered me to follow them.

When we came near the main body of the enemy the Indians gave a live-shout, as they call it when they bring in a prisoner alive (different from the shout they give when they bring in scalps, which they call a dead-shout). The other Indians ran to meet us. One of them struck me across the side with a cutlass; he cut through my clothes, but did not touch my flesh. Others ran against me with their heads. I asked if there was an interpreter among them. "I am one," a Frenchman cried. "Is this the way you treat your prisoners-let them be cut and beaten to pieces by the Indians?" I asked. The interpreter told me to come to him, but the Indians would not let me-one held me by one arm and another by the other. A difference arose among the four Indians that had captured me and they began to fight. Seeing this, their commanding officer came and took me away. He brought me to the interpreter. This fellow drew his sword and pointed it to my breast. "Tell the truth," he ordered, "or I will run you through. How many men are in your scouting party?" fifty," I told him.

"Where did they go?" "You have so many men that I suppose you can tell better than I," I replied. "You tell me wrong," he said. I know of more than one of your men that were slain were that many officers," he said, and he led me to a body. Lieutenant Kennedy. I saw that he had been severely tomahawked by the Indians. The interpreter asked me if he was an officer and I told him he was a lieutenant. Then he took me to another, who I told him was an ensign. From them he led me to Captain Spikeman, who was lying in the place I had left him. The Indians had cut off his head and fixed it on a pole.

I begged for a pair of shoes and something to eat. The interpreter told me I should have what I needed when I got to Ticonderoga, which was only a mile and a quarter off, and then delivered me to the four Indians who had captured me. The Indians gave me a piece of bread and put a pair of shoes on my feet.

About this time Robert Baker, mentioned above, was brought where I was. Though we were in such a distressed condition we were extremely glad to see each other. He told me of five other Rangers that had been taken prisoner.

Now we were ordered to march on toward Ticonderoga. Baker replied that he could not walk. An Indian pushed him forward, but he could not go, and he sat down and cried. At this, an Indian took him by the hair and was going to kill him with his tomahawk. I was moved with pity for him. Weak as I was, I took his arms over my shoulders and was able to get him to the fort.

Upon our arrival we were immediately sent to the guardhouse. About half an hour later we were brought before the commanding officer. He questioned us separately through his interpreter and then sent us back to the guardhouse. The interpreter came and told us that we were to be hanged the next day because we had killed the seven prisoners we had taken on the lake. Afterwards he was so kind as to tell us this was done only to terrify us.

About an hour later a doctor and his mate came and dressed our wounds, and the commanding officer sent us a quart of claret. We lay on the floor without blankets all night.

The next day I was put into the hospital. I remained here till the nineteenth of February, when the Indians insisted on having me to bring to their home and broke into the hospital. But the sentinel called the guard and turned them out. After this the commanding officer persuaded them to let me stay till the first of March. By that time I was able to walk about the fort and I was quartered with the interpreter.

One day, while I was in the interpreter's lodging, ten or twelve Indians came in with scalps they had taken, to have a war dance. They set me on the floor, put seven of the scalps on my head, and danced round me. When the dance was over they lifted me up in triumph. After they put me down, I went and stood by the door. Suddenly two of the Indians began to dance a live-dance, and one of them threw a tomahawk at me. Fortunately I had been watching him and I dodged the weapon.

I lived with the interpreter till the first of March, when General Rigaud came to the fort with about sixteen hundred men in order to make an attack on Fort William Henry. Their plan was to scale the walls and I saw them making scaling ladders for this purpose. The day before they marched the general sent for me. "Young man," he said, "you are a likely fellow. It's a pity you should live with such an ignorant people as the English. You had better live with me." I told him I was willing to live with him. "You shall," he answered, "and go with me wherever I go." "Perhaps you will have me go to war with you." "That is just the thing I had in mind. I want you to guide me to Fort William Henry and show me where I can scale the walls." I told him I was sorry that a gentleman should ask such a thing of a youth, or try to draw him away from his duty. He said that he would give me seven thousand livres on his return. But I replied that I was not to be bought with money, to be a traitor to my country and help in destroying my friends. He smiled. "In war you must not even show consideration for your father or mother."

When he found that he could not persuade me with all the alluring promises he had made, he ordered me back to the fort. Then he had two other prisoners brought before him. To them he made the same proposals he had to me, and they consented.

The next day I went into the room where these men were and asked them if they had been with the general. They said they had, and that they were to have seven thousand livres apiece as a reward for their services. "Is that the value of your fathers and mothers, and of your country?" I asked them. "We are obliged to go."

"The general cannot force you. If you take part in this

attack, you had better not return among your own people. If you do, and Baker and I live to get home, we will do everything we can to see you hanged."

At this time a smith came and put irons on my feet. But the general gave each of those two men a blanket, a pair of stockings and shoes. They were taken out of the guardhouse and marched with the French as guides.

The general did not succeed. He only burnt our bateaux, etc., and returned to Ticonderoga. Nor did the two poor fellows ever have their reward. Instead, they were sent to the guardhouse and put in irons.

Soon after this I was taken out of irons and went to live with the interpreter again. On the twenty-seventh of March the Indians came and took me with them, to go to Montreal. They tied my arms with a rope and set me to draw a large sled loaded with provisions. By the time we got to Crown Point I was so lame that I could not walk. The Indians went ashore and built a fire, and then told me I must dance. I obeyed rather than be killed.

When we set out again I knew I could not draw the sled much further and I did not know how to get rid of it. A strange fancy came into my head. I invited three squaws to sit on my sled and then I pleasantly told them I wished I was able to draw 'em.

All this delighted the Indians. They freed me of the sled and gave it to other prisoners. They stripped me of all my clothes and gave me a blanket. And the next morning they cut off my hair and painted me like one of themselves. With needles and Indian ink they pricked on the back of my hand the form of one of the scaling ladders which the French had made to carry to Fort William Henry. I understood they were vexed with the French because of their failure to capture it. We traveled about nine miles on Lake Champlain. When the sun was two hours high we stopped and the Indians made a fire. Then they took one of the prisoners that had not been wounded, and were going to cut off his hair as they had done mine. He foolishly resisted them, so they prepared to burn him. But the commanding officer prevented it at this time. However, the next night they made a fire, stripped him and tied him to a stake. The squaws cut pieces of pine, like skewers, and thrust them into his flesh, and set them on fire. Then the Indians began to whoop and dance round him. My captors ordered me to do the same. Love of life obliged me to obey, for

I could expect no better treatment if I refused. With a bitter and heavy heart I pretended that I was merry. They cut the poor man's cords, and made him run backwards and forwards. I heard him cry to heaven for mercy. Finally, in extreme anguish and pain, he pitched himself into the flames and died.

From there we traveled without anything worthy of notice happening till we came to an Indian town about twenty miles from Montreal. When we were about a gun's shot from the town the Indians gave as many live-shouts as they had prisoners and as many dead-shouts as they had scalps. The men and women came out to meet us and stripped me naked. After this they pointed to a wigwam and told me to run to it. They beat me with sticks and stones all along the way. Next day we reached Montreal, where I was brought before Governor Vaudreuil and questioned. Afterwards I was taken into a French merchant's house.[39] [Brown was later freed and returned to his home after serving nearly two years in slavery.]

Thomas Brown

Francois-Pierre de Rigaud, de. Vaudreuil (1703-1779) (Library of Congress)

British Defeat at Fort William Henry – August 1757

Lord Loudoun arrived to take command of British forces in America after the death of General Braddock. Britain planned to take Quebec. To do that, the British planned to first target Louisbourg, but this would free up French forces on the Saint Lawrence since they were too far to affect an attack on Louisbourg. To protect the frontier, the British placed General Daniel Webb in command of 2,000 regulars and the colonies would provide another 5,000 militia. Fort William Henry and the French fortress of Carillon were only a few days apart using the waterway of Lake George. The French had not been idle. Montcalm guessed that the British might target Louisbourg and this would give him an opportunity to deal with Fort William Henry. In March 1757, a French force moved on Fort William Henry and laid siege to it destroying watercraft and outbuilding before withdrawing. By summer the French had built up a force of 8,000 troops at Carillon including Indians that they had difficulty in controlling. Webb responded by reinforcing Fort William Henry with a thousand troops raising the garrison strength to 2,500. Many of these were ill with small pox. On 30 July the French moved on Fort William Henry. Montcalm called upon the British commander, Colonel George Monro to surrender and he refused. The French laid siege to the Fort and cannon fire breached the walls with little damage done by the British return fire. On 7 August Montcalm again called upon Monro to surrender. The terms were agreed and allowed the British to withdraw to Fort Edward carrying arms and one cannon without any ammunition. Those who surrendered agreed to refrain from fighting for 18 months. Montcalm endeavored to make his Indian allies including the Abenaki understand the terms without success. They had already started butchering the British sick and wounded. The massacre of the defenseless soldiers, women and children went on for hours while the French made efforts to stop the bloodshed without success. The estimates of those killed, wounded or enslaved by the Indians run from 200 to 1,500. A newspaper in Boston reported the event.

> Boston, Aug. 15th
> Yesterday an Express arrived here from Albany, which Place left last Thursday Noon, with the Following Account, viz.
>
> After a most gallant and obstinate Defence made by the Garrison at Fort William-Henry, and in the Lines under the Command of Lieutenant Monroe, and Lieut. Col. Young second in Command; after all their Ammunition was expended, and most of their Cannon and Mortars burst, the brave Officers and Soldiers were forced to submit to Numbers (the French Army estimated to be 12,000 Regulars, Indians and Canadians, and were well served with a Train of Artillery) But such was their superior Spirit, that they would accept of no other Articles of Capitulation, but the very honourable Terms of Marching off the whole Garrison upon Parole, and not to bear Arms under eighteen Months. The French did not show that true Vigour and might be expected from the Superiority of Numbers; but did exert every bad one by way-laying the defenceless Garrison after the French Guard had left them, by Scalping great many, striping all the Officers, and other Acts of Cruelty: so that the brave Col. Monroe came in Stript at the Head of his Garrison to Fort Edward. Fort Edward was not yet invested on the 11th in the Morning; and if our Reinforcements do get up Time enough to General Webb, he will hope to make a Stand there: Lieut. Col. Young is Wounded.[40]

After the massacre, most of the Indians headed home and Montcalm was later successful in obtaining the release of 500 of the people seized by the Indians. He did not follow up with an attack on Fort Edward due to confusion caused by the massacre and the departure of his Indian allies. When he learned of the French movements, William Johnson moved to reinforce Fort Edward and he arrived there on 6 August. These reinforcements were not needed since Fort Edward was no longer threatened.

The fall of Fort William Henry had consequences. General Webb was recalled for his actions or perhaps the lack of them. Johnson called him a coward. Lord Loudoun was recalled, primarily for his failure to take Louisbourg. He was replaced by General Abercromby. Colonel Munro died in November 1757 of apoplexy. James Fenimore Cooper wrote a book about it, a classic, *The Last of the Mohicans*. This was a fictional account. There was no punishment of the Indians until two years later when Rogers' Rangers attacked the Abenaki. There are unknowns. The exact number of British butchered by the Indians is not known. The British were occasionally accused of using germ warfare on the Indians, i.e., small pox to which Indians were highly susceptible. More commonly, the Indian small pox epidemics were caused by contact with white small pox victims such as those the Indians butchered at Fort William Henry and prisoners taken by the Indians.

> Disease, which Jonathan Carver [the explorer] saw as God's revenge on France's Indian allies for the killings, had been much less partisan. Rural Americans who had not been inoculated were vulnerable to smallpox, which thrived with armies and was one of several deadly diseases in urban prisons. A few American troops who had been at Fort William Henry, such as ranger captain Richard Rogers, whose body was reportedly dug up and scalped by unsuspecting Indians, had died of the disease before the siege began. During the fighting, smallpox and gunfire were lethal allies challenging English life and morale. At least one uncaptured New Hampshire soldier died of smallpox on his way home. This epidemic, originating in Canada in 1755, had still been rampant enough early in 1757 to deter some Indian allies from joining the French expedition. At least twenty-seven parolees either survived an attack of the disease in Canada or showed symptoms on their passage from Quebec to Halifax. Smallpox and other diseases probably killed most of the forty prisoners who are thought to have died in Canada and France, and likely killed some of the fifty-three last heard of while in Canadian or French custody.[41]

Any contact between whites and Indians could lead to smallpox. Indian prisoners captured by Robert Rogers often died from smallpox such as some reported by the press.

> New York Jan 28. By several persons who come to town last week from Albany, we learn that all was quiet and well at the several fortresses of Niagara, Crown-Point, &c. That Maj. Rogers was returned from New-York having left a young Indian Lad (one of the prisoners he bro't off from St. Francois) to be put to school to be instructed in English language: ----- That the two girls which he also bro't off: died lately with the small-pox at Albany: These children it is said, were relatives of Mrs. Williams, who was taken captive when in her infancy, and educated and married in Canada.[42]

Mutiny on Rogers' Island – 6 December 1757

The Americans are in general the dirtiest, most contemptible cowardly dogs that you can conceive. There is no depending upon 'em in action. They fall down dead in their own dirt and desert by battalions, officers and all. Such rascals as those are rather an incumbrance than any real strength to an army.[43]

James Wolfe, 20 May 1758

The Hudson River in December South of Rogers' Island (Author)

Rogers' Island is located in the Hudson River near Fort Edward and on 6 December 1757 it was bitter cold, as usual. Corporal punishment for such offenses as sleeping on guard duty flourished on Rogers' Island. The frequency of floggings and other punishments rankled the troops. Earlier that year colonial and British troops were merged under the same rules and articles of war. This meant that the colonials including the rangers were now subject to the same corporal punishments as the British soldiers. Punishments such as running the gauntlet through thirty or more soldiers wielding whips were imposed for offenses such as sleeping on guard duty. Riding the wooden horse was used in which a transgressor was placed astride an elevated horizontal tree trunk with muskets hanging from his legs. The weight proved a source of excruciating pain and often dislocated joints. Flogging was commonly used for lesser offenses such as sitting down while on guard duty, drunkenness, cheating at cards, and similar offenses.[44]

The British loss at Fort William Henry added to the discontent, since the rangers blamed the British regulars and commanders for the loss and viewed them with contempt. The mutiny was touched off by the flogging of two rangers for illegally procuring rum, something commonly done by soldiers. Why these two rangers were singled out is unknown. Some of the troops probably after consuming their illegally procured rum spilled out of their huts and headed for the guardhouse to free all prisoners confined therein. A riot ensued when the Officer of the Guard threatened to shoot any ranger who touched the guardhouse. The shouts and jeers of the crowd were so loud that they carried across the snow to Fort Edward where the commander, Colonel Haviland, ordered an officer to Rogers' Island to investigate. After reporting the melee, the officer returned to Robert Rogers with orders from Haviland to send six ringleaders over to Fort Edward for interrogation. Rogers complied. What followed was a long delay while Rogers was out on a mission and he asked General Abercromby to intervene and direct the release of the six mutineers. Abercromby recognized the value of the rangers and in view of Rogers recent successes put an end to the affair. When Rogers return to Fort Edward on 25 January 1758, the mutineers were released to him and this ended the incident.[45]

The Battle on Snowshoes – 13 March 1758

Mary Cochrane Rogers, the Great-Great-Granddaughter of Robert Rogers provided a narrative of this battle based on the Journal of Robert Rogers.

Lake George was frozen and the snow was four feet deep in the woods, when on March 10, 1758, Colonel Haviland, commanding at Fort Edward, sent Major Rogers with one hundred and eighty men to reconnoitre the French position at Carillon. Rogers and his Rangers marched from Fort Edward in snow shoes to the half-way brook, in the road leading to Lake George, and there encamped the first night.

On the 11th they proceeded as far as the First Narrows on Lake George and encamped that evening on the east side of the lake. At sunrise of the 12th they marched from their encampment. When they had gone some three miles, the Major saw a dog running across the lake. Thinking that the Indians might be lying in ambush, he sent a detachment to reconnoitre the island. None, however, could be seen. To prevent the enemy from discovering his force, Rogers halted at Sabbath-Day Point, on the west side of the lake. From the hills he looked northward over the lake with his perspective glass, but could see no signs of French or Indians. As soon as it was dark the party advanced down the lake. Lieutenant Phillips and fifteen men, laying aside their snow shoes and putting on skates, glided down the lake, as an advanced guard. The main body, flanked on the left by Ensign Ross, marched under the west shore. It was a very dark night and the band of rugged foresters kept close together to prevent separation. In this manner they continued their silent march close to the mountains fringing the lake until within eight miles of the French advanced guards, when they were in- formed by Lieutenant Phillips, who had hastened back, that a fire had been discovered in the woods on the east shore.

The Rangers, after hiding their sleighs and packs in a thicket, marched to attack the enemy's encampment, but when they reached the place no fires were to be seen.

They did not know that the French had discovered their advanced guard and, putting out their fire, had carried the intelligence to Ticonderoga. The Rangers then returned to their packs and there lay the remainder of the night without fire, so that no column of blue smoke would reveal their hiding place. At sunrise of the 13th the Rangers left the lake and on snow shoes struck into the woods on the west side, keeping on the back of the mountains that overlooked the French advanced guards.

They halted at noon at a point nearly west of the mountain- that from that day was to bear the name of Rogers – and some two miles from the French lines. · Little did they know what that tragic afternoon held in store for them? Here they refreshed themselves until 3 o'clock, that the day scout from the fort might return before they advanced, since the Major intended at night to ambuscade some of the roads in order to trap the enemy in the morning.

Once more they began their toilsome march, one division headed by Major Rogers, the other by Captain Buckley; a rivulet at a small distance was on their left, and a steep mountain on their right. They kept well to the mountain, for the Major thought that the enemy would travel on the ice of the rivulet since it was very bad travelling on snow shoes. When they had gone a mile and a half a scout from the front told Rogers that the enemy was approaching on the bed of the frozen stream,-ninety-six of them-*chiefly savages. The Rangers, concealed by the bank of the rivulet,* immediately laid an ambush, gave the first fire and killed above forty Indians whom they scalped on the spot. The rest retreated, followed by about one-half of the Rangers, who were exulting over their victory, only to be suddenly confronted by more than six hundred Canadians and Indians fresh from Fort Ticonderoga, under Durantaye and Langry, French officers of reputation, who were fully prepared to meet four hundred Rangers, of whose movements they had been apprized both by the prisoner taken and by the deserter from Putnam's men. Rogers ordered a retreat, which he gained at the expense of fifty men killed; the remainder he rallied and drew up in good order. They fought with such intrepidity and bravery that they obliged the enemy "tho seven to one in number," to retreat a second time, but Rogers had not sufficient numbers to follow up the advantage. The enemy then rallied and, recovering their ground, fought with great tenacity and determination, but were so warmly received that they were put to rout the third time. Finding the Rogers party so much inferior to themselves in number, the enemy again rallied and renewed the fight with vigor for some time. A body of two hundred Indians were now discovered going up the mountain on the right in order to gain the rear of the Rangers. Lieutenant Phillips with eighteen men gained the first possession and beat them back. Lieutenant Crafton with fifteen men stopped the French on the left from gaining the other part of the mountain. Two gentlemen volunteers hastened up and supported him with great bravery. The enemy now pushed so closely on the front that the combatants were often not twenty yards apart, and sometimes were mixed together. Lieutenant Phillips, surrounded by three hundred Indians, surrendered under promise of good quarter, but a few minutes later he and his whole party were tied to trees and hacked to death in a most barbarous manner, The savages maddened, it is said, by the sight of a scalp they, found in the breast of a man's hunting frock, revenged themselves on their victims by holding up their scalps. The Rangers were now broken and put to flight, each man for himself, while the Indians, closely pursuing, took several prisoners.

My great-great-grandfather in his modest narrative does not mention his own hairbreadth escape. The Rangers, when put to flight, retreated in the best manner possible. Rogers was singled out by the French; the Indians, closely pursuing, ran him up the steep mountain then known as Bald Mountain, since Rogers Rock, to its face, and there on the brow of the precipice he threw away his knapsack and clothes together with his commission. There was but one chance for his life, and death was preferable to capture and torture by the savages.

Slowly the sun is setting over the mountain tops, gilding the lake below, as down the face of the precipitous rock for more than a thousand feet he slides in his snow shoes to the frozen lake below, and there, quickly changing his snow shoes for skates, glides over the vast white desert. Scarcely had he disappeared from sight when the foremost warrior reached the cliff sure of his prey-"No Rogers!" There were his tracks! Other warriors came running up to the cliff sure of the prize – Rogers' scalp – for the enemy dreaded him, and with reason-and gazed upon his tracks.

Soon a rapidly receding form on the ice below attracted their notice, and the baffled savages, seeing that the famous Ranger had safely effected the perilous descent, gave up the chase fully persuaded that Rogers was under the protection of the Great Spirit. The Indians have a superstition, that the witches or evil spirits haunt this place, and seizing upon the spirits of bad Indians, on their way to the happy hunting grounds, slide down the precipitous cliff with them into the lake where they are drowned. Atalapose is their word for a sliding place.

During the one and one half hours of battle the Rangers lost eight officers and more than one hundred privates killed on the spot. The enemy lost one hundred and fifty killed and some one hundred and fifty wounded, mostly Indians. Was Colonel Haviland as indifferent and shortsighted as to send Robert Rogers with his brave Rangers to meet this impossible situation at such a great loss of life, or was he influenced by improper motives? Evidently Rogers's suspicions were awakened, for the clause, "but my commander doubtless had his reasons, and is able to vindicate his own conduct," is italicized in his journal.

This is what Major General John Stark, the friend and companion of Rogers says, though not in the engagement, of Colonel Haviland's act: "This officer was the same who sent him (Rogers) out in March, 1758, with a small force, when he knew a superior one lay in wait for him. He was one of those sort of men who manage to escape public censure, let them do what they will. He ought to have been cashiered for his conduct on that occasion. He was one of the many British officers who were meanly jealous of the daring achievements of their brave American comrades, but for whose intrepidity and arduous services, all the British armies, sent to America during the seven years' war would have effected little toward the conquest of Canada." Rogers was saved by a miracle and by his own daring. Thus ended his brave but unfortunate battle on snow shoes.

General Montcalm in a letter dated less than a month after the encounter, says: "Our Indians would give no quarter; they have brought back one hundred and forty-six scalps."
We cannot with certainty say what Rogers, at this time twenty-six years of age, might have done had he had four hundred strong- but there is every probability that he would have put the enemy to rout.[46]

Mary Rogers, 1917

In Boston a letter on the battle was published in the press.

BOSTON March 27. Extract of a Letter from Albany, dated March 20.
–Major Rogers has been attack'd by a thousand French and Indians: He had two Hundred Men with him and Ten Officers, one of which he and a Lieutenant and fifty seven Men only escaped. He says he hath killed at least two hundred Men and brought eight Scalps with him.[47]

British Assault on Carillon Repulsed – 8 July 1758

George Augustus Howe (1725-1758) (Library of Congress)

The British were determined to take Carillon and to this end launched an attack with overwhelming forces against the French under General Montcalm. General Abercromby commanded British forces and his deputy was Lord George Augustus Howe, a much more able commander.

> Lord Howe was everything that the stuffy and ineffective Abercromby was not, and British regulars and colonials alike so came to revere him. "Lord Howe was the idol of the army," a provincial carpenter wrote, "in him they placed the utmost confidence." From the few days I had to observe his manner of conducting, it was not extravagant to suppose that every soldier in the army had a personal attachment to him. He frequently came among the carpenters, and his manner was so easy and familiar that you lost all that constraint or diffidence we feel when addressed by our superiors, whose manners are forbidding."[48]

Howe ordered Rogers forward to thoroughly scout Carillon and "discover the enemy's forces in that quarter."[49] Rogers did this and on 5 July 1768 Howe's army took to its boats and sailed north down Lake George to Carillon. Howe and Rogers were in the lead boat. On 6 July the British army was ashore and moving through dense woods when it collided with the French advance guard. Heavy firing broke out and when the smoke cleared the French had fled and Howe was found dead, shot through the chest.

James Abercromby (1706-1781) (Wikipedia)

    Abercromby was now in command and under his leadership, the attack turned into a nightmare. The British force of 15,000 troops attacked one kilometer from Carillon on a slight rise against Montcalm who had 4,000 troops. Abercromby used no artillery preparation. Montcalm's troops were entrenched and no effort was made by the British to flank the position relying instead on a frontal attack with devastating consequences. The British sustained over 2,000 casualties while the French lost less than 1,000. The Battle of Carillon was the bloodiest battle of the French and Indian War. The British returned to Fort Edward. Because of this disaster Abercromby was replaced by General Jeffrey Amherst in September, 1758.[50]

Jeffery Amherst (1717-1797) (Library of Congress)

In Boston, a letter was received and published by the press.

> BOSTON July 17, EXTRACT OF a Letter from Albany dated July 10, 1758.
> Our Army, consisting of 16,000 Men, set off from Fort William Henry the 5th Inst. And landed at the Narrows the 6th in the Morning without any opposition; a large Division with Lord Howe at their Head moved towards the Fort but were met within about two Miles of Ticonderoga, at the Saw-Mill, by a large Body of the Enemy, on which a hot Engagement ensued: at the beginning Lord Howe was shot dead, it is said by a French Officer, who it is said Capt. Henry Piney immediately shot: His Lordship is universally lamented both by the Army and all others. . .
> 'Tis said Major Rogers has taken an Express going from the Fort to Crown-Point, the purport of whose Dispatch was, That the English had landed with a large Army, and that unless they had speedy Reinforcements, the Fort would be able to hold out but a short Time. --- We have now a fair prospect before us of revenging the many bloody Murders committed by our perfidious and Blood thirsty Foes.
> Just as the Courier was setting out off from Albany, he heard there was an Express from the Army, with an Account that Major Rogers had surrounded and taken Prisoners a Party of some 500 French, and 8 Pieces of Cannon --- The Body of the Right Honourable Lord George Viscount Howe, was brought to Albany last Monday. A Letter from the Lake mentions that there were but 25 of our Men killed.[51]

While the Carillon was under attack the Siege of Louisbourg occurred to the north. In order to attack Quebec, the British would need to seize Fortress Louisbourg. Louisbourg would block any attempt by the British to sail up the Saint Lawrence for an attack on Quebec. The loss of Quebec could end the French empire in North America. A massive British naval fleet assembled and departed from Halifax on 29 May 1758. Heavy seas and weather delayed the siege but on 19 June the British opened fire. The siege continued until 26 July when the French surrendered Fortress Louisbourg opening the way for a campaign against Quebec the following year. In Boston the news reported the victory.

> BOSTON Aug. 21. A Letter from Gabbarous-Bay, dated July 29,1758.
> I have now the Pleasure to write you, that Saturday Morning the Grenadiers Guard, under British Colours, upon the Walls of Louisbourg, which is a fine Tune the French has not danced to for some Time; but now the Time for 'em to pay the Fifers. . . . it was well they surrendered as they did, for we had 3 large Batteries of 32 and 24 Pounders just finish'd to open the Night and next Day should have storm'd.[52]

Battle of Fort Anne – 8 August 1758

On 2 August 1758, Rogers was ordered to sweep east to Wood Creek and then turn south, back to Fort Edward. They had ten days of rations. The force of 400 rangers, 150 light infantry, and 100 regulars moved toward Wood Creek. Major Israel Putnam commanded the rear guard. They had camped on the site of Fort Anne, an old fort that had been burned to the ground in 1711. They were seen by Indians who were allied to the French, but the British moved on without event. They returned to Fort Anne and on the morning of August 8 engaged in target shooting unaware that nearby, a French-Canadian-Indian force of 450 under Captain Joseph Marin de la Malgue was passing and heard the shots. Marin set up an ambush and at 7AM Rogers force walked into the trap. Putnam was wounded and several were captured including Lieutenant Worster who took eight bullets, was scalped, but lived to tell the tale.

Rogers sent runners to Fort Edward for help and charged into the fray. At a critical point in the fighting, he shot one Indian at point blank range and screamed "Come up you French dogs . . . fight like men!" In the close quarters of the fighting, everyone heard him and it broke the back of the French ambush. The French fled. Rogers scalped Marin who appeared to be dead. Marin was a serious loss to the French since he was one of their two top partisan leaders. There were many losses among Rogers troops and they returned to Fort Edward rather than pursuing the French. After so many recent losses, this was a needed victory for the British and it was reported in Boston and newspapers in other towns.

> By Courier from Albany arrived last Friday, we have the following Account, That Major Rogers had been sown to South-Bay, and discover'd nothing of the Enemy only two Canoes, which having the start of him got off clear: - - That on his Return to Fort Edward, on Tuesday the first Instant, he was Way-laid by 530

Indians between said Fort and Fort Anne, on which a smart Engagement ensued, which lasted two Hours, when he oblig'd the Enemy to retreat, with the Loss of 72 killed which he Scalp'd (30 of which were Indians) and two Prisoners, one a Frenchman, the other an Indian, which he bro't back to Fort Edward. Roger's Party consisted of about 700 Men, 17 of which were kill'd and 33 missing, among the missing Capt. Putnam, who by a Flag of Truce has sent a Letter to Fort Edward acquainting, that he was a Prisoner at Ticonderoga, but mentions nothing of the Rest.

"Tis tho't a great many of the Enemy were killed as Rogers bro't off all his killed without being scalp'd and buried them.[53]

Israel Putnam (1718-1790) in the War of Independence
(Library of Congress)

British losses were heavy. Francis Parkman reported 49 English fatalities and "more than a hundred" killed of the enemy. Another source put the French total casualties at less than thirty. Putnam was reportedly saved from ritual burning by the Iroquois by intervention of a French officer and a providential thunderstorm. The report of Marin's death was greatly exaggerated. He survived as had Lieutenant Worster.[54]

Carillon (Fort Ticonderoga) Falls to the British – 27 July 1759

The British returned to Carillon in July, 1759. General Jeffrey Amherst advanced with 12,000 troops against General Bourlamaque who had 3,600 troops to defend the fort. For four days British artillery bombarded the fort from 23 to 26 July and on the last day the French spiked their guns, blew up the fort and withdrew to Isle-aux-Noix. The British moved into the fort on 27 July and renamed it Fort Ticonderoga.

The Atrocities

Many brutal murders were committed by the Indian allies of the French. The greatest loss of life occurred at Fort William Henry after it was surrendered by the British to the French and their Indian allies in August 1757. Between 200-1500 British men, women, and children were murdered by the Abenaki and other Indian allies of the French. Father Roubaud who was present at the massacre would also figure in the Saint Francis Raid that followed later in 1759.

> The assembled chiefs did not object to the terms and agreed to restrain their young warriors, but politeness may have been read as acquiescence. Even if these Indians discounted their own earlier rhetoric about eating and drinking enemies, they still claimed the right to pillage the fort and the entrenched camp after the English had left. Stores of war and provisions were, however, to be the property of the Canadian government, and the personal effects of the English officers and men were to be respected. The Indians were free to take what they thought fell between those categories.
> At noon, a French detachment arrived at the gate of the fort, where a brief ceremony of transfer was held, and the 450 English duty soldiers marched off to their entrenched camp. At

this point, a number of Indians ran in through the gate and gun embrasures in search of their promised booty. Members of the retreating garrison heard cries of "Murder" and "Help" from within the fort, where thirty sick and forty severely wounded had remained behind, some in the comparatively well-protected by isolated casements under the ramparts. Pere Roubaud, who did not explain how a missionary came to be inside the fort so quickly, reported that a few of these unfortunate English were attacked and killed. Although other Indians scoured the fort without much success, Roubaud saw one warrior who "carried in his hand a human head, from which trickled streams of blood, and which he displayed as the most splendid prize that he could have secured." Roubaud, writing later, presented this as a foretaste of barbarities to come. Some of the seriously wounded, including Captain Ormsby, were saved, probably by the forceful intervention of the entering French garrison. Indians watched with suspicion and derision as the English soldiers carried their belongings and as wagons hauled the officers' baggage. The French had some difficulty protecting the military stores and provisions from the Indians. There were complaints that the French took the best for themselves and that the Indians had been deceived by the surrender terms. One English officer heard an Indian chief "violently accuse the French general with being false and a liar to them, that he had promised them the plunder of the English, and they would have it." Anger would be intensified by the envy directed at those few warriors who had a trophy to prove they had been active in a great battle. The English, now gathered in the adjoining camp they had defended so well, gained no clear picture of what had happened in the fort, but could imagine.

Some Indians had already been inside the English entrenched camp before the capitulation was signed, and it is unlikely that they had been at Montcalm's council of chiefs or had heard the terms explained by them. At noon, Montcalm had posted a guard of two hundred French regulars inside the camp. Monro ordered the destruction of all liquor in the camp, but reports vary on how thoroughly and by what methods the liquor disappeared. That afternoon, English officers entertained their French counterparts with an impressive spread of delicacies, served with wine and beer. Indians were inside the camp throughout the afternoon, acquiring what they could and being considered troublesome and dishonorable thieves by both the English and the French. There was persistent difficulty about the English officers' baggage. European officers carried what any warrior would have regarded as an enormous amount of personal baggage. Some American officers, judging from their claimed losses, patronized the Albany clothiers in order to assert their status with multiple uniforms of velvets and silks in scarlet, blue, or green, topped with lace-trimmed beaver hats. Even warriors who exactly understood the terms of the surrender could presume that much legitimate booty was being unfairly protected as personal belongings. Some English officers offered money to Indians to leave their belongings alone. Other confrontations turned nasty, and Montcalm was called to settle matters. He used "entreaties, threats, flattery, conferences with chiefs, the intervention of officers and interpreters who have any authority with these barbarians." He left for his own camp about nine o'clock that night, after the Indians had been cleared from the camp. It was announced that the parolees would leave the camp at first light, but this display of French confidence masked well-founded fears.[55]

The press was slow to report details of the massacre since in many cases such as the *New York Gazette*, printers had been called up for militia duty.[56]

> When the New York papers resumed publication, their conflicting reports included a major story printed by government order. This was the most extensive newspaper version of the slaughter, offered in the most graphic prose. "Indian blood hounds" were said to have killed and scalped many officers and men, and killed or captured the blacks and Indians. "The throats of most, if not all the women, were cut, their bellies ript open, their bowels torn out and thrown upon the faces of their dead and dying bodies: and, it is said, that all their women were murdered in one way or another." The gruesome details gathered, invented, or improved on by this "authority" included the view that all the children had been

taken by the heels and had their brains dashed out against stones or trees. Readers were reminded of the murder of the wounded in Braddock's army and in the defeated garrison at Oswego, and were told that the survivors of Parker's expedition were not likely to be spared. Nor were readers to forget the innocent who were daily killed and captured along the frontier. The tirade ended by urging that no French prisoners be taken, no capitulations negotiated, and no quarter asked. Every armed man was to sell his life as dearly as he could. This panicked version of the Fort William Henry tragedy survived in American legend.[57]

Indian murdering was later summarized by the press in Boston.

. . . St. Francois Indians, both in this and former wars, have been severest savages to the frontier settlements of the Massachusetts and New-Hampshire, than any other whatsoever; and have been guilty of more inhumanities, bloodshed and murdering, than perhaps any tribe on the continent: providence never design'd that those bloodthirsty heathen should go down to the grave in peace.[58]

The Indian atrocities were one of the factors that led to the most famous raid of the war described in the following chapter.

2. The Saint Francis Raid

Remember the barbarities that have been committed by the enemy's Indian scoundrels on every occasion, where they had an opportunity of showing their infamous cruelties on the King's subjects, which they have done without mercy. Take your revenge, but don't forget . . . it is my orders that no women or children are killed or hurt.[1]

Lord Jeffrey Amherst

The Kennedy Party

Jeffery Amherst took command of British forces in 1758 after successfully conquering the French fortress of Louisbourg. An attack on Quebec that could end the war was planned. General James Wolfe was sent on the Quebec expedition that started on 1 May 1759. Once Wolfe was dispatched, Amherst was eager to know progress since other attacks were planned that relied on Wolfe's success. Wolfe's messages back to Amherst were intercepted and tension mounted over the fate of Wolfe.

James Wolfe (1727-1759) (Library of Congress)

Messengers sent to Wolfe took a long route that was taking too much time. Captain Quinton Kennedy of the 17th Foot stepped forward and volunteered to go to Wolfe by a faster route than had been used by others. Amherst quickly accepted. Kennedy was well qualified for the task. He was cool under fire and had participated in successful raids in the wilderness. Like Rogers, readers on both sides of the Atlantic followed newspaper accounts of his exploits. The following account appeared in the Boston press on 27 August 1759.

> Extract of a Letter from Crown Point Aug. 10. "Capt. Kennedy with a few Indians, has taken in Hand to go hence, thro' the Woods to Quebec. They went off Yesterday, and in their Way going down the Side of the Lake saw two Sloops and a Schooner about 20 Miles from this Place, one of the Sloops carrying 24 Guns; whereupon Captain Kennedy immediately sent one of his Men back to inform General Amherst thereof; and the General upon receiving the Advice, directly order's Gages' Light Infantry, Roger's Rangers, and a Company of Grenadiers off, to seek the enemy, in Whaleboats, one of the Reddoes and three Row-Gallies. This Morning another Reddoe went off, and 300 Men more; but we have not yet heard from the first Division."[2]

In August 1759, Kennedy's party, that included Stockbridge, Indians left Crown Point to find Wolfe.[3] Kennedy would travel via the Saint Francis Abenaki village under a flag of truce claiming to be emissaries sent to negotiate a prisoner exchange. The Kennedy group was intercepted by a party of Abenaki Indians guarding the northern end of Lake Champlain. The Kennedy party was taken as prisoners of war and turned over to the French. Amherst was infuriated by this breech of international etiquette and vowed revenge against ". . . the enemy's Indian scoundrels." He called in Rogers on 12 September 1759 and ordered him to "Take Revenge."[4] This was good news for the rangers. They had scores to settle. Amherst's specific instructions to Major Robert Rogers, sent from his camp at Crown Point on September 13, 1759, read as follows:

You are this night to set out with the detachment as ordered yesterday, viz. of 200 men, which you will take under your command, and proceed to Misisquey [Missisquoi] Bay, from whence you will march and attack the enemy's settlement on the south-side of the river St. Lawrence, in such a manner as you shall judge most effectual to disgrace the enemy, and for the success and honour of his Majesty's arms. Remember the barbarities that have been committed by the enemy's Indian scoundrels on every occasion, where they had an opportunity of showing their infamous cruelties on the King's subjects, which they have done without mercy. Take your revenge, but don't forget that tho' those villains have dastardly and promiscuously murdered the women and children of all ages, it is my orders that no women or children are killed or hurt. When you have executed your intended service, you will return with your detachment to camp or join me wherever the army may be. Your's, &c.[5]

Jeffrey Amherst

Newspapers reported the Kennedy affair after the battle of Quebec was over. The report supported the myth that Kennedy was on a peace mission.

BOSTON Feb. 11. We are credibly informed, that notwithstanding the many reports that have been spread some Time ago of Capt. Kennedy's being sent by Gen. Amherst with an Express to General Wolfe, that it was not so, but that he was sent a Flag of Truce to the Indian Town of St. Francis, with overtures of Peace, proposed to them by Gen. Amherst, and try to bring them over to English Interest: But they, contrary to all the Rules of War, (even the Savages themselves have heretofore held Flags of Truce sacred) immediately on his arrival, seized Capt. Kennedy, and the few others that were with him, and carried them Prisoners to Montreal: Intelligence of which afterwards coming to the General's Ears, he was so exasperated against them for their inhumanity, that he immediately propos'd the destruction of their Town to Major Rogers, who willingly undertook the Adventure.[6]

While the proximate cause of the raid was the Kennedy affair, there were other reasons some of which had little to do with the Abenaki tribe. Amherst believed that a clear British victory at Saint Francis would dispel the myth that persisted among the British troops of the invincibility of the Indians in the wilderness that had grown since Braddock's disastrous defeat that had cost two-thirds of his force. Destruction of Saint Francis would also avenge the Indian massacres on the frontier and would reduce Indian raids.[7] A witness described the ambush of a British woodcutting party within sight of their camp on Lake George.

> They killed and scalped six, wounded two, took four prisoner, and only four of the whole party escaped. They showed themselves plainly to the whole army after they got the scalps, gave a hollow *[sic]* and then made off to their bateaux, which were not more than two miles from the head of the lake. A large party was ordered out after them but in vain. They butchered our people in a most shocking manner by cutting pieces of flesh out of their necks, thighs and legs.[8]

Rogers was a favorite of the press.

> NEW-YORK June 16. By the Albany post arrived last night we have advice that the brave Major Rogers has had another brush with the French: He, with 200 Rangers being out on a Scout landed about three miles from Nut-Island, the 4th instant, but were soon attacked by 300 of the enemy, when a smart engagement immediately commenced, and ended greatly to the disadvantage of the French, they being soon obliged to fly, having between 40 and 50 men killed and wounded. The Major brought off three Indian scalps, but had 10 men killed and 9 wounded: Among the former were Capt. Johnson of the Rangers, and Ensign Wood of General Monckton.[9]

Rogers was pleased. For three years he had been petitioning for an attack on the Abenaki who had been attacking colonial settlements.[10] The rangers at Crown Point now had ample forces available since Captain John Stark had just returned from a road building effort in New Hampshire. Eight of Rogers' ten companies would be represented in the raid. David Brewers' Company was at Fort George near Fort William Henry and would not go along. John Stark would not be on the expedition since he and his troops were exhausted from their road building effort. Amherst insisted that a force of rangers remain at Crown Point and John Stark would command them. Rogers would lead a mixed force in the attack on Saint Francis. Of the 200 troops on the campaign, he would have 132 rangers including 24 Stockbridge Indians. The rest would be colonial and regular volunteers.[11]

Saint Francis Village

Saint Francis Village (also known as Odanak) was located at the confluence of the Saint Lawrence and Saint Francis Rivers in the French province of Canada not far from its border with the New Hampshire. By 1759, it was located on a bluff overlooking the Saint Francis River. It is midway between Montreal and Quebec. The original Abenaki homeland included a large part of southeastern Canada, all of present day New Hampshire, all but the southwest corner of Vermont as well as the northeastern part of New York and the northern part of Massachusetts. The Abenaki roamed over this entire area hunting and fishing which may account for the friction that developed between the British settlers and the Indians. Saint Francis was established as a Jesuit mission in the late 1690s where a church dedicated to Saint Francis was built and the Abenaki people were offered protection by the colony of New France. This clearly was not a typical Indian village and it was described as containing European-style homes surrounding a church.

> Odanak or St Francis consisted of sixty framed and windowed houses covered with boards and stone, twelve built in the French style with lofts and cellars and grouped round a square. The rest were log cabins and plank-built dwellings, with unglazed 'windows', some just black holes, others covered with paper on which were painted fish, birds and animals. There was a Jesuit church and, nearby, the Council House, solidly constructed for defence with embrasures and notched musket holes. In the clearings by the houses were cultivated patches of corn, melon and pumpkin.[1]

> Monsieur Franquet, a French engineer who visited the village in 1752, observed that most [of the fifty-one] homes were constructed of squared log timbers covered with lengths of bark or rough-cut boards. At least 12 were one or two-story French-style wood-frame houses with clapboards; 3 houses were built of stone. They were

arranged in rows around a central square, with a church and a large Council House. Simôn Obomsawin's family lived in a two-story French-style wood-frame house.[2]

It had several hundred souls including the Abenaki as well as other tribes. Europeans were also resident either those captured in Indian raids or others who resided there by choice. The village was supported by the French. The Abenaki raided British settlements and in return were rewarded with gold by the French for British prisoners. Gold candelabra and other trinkets were provided by the French for the church. War against the British was a profitable endeavor for the Abenaki, but all good things end and the Abenaki would discover that there was a penalty side of the war.

Rangers Depart Crown Point – 13 September 1759

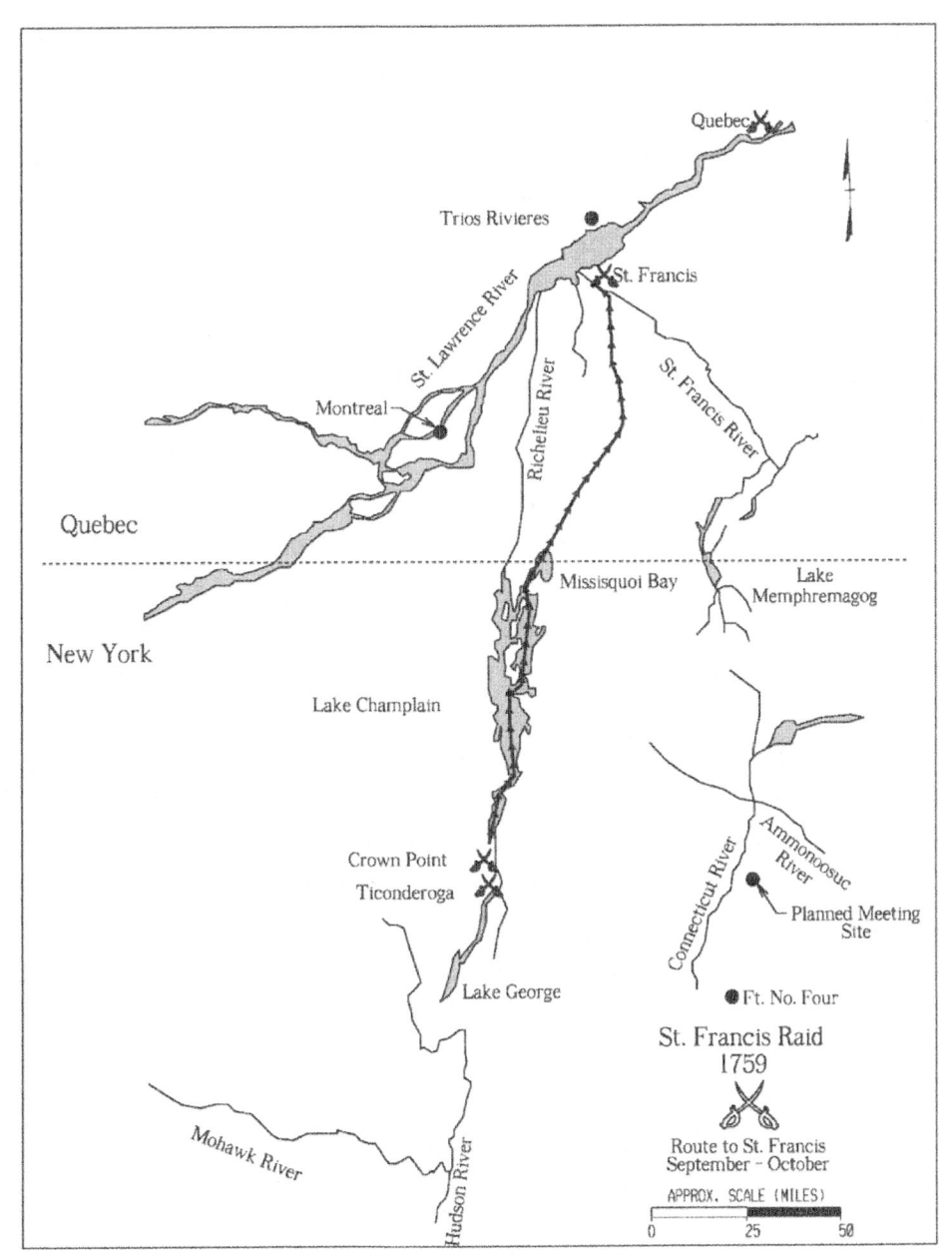

The Route to Saint Francis (Connor Eggleston)

Having received his orders from General Amherst, Rogers assembled his rangers at Crown Point, a straight line distance of 150 miles from the Saint Francis village.[3] The actual distance traveled would be over 200 miles. They would draw rations for thirty days. Rogers would have a mixed force for this raid. In addition to his rangers and others, Mohawk Indians would be on the expedition.[4] Rogers did not trust the Mohawks because they were loyal to Sir William Johnson who wanted a share of the credit for the raid. Amherst ordered him to take the Mohawks anyway. Rogers thought that Amherst had been tricked by Johnson and his misgivings about the Mohawks would be proven as well-founded during the expedition.[5] Rogers would follow a water and land route starting on Lake Champlain at Crown Point to Missisquoi Bay. From there he would move overland to Saint Francis. The water route was the easy part except when he reached the northern lake. Here, the French patrolled with a brigantine, a schooner, gunboats and other ships. The ranger whaleboats were no match for any of these.[6] This would be a very difficult mission for the rangers. The Abenaki knew the terrain and Montreal was near Saint Francis so the French could quickly reinforce the village if they knew of the raid. Once the attack occurred, Rogers could expect a quick reaction from Montreal with troops pouring after him. They were moving into uncharted territory with few reliable guides to chart their course.

Once it was dark, Rogers departed, as a major event was occurring to the north. At Quebec, British General Wolfe had the fortress under siege and in an early morning attack the French were defeated. Both General Wolfe and the French commander General Montcalm were killed in the battle, a great and decisive victory for the British.

Death of General Wolfe at Quebec (Library of Congress)

Word of this did not reach Crown Point until days after Rogers' departure. As a result of the British victory at Quebec, there was movement of French troops toward Lake Champlain searching for any additional British activity. The French did not suspect the raid on Saint Francis at this time. Unrelated to the raid, on 11 September, Ranger Joseph Hopkins made an unsuccessful attempt to burn the new French sloop, the *L'Esturgeon*, at Isle aux Noix. As a result, the French were on alert for further such attacks.[7] Amherst and Rogers held the raid as a closely guarded secret and Amherst circulated rumors as to the destination of the rangers to deceive French spies. The weather was stormy and raining for most of the journey. The rangers occupying seventeen whale boats rowed north from Crown Point on 13 September.

They rowed cautiously to avoid detection and remained within sight of each other stopping frequently to listen intently for any sound of French vessels. Rogers sent scouts overland to look for any French boats and they returned indicating that they had sighted the French a few miles north near the mouth of the Otter River where Lake Champlain narrows a bit. The rangers reached South Otter Bay and its shoals where they spent their second night dragging the boats across the shallows. Scouts saw three French sloops near Diamond Island and the rangers spent that day concealed waiting for the sloops to depart. One sick Stockbridge Indian was sent back to Crown Point.

The Gunpowder Explosion

On the following day disaster struck when Captain Samuel Williams (also spelled Willyamos in some sources), a regular officer, managed to blow himself and several others up in a gunpowder explosion while they were at the Otter River. It was reported as "a keg of gunpowder accidentally took fire."[8] The reason for the explosion remains a mystery. One theory is that the French planted "decoy boats" rigged with explosives to kill any British soldiers who discovered them. Another is that Williams got into an altercation with the Mohawks that ended when they blew a keg of gunpowder.[9] The prevailing theory is the one that blames the "decoy boats". This stemmed from an earlier ranger attempt to blow up a French vessel. To counter future efforts the French rigged several boats with explosives set to explode when tampered with. Lieutenant Campbell in his journal noted. " . . . While I was scouting ye French fleet from ye point with Major Rogers, ye Scot & 1 other from Montgomery's had a very uncommon accident from an explosive boat with Captain Williams. All 3 were badly wd. Capt Williams suffer'd a badly torn hand and arm . . . "[10] Newspapers had a different explanation for Captain Williams' injury.

> BOSTON Oct. 1. By the Courier which came in last Saturday from Albany, we have Accounts, . . . We also hear from Albany, that Major Rogers was gone out on a Scout with 250 Men, and that two Days after he set off one Captain Williams of the Regulars, who went out with Rogers's Party, by some Accident, his Gun went off and tore his Hand and Arm to such a Manner that he with 4 or 5 Men return'd back to Crown-Point, which was the last Account they had received from Rogers, when the Courier left Albany, which was last Tuesday so that we imagine they can be no truth in the Account under the New-York Head, of Rogers's having taken and scalped 200 of the Enemy.[11]

Whatever the cause, Williams was badly burned along with others. This was no loss to Rogers since he did not trust Williams and they were at odds over a disagreement a few months earlier. Lieutenant James William Dunbar replaced Williams as commander of the British regulars. Rogers respected Dunbar.

More bad news followed: two rangers were wounded in an accidental firearms exchange. Next, provincial militia under Captain Butterfield started to report sick. Finally, the Mohawks refused to accomplish their scouting duties and Rogers had his chance to send them home. In all, Rogers lost forty-one men, none to enemy action. The sick, Mohawks, and injured were sent home.[12]

Grand Isle

On 20 September Rogers camped near Grand Isle. It was here that the rangers observed French boats searching for them. The French were methodically searching from cove to cove. It is not clear if the search was based upon solid intelligence of the planned ranger attack at Saint Francis or if it was caution after the loss of Quebec. The rangers waited and remained concealed that day. The miserable weather helped and they were not seen by the French. They continued their journey and reached Missisquoi Bay early on 23 September, ten days after their departure from Crown Point. The boats were hidden with return voyage supplies guarded by two Stockbridge Indians. Rogers issued his instructions "to lie at a distance in sight of the boats and there to stay until I [Rogers] came back, except that [if] the enemy found them; in which case they were with all possible speed to follow my track."[13] On 23 September the rangers with great haste moved overland in the uncharted wilderness northeast toward the Saint Francis village. They had one hundred miles to go carrying two weeks of provisions. They would average nine miles a day. Five days of rations were left with the boats.

Loss of the Boats

Bad luck intervened. A French scouting party found a British oar floating in Lake Champlain and sounded the alarm. Another account indicates that an alert Abenaki heard the faint splash of an oar in the night and reported this to the French Commander at Isle au Noix, General Francois-Charles de Bourlamaque.[14] Whatever the reason, the French launched a thorough search in the area. The next day a larger French force which numbered nearly 400 discovered the boats. The whaleboats had "Rogers' Rangers" painted on the bows and that left no doubt as to the identity of the intruders. This blunder by Rogers has never been explained. Bourlamaque knew that the rangers were heading for either Chambly, Maska, or Saint Francis village, but which one? Bourlamaque covered all possibilities by sending runners to the Governor of Montreal, Francois-Pierre de Rigaud de Vaudreuil and General Francois-Gaston de Levis, now commanding French forces after the fall of Quebec and death of General Montcalm. He also sent a runner to Father Roubaud at Saint Francis.[15] On 1 October a force of 100 French and Abenaki Indians set out from Saint Francis to intercept Rogers.[16]

Most of the whaleboats were destroyed, but the French kept some for their own use. The two Stockbridge rangers left behind to guard the boats moved quickly to find and inform Rogers. Meanwhile, Rogers was moving through difficult swampy terrain when he received word on 25 September from Indian scouts that the boats had been taken. Rogers still had fifty miles to go and his options were not good. He was behind enemy lines and would have no supplies for his return to Crown Point. Further, the French had picked up his trail and were in pursuit. He concluded that the Abenaki had been alerted about his raid. The element of surprise may have disappeared. A force of 200 French were now on Rogers' trail. Rogers summarized in his journal.

> This unlucky circumstance . . . put us in some consternation . . . Being so far advanced in their country, where no reinforcement could possibly relieve me, and where they could be supported by any numbers they pleased, afforded us little hopes of escaping their hands. Our boats being taken, cut off all hope of a retreat by them; besides the loss of our provisions left with them, of which we knew we should have great need at any rate, in case we survived, was a melancholy consideration.[17]
>
> ***Robert Rogers***

Council of War

Rogers shook off his pursuers and held a council of war with his captains. They decided to continue with the mission and would send word back to General Amherst about the loss of the boats. The lamed Lieutenant McMullen and six ailing rangers would return to Crown Point by the most direct route to ask Amherst to send provisions for 150 men to an abandoned fort sixty miles north of Number Four. Rogers knew that they could not make it any further than that point without provisions. Rogers was now down to 153 troops.[18] They would alter their return by heading due south from Saint Francis to Fort Number Four along the Connecticut River. This would avoid any French forces waiting for them at the boats. Bourlamaque had reinforced the forces at the boats to 360.[19] Wherever the rangers were heading, he thought that he would catch them upon their return.

Although lame, McMullen left immediately and reached Crown Point on 3 October after a difficult trek of over 100 miles. This was quite an accomplishment since he and the men with him were sick or lame. After the raid, McMullen would be promoted to captain in recognition of this feat. Amherst ordered Ranger Lieutenant Samuel Stevens to Number Four with instructions that supplies be left at the specified point. Stevens was to wait there for Rogers' or until there was no possibility of his arrival. This last point would cause trouble later.

> Herewith you will receive a letter from me to Mr Bellows at No. 4. . . . Who is thereby directed to furnish you provisions sufficient to victual Major Rogers and his party . . . and with said provisions, and a competent number of men, which Mr Bellows is likewise ordered to furnish you with, to be aiding . . . in conveying them to Wells River. You will proceed thither, and there remain with said party as long as you shall think there is any probability of Major Rogers returning that way.[20]
>
> *Jeffrey Amherst*

Rogers immediately continued from the northern end of Lake Missisquoi toward Saint Francis Village through the most difficult part of their journey. They were now entering a marshy area where there was no firm ground. The constant moisture was causing trench foot, chilblains and fever. They started to lose stragglers. Worse, they did not know if these were losses from accident or from a pursuing enemy. Four had vanished by 3 October and more would disappear as they moved toward Saint Francis. On 4 October they reached the first firm ground since leaving Lake Missisquoi and the following day they hit the Saint Francis River, about forty yards wide at this point. They had to cross and used a human chain to do so. Rogers used the strongest man to anchor the near shore and inched out into the flow to the other side. Once secure, others used the human chain to cross. At the deepest part of the river some of the shorter men found it over their heads. Some were wrenched free from the chain by the current. Men and muskets were lost in the crossing. When the rangers finally emerged from the river, they were on dry ground within a short easy distance from Saint Francis Village. Rogers called the role and found that he was down to 142 troops, five without muskets.[21]

At the same time that McMullen reached Crown Point, Rogers approached Saint Francis village. His move through the swamps threw pursuers off of his trail. After struggling in the swampy bogs the French and Abenaki gave up the chase. Rogers had eluded pursuers and on 3 October Abenaki women washing in the Saint Francis River observed wood chips floating down the river. These may have come from Rogers' Saint Francis River crossing in spite of his effort to leave no trace at the river.[22] He had stopped chopping trees at the river because of the loud noise that this produced.[23] The chips in the river should have caused an alarm, but did not.

The Fight at Saint Francis – 4 October 1759

As the rangers closed in on Saint Francis, they saw smoke from camp fires that led them to the camp and it appeared that the Abenaki remained unaware of Rogers' approach. Rogers reached the camp late on the 3rd of October. Many of the warriors were absent on a hunting expedition. Others were with the French pursuing the rangers. By that time there were as many as 200 Abenaki remaining in the village of an original population of 500.[24] Rogers donned Indian garb and slipped into the camp to reconnoiter. Rogers observed dances going on apparently part of a harvest or wedding celebration, but the reason for the dancing has never been confirmed.[25] Incredibly, the Abenaki appeared unaware of his arrival. They were reeling around in the streets drunk and the noise masked the movement of the rangers. Rogers made a reconnaissance of the village at 8 P.M.[26]

Rogers returned to his troops to organize the attack. He was not the only person to enter the camp that night. A turncoat Mohegan Indian named Samadagwis who was with the rangers slipped in to warn the Abenaki of Rogers' arrival. Some heeded the warning and moved their wives, sick people and children away to a camp several miles from the village.[27] The warriors then returned to fight Rogers.[28] Apparently the rest were too drunk to comprehend what was going on. The celebration had been going on for days and proves beyond any doubt that the Abenaki knew how to celebrate.

By now, Rogers' party was down to 142 troops. At 3 AM on 4 October, Rogers divided his troops into companies and set his best shooters in locations where they could cut off fleeing Abenaki. The troops dropped their knapsacks, fixed bayonets and prepared for the assault.[29] At about 5AM, half an hour before dawn, Rogers launched his attack after surrounding the village.

The Abenaki were caught sleeping after a long night of celebration. The celebrations were so loud that some of the villagers had moved their bedding to an island below the village just to get some sleep.[30] There was no organized defense and it became a slaughter. At this point, the nearest French and Abenaki forces were those that had given up the chase and were now 15-18 miles away at the Yamaska River without any clue as to where the rangers were located.

Over 600 settler scalps, mostly English, were displayed in the village.[31] The rangers were in no mood to grant quarter to anyone as they broke down doors and killed everyone in sight. Amherst's caution against killing women and children was soon forgotten. Buildings were torched and everything was burned except for three storage warehouses that contained corn needed for the trek to Number Four. Captain Ogden was posted at the river to cut off any fleeing Abenaki. It was here that many of the Abenaki casualties occurred. Those who tried to swim were shot as well as those who tried to launch canoes. Rogers had achieved surprise.

Many inhabitants tried to hide in attics in order to escape the rangers and they died in the flames. The church was ransacked for treasure before it was burned. At least one account indicates that a priest would not come out and died as the church burned. The church bell continued to ring as the church burned, adding to the chaos.[32] "By about 6:10 a.m. the firing ceased. Saint Francis was now a smoking ruin, the air thick with smoke and the stench of burning flesh."[33]

As the sun rose, Rogers ordered the rangers to load up on corn and burn what remained of the village. Not all of the warehouse corn was destroyed. Some was left for the Abenaki survivors. This was a mistake.[34] As soon as Rogers departed, the women started grinding corn for their returning warriors. They produced a ration of burnt corn mixed with maple sugar and tallow. This was an ideal ration for life on the trail. It was light-weight and small. Two handfuls mixed with water could sustain a warrior for a day.[35] On the other hand, the rangers packed dried corn on the cob from the warehouses which meant that most of the space and weight in their packs was from the cob. There was no time to be picky. The rangers grabbed what they could as fast as they could in order to escape.

Rogers' report to General Amherst provides additional details.

> Sir,
> The twenty-second day after my departure from Crown Point, I came in sight of the Indian town of St. Francis in the evening, which I discovered from a tree that I climbed, at about three miles distance. Here I halted my party, which now consisted of 142 men, officers included, being reduced to that number by the unhappy accident which befell Capt. Williams, and several since tiring, whom I was obliged to send back. At eight o'clock this evening I left the detachment, and took with me Lieut. Turner and Ensign Avery, and went to reconnoitre the town, which I did to my satisfaction, and found the Indians in a high frolic or dance. I returned to my party at two o'clock, and at three marched it to within five hundred yards of the town, where I lightened the men of their packs, and formed them for the attack. At half an hour before sunrise I surprised the town when they were all fast asleep, on the right, left, and center, which was done with so much alacrity by both the officers and men, that the enemy had not time to recover themselves, or take arms for their own defence, till they were chiefly destroyed, except some few of them who took to the water. About forty of my people pursued them, who destroyed such as attempted to make their escape that way, and sunk both them and their boats. A little after sunrise I set fire to all their houses, except three, in which there was corn, that I reserved for the use of the party.
>
> The fire consumed many of the Indians who had concealed themselves in the cellars and lofts of their houses. About seven o'clock in the morning the affair was completely over, in which time we had killed at least two hundred Indians, and taken twenty of their women and children prisoners, fifteen of whom I let go on their own way, and five I brought with me, viz. two Indian

boys, and three Indian girls. I likewise retook five English captives, which I also took under my care.

When I paraded my detachment, I found I had Capt. Ogden badly wounded in his body, but not so as to hinder him from doing his duty. I had also six men slightly wounded, and one Stockbridge Mohegan Indian [Samadagwis] killed.

I ordered my people to take corn out of the reserved houses for their subsistence home, there being no other provision there; and whilst they were loading themselves I examined the prisoners and captives, who gave the following intelligence: "That a party of 300 French, and some Indians, were about four miles down the river below us; and that our boats were way-laid, which I had reason to believe was true, as they told the exact number, and the place where I left them at: that a party of 200 French and fifteen Indians had, three days before I attacked the town, gone up the river Wigwam Martinique, supposing that was the place I intended to attack;" whereupon I called the officers together, to consult the safety of our return, who were of opinion there was of no other way for us to return with safety, but by No. 4. On Connecticut River.[36]

Robert Rogers

Hard decisions faced the troops: should I load up with corn or treasure such as the gold candlesticks from the church? Some such as Barnes,[37] the prisoner freed during the raid, chose loot and would later regret it. Rogers learned from the few prisoners that were taken that a French force of 400 was expected at Saint Francis the next day.[38] There was no time to lose. They would leave immediately with their loot, as much corn as could be carried and six Abenaki prisoners.[39] While Rogers ordered the troops to load up on corn, not loot, many seized treasure for their own use. Rogers carried back loot to be turned over to the Crown. General Amherst was impressed when he saw the return of the rangers to Crown Point. "Several of [Rogers'] detachments are come in loaded with more Indian riches than I thought any of their towns would have contained. . . ."[40] A summary of the loot was compiled later.

At this point it was a successful raid, but this would change. Rogers lost one killed (the scout, Samadagwis) and six wounded. He claimed over two hundred Abenaki dead, but this was an inflated figure. French would later claim that thirty-two were killed, mostly women and children. The true number is somewhere between the two estimates. A total of 50 dead appears to be a reasonable number considering the element of surprise enjoyed by the rangers and many bodies not counted because they were burned in the fires or carried down river.[41] Scotsman Robert Kirkwood who was in the camp at that time would later state. "This was I believe the bloodiest scene in all America, our revenge being complete."[42] Rogers now had to deal with prisoners and rescued captives. Bringing prisoners along for the return was a huge mistake since it slowed the column and added dissension among the troops.

The rangers would move south toward Number Four, a straight line distance of two hundred miles through unmapped wilderness. This was a bad time of year to be moving through the woods. Wild game were hard to locate and scarce. Some say that a sort of natural phenomenon had occurred that had caused wild game to flee the region.

The Return-5 October 1759

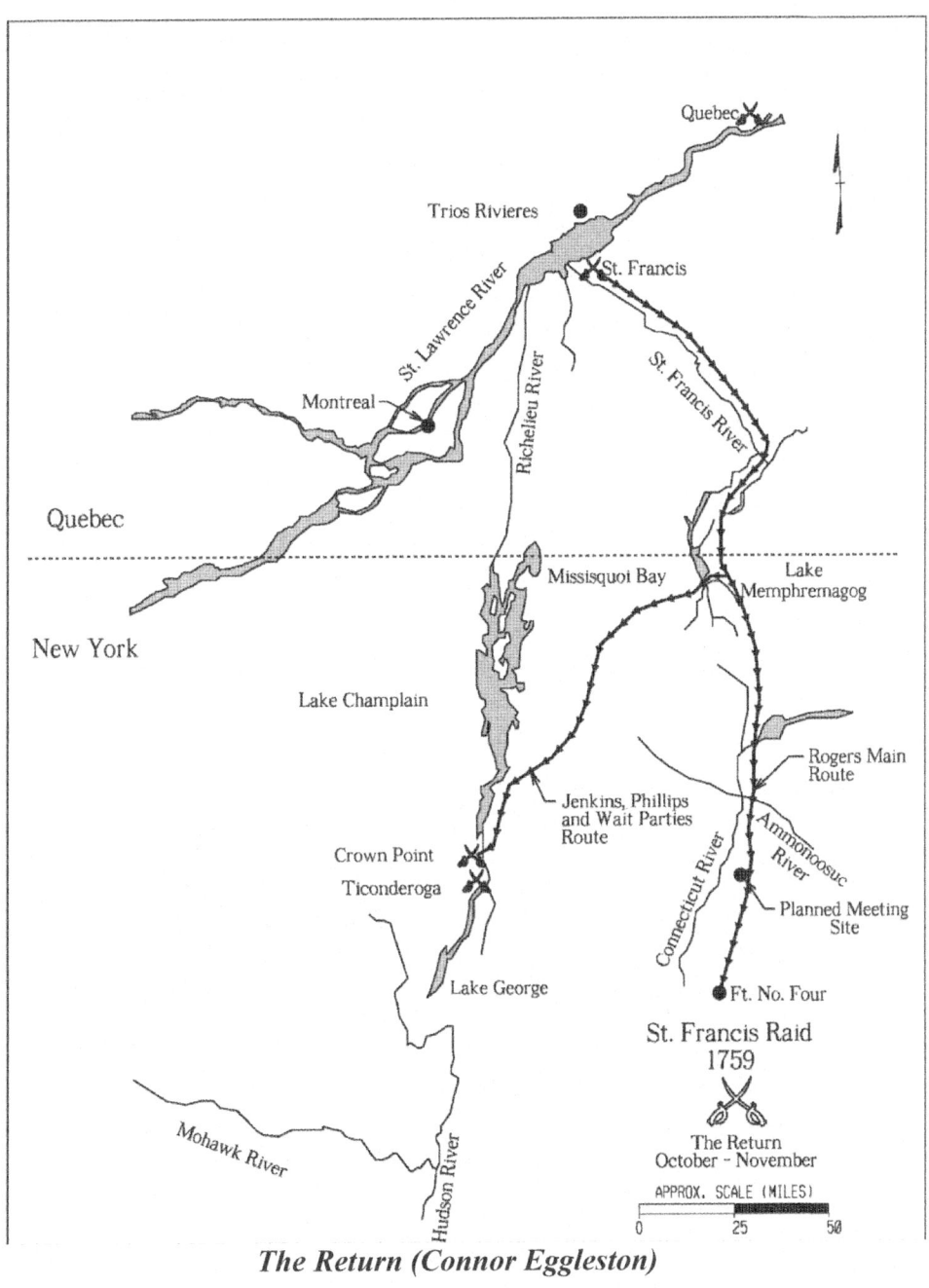

The Return (Connor Eggleston)

While Rogers had lost very few people thus far, the return would be difficult and forces were assembling to defeat his small force. Rogers called a quick conference of his officers confirming that they would now move to Lake Memphremagog. To confuse the enemy, he released some of the prisoners telling them that he was moving in the opposite direction.[43]

News of the raid travelled quickly throughout the province. It reached the French at Trois-Rivieres on the Saint Lawrence River, north of Saint Francis, by noon on the day of the attack. The raid caused quite a commotion among the French. The honor of France demanded a strong response, etc. Bourlamaque sent another 300 men to join those at Missisquoi Bay who were waiting for the ranger return. It was a wasted effort. He was unaware that Rogers had changed his route for return. At Trois-Rivieres a pursuit party of experienced fighters was organized. This reached Saint Francis on 5 October, a day behind Rogers.

Major Jean Daniel Dumas was one of Rogers' pursuers. He was commander of the French Canadian Marines and was at nearby Three Rivers when word arrived of the raid. He was considered the hero of the Monongahela where he had distinguished himself in the battle against Braddock. At Saint Francis a pursuit party was quickly organized and included Chief Gill whose wife had been kidnapped by Rogers. Gill was outraged and bent on revenge as were others that composed the pursuit force of 200 French, Canadian and Abenaki. Father Roubaud summarized. "... I have gathered my savages and the next day we pursued the assailants...."[44]

The First Day

The rangers started their return on the east side of the Saint Lawrence River moving south and then west to Lake Memphremagog. Rogers made good progress during the first eight days reaching Lake Memphremagog, seventy miles from Saint Francis. Rations were starting to run out and Rogers reluctantly agreed to break up his command into parties of ten to twenty men each. These smaller groups were more likely to successfully forage for food. Smaller groups were also more likely to be trapped and annihilated by the French. Vengeful pursuers could track down and destroy them. Rogers underestimated the speed and determination of the French and Abenaki. They were outraged by the destruction of Saint Francis and were bent on catching up with the rangers and destroying the lot. They pushed hard with few breaks and closed the gap between the rangers and themselves. They were also better supplied and rested than the rangers who started their return in a state of exhaustion. The rangers had a one day head start when they left Saint Francis and this lead had disappeared. The French and Abenaki were closing in.

The rangers divided into eleven parties and continued their return. Following rangers led the parties: Avery, Bradley/Hoit, Campbell, Cargill, Dunbar/Turner, Evans, Farrington, Jenkins, Phillips, Waite, and Rogers. Each leader would decide his own route back. Some would follow Rogers trek while others split off into other directions. Each of the party leaders had a compass set in the end of his powder horn. This was essential in navigating during the journey. The prisoners and repatriated whites were distributed among the parties. The pursuers realized that Rogers had split up his command and they planned to attack and destroy each party, but they did not detect that three parties (Jenkins, Phillips, and Waite) had headed southwest toward Crown Point. These parties got a free ride without interference from the pursuers but would face other challenges. The fate of each party has been reconstructed centuries after the event. Burt Garfield Loescher extensively researched Robert Rogers and his parties after the Saint Francis Raid.[45]

The Avery Party

Ensign Elias Avery and his party included six provincials and three rangers (Ballard, Hewit and Lee). Avery followed Rogers, headed south toward the Connecticut River. On 13 October the party ran into trouble. Avery and two others were out hunting while the others set up camp and rested. The party was starving and their diet of mushrooms and beech leaves had left them in a weakened state. They were unaware that the pursuit party had closed in until they looked up into the faces of Abenaki warriors that were dyed blood red, a horrifying sight. There was no resistance. The captives were stripped and tied to trees. The three rangers with their green uniforms and bonnets drove the Abenaki into a rage. Samuel Ballard was selected for torture and was repeatedly stabbed until he expired. This seemed to appease the Abenaki and the six terrified survivors were cut loose and led back toward Saint Frances. After two miles the group stopped and encamped for the night. The two surviving rangers, Hewit and Lee knew what to expect at Saint Francis and they slipped away from the camp during the night leaving the others behind. They found their way to the Rogers' party as did Avery and the other two members of the hunting party.[46]

The Bradley/Hoit Party

Sergeants Benjamin Bradley and Stephen Hoit (together) and seven other rangers headed south toward the Connecticut River. Upon reaching the river they followed the east bank hoping to meet Rogers and the promised supplies. The party became lost and all succumbed to starvation except for Duke Jacob.

It would seem that the hand of Providence intervened for Jacob. Out of the wilderness appeared a hunter from Stevenstown, who had set up a camp by the side of Gorge Brook near its conflux with Baker River. In the huge meadow in the head of Jobildunk Ravine beyond the ridge, he had set his traps for beaver and set up Indian culheags for sable on the mountainside. While visiting the latter the morning after Jacob's collapse, he fell upon his footprints crossing his line. He found Jacob at the foot of the cascades on Baker River. Carrying the emaciated form over his shoulder he returned to camp. Jacob responded to the hunter's food and care, and in a few weeks was helping him with his traps.

They returned to Stevenstown when the snows came to the valley. The incredible story of Bradley's party is substantiated by the fact that the remains of the party were later discovered, and there was the lone survivor, Jacob, to tell the tale.[47]

The Campbell Party

Lieutenant George Campbell's party of thirteen included Jane Chandler a white raised by the Abenaki and taken prisoner by Rogers during the raid. Campbell noted that his troops had run out of food completely before reaching Lake Memphremagog. They moved south from Lake Memphremagog eventually reaching Holland Pond in Essex County, Vermont. It was here that Chandler attempted to mislead the party by showing them an "Abenaki shortcut" that in fact sent them circling around the pond for three days before her deception was discovered. The enraged Stockbridge guides were determined to kill her but Campbell intervened and she was spared. Chandler later disappeared and was not seen again. Campbell kept a diary and after Chandler disappeared he "Order'd ye party away from ye acurs'd Pond." Starvation set in as the party worked its way toward the Connecticut River. Campbell noted ". . . Sparrow & Hartwell had found some birds eggs in ye bogs & popp'd them raw into their gullets without sharing, which most caused a fight amongst ye party. Ye men are losing their reason for want of food." "One Ranger was discover'd eating his own stool which I sought to forbare & was acurs'd by ye crazed men, for I knew Smith for a most respectable Ranger in ye past." They eventually reached the Connecticut River and found a boat of provisions sent by Rogers from Number Four. Campbell noted "I Daresay, it was ye most welcome sight these eyes will ever view."[48]

The Cargill Party

Lieutenant Abernethy Cargill headed south toward the Connecticut River. Cargill chose a slightly different route than the others and moved from the east bank of Lake Memphremagog to the Barton River and followed it south discovering a nearly hidden lake in Orleans County, Vermont. The lake was rich with fish and the troops quickly fashioned fishing poles and went to work hauling in fish in large numbers. A stop-over here was a risky business since they had no clue how close the pursuers were or if they were even followed. Hunger overcame these concerns and the supply of fish seemed inexhaustible. After fully satisfying their hunger, the Cargill Party moved on to the Connecticut River to what became known as the "rendezvous of starvation." Lieutenant Stevens was not there with promised supplies and they were again starving until Rogers arrived with canoe loads of provisions.[49]

The Dunbar/Turner Party

Lieutenants William Dunbar of Gage's 80th Light Infantry and George Turner of Rogers' Rangers headed south for the Connecticut River. The party included eighteen men, eleven from the 80th and seven rangers. They were closely followed by Major Dumas with a force of over a hundred Canadians and Abenaki under the vengeful Chief Gill. The

Dunbar/Turner Party was overtaken by their pursuers at the end of the day after they had completed a long uphill march. They were overwhelmed by Dumas but made a valiant stand for a short time before being driven into the swampy end of a nearby lake. In the hand-to-hand fighting that followed, the vengeful Abenaki and Canadians surrounded and destroyed the party. Only three privates in Dunbar's force were taken prisoner and Sergeant Lewis escaped. The mutilated bodies of the rest washed downstream into the Pherrins River. The seven rangers escaped in the darkness although Turner and several other rangers were wounded. The prisoners were returned to Saint Francis where they were tortured and killed along with the survivors of Avery's Party. The survivors the Dunbar/Turner Party escaped moving south to the headwaters of Moose River. Along the way three survivors were attacked and killed by wolves while hunting. The others eventually reached the Connecticut River and where they were met by Rogers who had brought provisions.[50]

The Evans Party

Sergeant John Evans' party of Rogers' Rangers left the fold of Major Rogers' parent detachment at present-day Sherbrooke. A forlorn squad, hunger-bent with cramps, they stumbled along, seeking game that was not there. Sergeant Benjamin Bradley's squad, who had looted the church, was close to the Evans group, and eventually joined them. The two squads evidently stayed close together until they reached the Connecticut. From Sherbrooke, they followed directly south, across the Massawippi River, crossing Highway 5; continuing south through present-day Hatley, then Barnston and through the Barnston Swamps to the Niger River, which they followed.

They finally reached the Connecticut, via the Pherrins River, Island Pond and Nulhegan River, where Rogers found part of them at the ruins of Fort Wentworth, near the Upper Ammonoosuc River.[51]

The Farrington Party

Lieutenant Jacob Farrington headed south toward the Connecticut River with his platoon of ten rangers. Farrington was a skilled woodsman with an uncanny sense of direction. He led his party to the Moose River where they could go no further due to starvation. They had eaten their leather equipment and had nothing left when by chance they encountered an owl that was shot. They devoured this uncooked delicacy. Farrington and a few of his strongest survivors left the others to find Rogers and the promised provisions. Rogers found Farrington who guided him back to the other survivors. They arrived and found that most had died of starvation. Farrington lost half of his platoon during his return from Saint Francis. All died of starvation.[52]

The Jenkins Party

Lieutenant Jenkins headed southwest toward Crown Point.

After two centuries, the mysterious fate of Lieutenant Jenkins' party has been solved, thanks, primarily, to the French journal of Meloizes, and Lieutenant Campbell's diary. If superstition had held sway, the number in their party would have sealed their fate. There were thirteen: Lieutenant Jenkins of the provincials, ten Rangers and Provincials, including two Stockbridge guides, and two Abenaki prisoners, Chief Gill's wife, Marie-Jeanne and one of the teen-age Indian women. . . . From the beginning, hunger was their constant companion, although the "route was the best region for hunting," it being the hunting grounds of the Abenakis. . . . Lake Champlain was not very far away, and their location was too far north for succor from Crown Point. Near the Falls, five of the Rangers and Provincials left those too weak to travel. Following down the Missisquoi, searching for game, they found it in the form of five Abenaki horses pastured near "Missisquoi Castle," the ruins of an Abenaki fort on the river. Fortunately, their Abenaki owners were away hunting, so the Rangers, on the verge of starvation, cast their customary caution aside. They killed one horse and proceeded to cook it. The Abenaki owners were warned of the Rangers' presence in a roundabout way.

While hunting with a Frenchman at Missisquoi Bay, a group of squaws, while crossing the bay in canoes, had seen Rangers hunting ducks near the mouth of the Missisquoi. Concerned over their horses, some of the Abenaki took a shortcut by land to the old fort and discovered the Rangers were busily cooking part of a horse. Not knowing the size of the Ranger force, all but three Abenakis returned to Bourlamaque at Isle aux Noix, who sent a strong detachment after them. He might have spared his efforts, for the five Rangers and Provincials had already been surprised and captured by the three Abenakis who had stayed; their concern for their remaining horses being greater than any fear of a superior party of English.

They made a victorious entry into the camp at Isle aux Noix on the evening of November 2. When the Rangers told Bourlamaque of the remainder of Jenkins' detachment starving up the Missisquoi River, a party of the Missisquoi Abenakis went after them. Five days later they returned. They had been too late to save Lieutenant Jenkins from dying of starvation. They found the remaining six of his party, including the Abenaki girl prisoner. . . .Since their names are not known, this [their fate] cannot be definitely established.[53]

The Phillips Party

Lieutenant William Phillips and his party of six rangers headed southwest toward Crown Point. They escorted a German woman released at Saint Francis, two Abenaki girls and Chief Gill's youngest son, Xavier. Phillips' party reached the west side of Lake Memphremagog and then followed the Lamoille River to Lake Champlain. It had been a hundred mile journey of starvation. Desperation mounted and reached the point of a proposal to eat one of the prisoners. Fate intervened in the form of a muskrat that happened by and was killed. This sustained the group and saved a prisoner from a very unhappy ending. Langy's partisan group was close on the trail of the Phillips Party but the trail petered out and Langy missed the party. To improve the hunting, Phillips split his party sending most forward while he and four other rangers stayed back looking for game and acting as a rear guard. The last members of Phillips' party arrived at Crown Point on 12 November long after other groups had been rescued. All members of this party survived.[54]

The Waite Party

Captain Joseph Waite headed southwest toward Crown Point. This party was composed of twelve rangers including Sergeant Benjamin Waite, Joseph Waite's brother. They reached the west side of Lake Memphremagog and followed it south. Half way down Waite changed course and decided to head for the Connecticut River rather than directly for Crown Point. They stopped at lakes and fished as the Cargill Party had done. This sustained them and was about all that exhausted and starving men could do. AS they continued small lakes with sustaining fish petered out and death by starvation loomed near. When they were about twenty-five miles from the Connecticut River Waite decided to leave the party under the command of his brother while he moved ahead with a few rangers to look for game. When Waite finally reached the Connecticut River he saw a deer and fired. He would later claim that it was the luckiest shot of his life. It saved him and his party. He and his small group feasted on venison and left the remaining carcass hanging in a place where it would not be missed by his brother, Benjamin. Waite would later settle at this place and today it is called Waitsville, Vermont. His brother and the remaining members of the party found the deer and also were saved. All members of the Waite Party survived the trek from Saint Francis.[55]

The Rogers' Party

Rogers' party was in the lead with most of the troops and he headed south toward the Connecticut River. Soon after they departed he ordered a small detachment on a detour to build a large fire to make the Abenaki think that the main body was camping there. He then set up an ambush for the pursuers as they rushed forward. He sprang the trap and inflicted such heavy casualties that they gave up the pursuit. Hunger set in as Rogers led the party toward the Connecticut River. The diet of minnows, beechnuts and an occasional squirrel kept them alive.[56]

Rogers finally reached the Connecticut River on 20 October. The group was exhausted and starving. It was during the trek to the Connecticut River that few first-hand accounts of the flight are seen. Starving and exhausted troops have little time to record what they observe. Rogers' journal has a few terse remarks about the trek to the Connecticut River. " . . . many days tedious march over steep rocky mountains or thro' wet dirty swamps, with the terrible attendants of fatigue and hunger."[57] They finally reached the Connecticut River and quickly moved to the rendezvous point where they expected to find Lieutenant Stevens.[58]

Where is Stevens? After nine days of difficult travel south along the Connecticut River, Rogers' company reached the rendezvous point set to meet Stevens and his supplies on 20 October. They found a burning fire, but no supplies and no Stevens. As ordered by Amherst, Lieutenant Stevens had moved from Number Four with supplies to the rendezvous point. He had set up nearby and daily sent men to the rendezvous point to fire guns and wait for Rogers. After several days of this, Stevens gave up and returned to Number Four with the supplies. Amherst noted in his journal that Stevens should have waited longer and Stevens was later court-martialed and dismissed from the service for his failure to wait for Rogers.

Rogers ordered that a raft be built while they waited in vain hoping that Stevens would appear. Rogers planned to float down the river with three men to Number Four and he promised his men that he would return with supplies in ten days. He left Lieutenant Grant in charge and launched his raft. Rogers had difficulty steering the raft and at one point was barely able to get it to shore.

> On 31 October they came on a party of woodcutters, who gave them food and shelter and helped them to the fort. Within half an hour of arriving at Number Four, more dead than alive, the exhausted Rogers had sent provisions upriver to Grant and the Rangers, where they arrived four days later, ten days after Rogers had left them and to the very day he had promised. He also sent canoes with provisions to help any stragglers on other rivers such as the Merrimack, and it was as well that he did.[59]

Other companies were scattered along the withdrawal route and beyond. On 2 November the French waiting at Missisquoi Bay heard English voices and investigated finding five survivors of Rogers' Rangers whom they took prisoner. A search in the area located three more of Rogers' men. Since they were carrying human flesh, the French cut their throats and left their bodies to rot. At the same time General Amherst learned that Rogers' Saint Francis Raid had been successful from a French officer who arrived under a flag of truce.[60]

After his arrival at Number Four Rogers wrote his report to General Amherst and waited until late November for other survivors to appear. On the 7th, Rogers' second in command arrived with Rogers' report of the raid. When the Rogers report arrived, euphoria reigned at Crown Point as word of the raid spread and Amherst sent congratulations to Rogers.

The parish priest at Saint Francis, Father Roubaud, sent his report to Bishop de Pontbriand at Montreal who forwarded the following to the Bishop of France on 5 November.

> The Mission of the Abenaki Indians of Saint Francois has been utterly destroyed by a party of English and Indians, who have stolen all the vestments and sacred vessels, have thrown the sacred Hosts on the ground, have killed some thirty persons, more than 20 were women and children.[61]
>
> ***Pere Pierre-Joseph Roubaud***

On 7th of November, a group of survivors was seen across Lake Chaplain from Crown Point. Help was sent and found six rangers, three prisoners, a white women freed from captivity, and a large amount of loot taken from Saint Francis. Rangers continued to straggle in during November at Number Four and Crown Point. Rogers was lionized in the press for his successful raid. Many of the Abenaki continued to serve the French during the remainder of the war. The raid greatly diminished the Abenaki raids in the British colonies. The pastor of the church, Father Pierre-Joseph Roubaud[62] returned to rebuild the church and Saint Francis was soon rebuilt. It stands, today, as a reminder of the raid.

The Cannibals

Rogers makes no mention of cannibalism in his journal for obvious reasons. Newspaper accounts also avoided the subject.

> Lieutenant George Campbell's group had gone through even worse nightmares than Rogers's detachment. Thomas Mante, who interviewed the survivors, gave this account in his later history of the war in North America: These were, at one time, without any kind of sustenance, when some of them, in consequence of their complicated misery, severely aggravated by their not knowing whither the route they pursued would lead, and, of course, the little prospect of relief that was left to them, lost their senses; whilst others, who could no longer bear the keen pangs of an empty stomach, attempted to eat their own excrements. What leather they had on their cartouch boxes, they had already

reduced to a cinder, and greedily devoured. At length, on the 28th of October, as they were crossing a small river, which was in some measure dammed up by logs, they discovered some human bodies not only scalped but horribly mangled, which they supposed to be those of some of their own party [Dunbar's Party]. But this was not the season for distinctions. On them, accordingly, they fell like cannibals, and devoured part of them raw; their impatience being too great to wait the kindling of a fire to dress it by. When they had thus abated the excruciating pangs they before endured, they carefully collected the fragments and carried them off. This was their sole support, except roots and a squirrel, till the 4th of November, when Providence conducted them to a boat on the Connecticut River, which Major Rogers had sent with provisions to their relief.[63]

The Evan's Party resorted to cannibalism when they also found the remains of the Dunbar bodies. Sergeant Evans of Concord recalled that after all leather accoutrements had been eaten he was still starving but refused to eat any part of the bodies that they found. Later one night he noticed a large knapsack that belonged to one of his comrades. He hoped that it might contain a few morsels of food. He slipped over and upon opening it to his horror he found that the knapsack contained three human heads.[64] He overcame his revulsion and cut pieces from a head eating them while the others continued to sleep. Decades later he was still guilt ridden over the incident but stated that these were the best morsels that he ever ate.[65]

The Jenkins Party also practiced cannibalism.

For such crazed and desperate men, it was but one step from devouring the dead to killing and consuming the living. The raiders had taken a handful of prisoners from amongst the villagers of Saint Francis; at least two of them — a grown woman and a young boy — were butchered for food.[66]

The murder and cannibalism of an Indian woman also feature in the *Memoirs of Robert Kirkwood*. She had been captured on the evening following the destruction of the village, being loaded with provisions from Saint Francis. In the coming days of strenuous marching, Kirkwood wrote, this prisoner proved of great service. Not only was she physically strong, and able to carry more than any three of Rogers' men, but she also displayed an admirable stoicism in the face of danger. Indeed, Kirkwood added, 'she bore it nobly, and was of infinite service in gathering roots and herbs, which she was better acquainted with, as she was bred among such hardships.'

Kirkwood observed that the captive was plump, having more flesh upon her than five of them. He claimed that Major Rogers several times proposed to *make away with her,* although the rest of the party would not consent. But Rogers was stronger, and in better spirits, than any of his men. When starvation reduced them to the greatest extremity, the major took matters into his own hands. Kirkwood told how Rogers 'followed the squaw who was gone out to gather roots, and there he kill'd and cut her up, and brought her to our fire, where he divided and cast lots for the shares which were distributed to each an equal part; we then broiled and eat the most of her; and received great strength thereby.'[67]

Kirkwood's memoir mentioning Rogers appears to be in error since Rogers was in a different party.

The Spoils of War

Some of the loot taken at Saint Francis was turned in to the British as the parties returned. More was kept by the troops or buried along the way back from Saint Francis. Treasure hunters have been looking for the loot ever since. The little church at Saint Francis was adorned with many priceless objects some of which came from the court of the French king, Louis XV and churches in France. Some of these were given as rewards for the British colonials murdered by the Abenaki. The treasures included a hand-embroidered cloth sewn by a lady in the court of the king, a two-sided banner with the Christ and Virgin Mary on alternate sides and framed in embroidery, a gift to Pere Roubaud by Queen Marie Leszcynska wife of Louis the XV of France. Some of these were proudly worn or carried by members of Rogers' Rangers as they paraded at Crown Point after their return from Saint Francis.

Louis XV
(Library of Congress)

Marie Leszcznska
(Wikipedia)

Other items included a ten-pound silver statue of the Virgin Mary, gold candle sticks and jewels such as a ruby described by Lieutenant Campbell: ". . . Rob Pomroy [Pomeroy] shewed [showed] me a Rube [ruby] ring he took from a savag [savage] big as yor [your] Iy [eye]. . . ." Both gold and silver coins were carried off in large quantities. Those items not carried away were destroyed when the church was burned.[68]

The fate of many treasures is revealed in the accounts of the returning parties. The Bradley/Hoit Party seemed cursed by their treasure. Bradley kept the Silver Madonna and Pomeroy had his Ruby Ring. Some say that the blood red ruby seemed to draw life from its wearer, Pomeroy. A body thought to be that of Pomeroy was later found but there was no trace of the ruby.

As they starved they cursed and blasphemed the Silver Madonna for their misfortune. When Bradley lay dying of starvation, to rid themselves of the curse, one of the party seized the Madonna from Bradley's grasp and threw it off a place called "Hardwood Ridge." Searchers have tried but failed to find the Madonna and many have tried over the last 250 years.[69]

The Evans Party also had treasure. Daniel Barnes buried the golden candlesticks at the foot of a huge birch tree on the way back from Saint Francis. In 1816 a farmer pulling stumps dug them up. One of the party buried gold coins and made a map of their location. In 1820 the map came into the possession of a treasure hunter who searched but never found the gold. Jackson Perry was born in 1820 on a Vermont farm near what was thought to be the location of the treasure. From his boyhood until his death in 1913, he witnessed many treasure seekers excavating near his farm. One excavation was forty feet long and six feet deep. It can still be seen. All of the treasure hunters left empty-handed.[70]

Members of the Farrington Party buried their treasure as a last act before they died of starvation as they waited for a relief party near Lower Waterford, Vermont. Volney Blodgett found a cache of old coins while pulling stumps on his farm near Waterford, Vermont. These are thought to be the treasure of the Farrington Party.[71]

According to a November 15, 1869 letter from E. Harrington to Louis Gill at Odanak the following items were found:

> In 1827, an incense vessel, believed to have been left by one of Rogers' men, was found on an island in the Watopeka river where

it empties into the St. Francis, at Windsor Mills, Quebec, and in 1838, one Robert Orme, of Vermont, found a large image of a saint at the mouth of the Magog river, and gave it to a priest then living in Sherbrooke.[72]

Saint Francis Epilogue

Of the 142 troops who reached Saint Francis Village, Rogers lost one killed during the raid, but another 60 were killed or died of starvation during the return. The fate of eight others who were captured is not known.[73] Those captured were not treated well. Many were dragged back to Saint Francis and "fell victim to the fury of the Indian women, notwithstanding the efforts of the Canadians to save them."[74]

The raid did not stop Abenaki attacks on British settlements, but it reduced the level of violence. It was months before another raid occurred and the attacks continued to diminish. More important since the raid struck deep into the heart of the French empire, the Abenaki morale plummeted and they blamed the French. Many of the Abenaki left the village and dispersed into the surrounding forest to avoid becoming casualties of future raids. The band of trust between the French and the Abenaki had been broken. At least one raid against the French-Canadians was staged by the Abenaki and French Canadians were butchered. Before the raid, the Cherokees had extended an offer to the Abenaki to join them in Carolina and now, many Abenaki joined a migration south for that purpose. The defeat of the French at Quebec persuaded the Abenaki that they were on the losing side and the prospect of vengeful New Englanders descending upon the Abenaki was a very real prospect. No one was safe from Rogers. The balance of terror had shifted. After the raid Father Roubaud left Saint Francis for Montreal. He was haunted by guilt over his decision to hand over the Kennedy party to the French and felt responsible for the destruction of the village. If he had sent Kennedy on his way rather than detaining the party, there may have been no raid. In 1760, Roubaud attempted to negotiate a peace treaty between the British and the Abenaki. Amherst entertained the offer and after negotiations, peace was offered in 1763. By then, Saint Francis was occupied by British troops and was in a virtual state of martial law until the British troops were finally withdrawn in that year. Saint Francis exists today and some of the descendents of the original inhabitants still reside there.[75]

Even though Rogers sustained severe losses in this raid, it made him a national hero. He received a promotion to the rank of captain in the British regular army. The promotion included permanency and retirement benefits. The press on both sides of the Atlantic lauded his feat.

> BOSTON Nov. 26. From Number IV. The following Particulars relating to the Destruction of the Indian Town of St. Francois, by a Party of Rangers, under the command of Maj. Rogers, may be depended on for truth, as it was taken from those who were present in the Action.
> Upon the 13th of Sept. Maj. Rogers marched from Crown-Point with about 200 men, and upon the 3d, of Oct. they came within sight of St. Francois, which the Major discovered from a tree, at about three miles distance, where he halted his detachment; consisting of 142 men, officers included, being reduced to that number by reason of some of the tired whom he sent back. . . . A little after sunrise the parties set fire to all the houses, except three, which the Major kept as a reserve, because in them was plenty of corn, but the rest were entirely consumed, and many of the enemy who had concealed themselves therein, which our men learnt from the crying and shrieking of those miserable wretches, when they perceived their houses on fire, and themselves like to be made the fuel: The sword without, which prevented all escapes, and the fire within rendered their situation most unhappy, most miserable: About seven in the morning the affair was over, in which they had killed some say 300, and some more, but by the lowest computation, there could not be fewer than 200 who were slain by the sword, by the fire and water: The party took about 20 prisoners, and retook 5 English captives. . . . That hath Maj. Rogers, with

little loss on his own side, almost wholly cut off one tribe and destroyed abundance of riches, it being extremely rich for a place of that bigness, having in it English goods, and vast quantities of wampum, and likewise considerable silver and gold, one ranger is said to bring off, 170 guineas, and another a silver image of ten pounds weight; but the hurry in which they set fire to their houses, could not give many an opportunity of bringing off more.[76]

What impressed people then (and now) was his personal leadership and courage as seen in the accounts of the raid. He was respected by his troops, shared their hardships and had their undying loyalty. He was certainly well qualified for this raid. He was young (28 years old) and physically fit. More important, he had experience fighting Indians and knew how to traverse difficult terrain. Unlike his British contemporaries, he could think like the French and their Indian allies giving him the ability to anticipate their moves. In other words, he was the perfect man for the job of attacking Saint Francis village. The Indians now called him Wobomagonda, the "White Devil." His star was on the rise.

3. On to Montreal

James Murray (1722-1794) (Wikipedia)

Great rejoicing in London followed the British victory at Quebec on 13 September 1759. General James Murray, the

British commander occupied Quebec and settled in for a long cold winter. He had 7,000 troops to defend Britain's new conquest and they were a fraction of the French, Canadian, and Indian forces that surrounded them and occupied the rest of New France.

Following the loss of Quebec in October, the French sought to regain supremacy in the New World by retaking Quebec. All French forces that could be spared were concentrated under Chevalier de Levis. As winter settled in General James Murray had all of the joy of cold weather in Canada while struggling to feed the civilian population of Quebec. He was isolated in a foreign country with supplies and reinforcements many miles away. To make matters worse, he was surrounded by a still competent enemy of French, Canadians and their Indian allies. Ensign James Miller recorded. "A severe winter now commenced while we were totally unprepared for such a climate . . . neither fuel, forage, or indeed anything else to make life tolerable."[1] Levis was determined to retake Quebec.

Lack of rations and fuel fed a rapid increase in disease. Dysentery and scurvy were rampant and a cold winter and unfriendly environment that year plagued the British as it had Rogers' Rangers during the Saint Francis Raid.[2] Murray would count over a thousand dead and 2,000 not fit for duty by spring.[3]

William Pitt (1708-1778)(Library of Congress)

In Europe the end of the year 1759 found Britain and its allies (principally Prussia) in a winning position in the Seven Years' War. The French planned invasion of Great Britain was thwarted by two British naval victories. At this time Lord William Pitt who had served as Prime Minister of Great Britain was now Secretary of State for the Southern Department and

Leader of the House of Commons. Lord Pitt in London was now in the position to issue instructions to the British commander in America, Jeffrey Amherst.

> . . . early in 1760, he [Lord Pitt] gave Amherst his instructions for the year. The war was by no means over. Amherst was the only general upon whom he could rely for American victories, and the substance of Pitt's instructions was the sole objective: take Canada. Amherst was no longer to be hampered by a schedule of details and expeditions written in London. He could take his own course. "It is His Majesty's Pleasure that You do attempt the Invasion of Canada . . . Accordingly as You shall from your Knowledge of the Countries through which the War is to be Carried. . . . Judge the same to be most Expedient."
>
> The Commander's chief assets as he faced the new campaign were his record of success and his personal popularity. Captain Robert Stewart, a colonial serving under Amherst, wrote to a Virginia friend, a Colonel George Washington, "I informed you how happy we are under the Orders of so consumate an Officer & so fine a Gentleman as our General appears to be and the genteel Politeness of His Behavior particular marks of which and indeed of real kindness he has been Pleas'd to Honr me with." . . .
>
> The colonists, proud of their freedom as British subjects, were increasingly disturbed at the attitude of the home Government in treating them as dependencies. In 1754, they had tried to form a Continental Congress, in which Benjamin Franklin had played a considerable part. That was defeated by their own jealousies, but the seeds of thought planted at that time were sprouting. The presence of a standing army in their midst, even for their own defense, was increasingly unwelcome. Amherst did not favor the quartering of officers and soldiers in the homes of the colonists except during special emergencies, when tents had failed to arrive or barracks were under construction. But the colonists objected to the move under any circumstances. In 1760, the Rhode Island Legislature sarcastically passed a bill compelling all public inns to provide quarters for all soldiers willing to pay twenty-five shillings per day.
>
> Even more overt and obnoxious was the policy of the Crown in

interfering with colonial legislation. Virginia had passed a so-called Two-Penny Act in 1758, having to do with the tax on tobacco. The act had certain inequitable features and the King nullified it. Whatever the merits of the arguments, the principle of the independence of the colonial legislature, composed of British subjects, was at stake. A test case was tried in 1760, when Patrick Henry, a fiery young lawyer gave birth to the radical sentiment, "a King, by disallowing acts of this salutary nature, from being the father of his people, degenerated into a Tyrant, and forfeits all right to his subjects' obedience."

In spite of the feeling against the army, Amherst was able to conciliate the colonies with praise of their patriotism, with apologies for quartering his troops and with promises of financial assistance by the Crown toward the pay of the Provincial forces. Unfortunately, he still had nothing more than promises to offer on financial matters. For the second time he approached the Province of New York for a loan. The Governor reminded him rather tartly that one of the things which was "wanting to facilitate the success of my application" to the legislature was "the nonpayment of the money lent last year for His Majesty's service, by which the paper currency of this Province was greatly increased." Nevertheless, supplies were obtained, and by the late spring, in spite of all obstacles, the Commander had gathered together nearly sixteen thousand men for the great project he had in mind. For the first time the whole issue in North America, in every detail, was in his hands. Following the plan which he and Pownall had discussed in the Governor's house in Boston two years before, he was now ready for a scheme, mammoth in its conception and daring all the hazards of the wilderness. He was to place three fingers at the throat of French Canada, each closing in simultaneously until the victim would be forced to yield.

Murray must advance upon Montreal from Quebec. The French would probably expect Amherst to come up Lake Champlain along the route which he had followed the year before. But Amherst was a tactician who believed in the value of the unexpected. He named Colonel Haviland in command of the Lake Champlain route. He himself would replace Gage at Oswego, and would advance to LaGalette. Then would come the master stroke of the campaign. LaGalette would not be a blockade to prevent a French retreat. It would be the start of the main offensive. He would transfer his army to boats and run the dangerous rapids down the St. Lawrence to the Island of Montreal. The French would not place their major defenses against the western route, because they looked upon the rapids as impassable and any attack by that route as hardly conceivable. Amherst believed it could be done and was determined to risk it.[4]

As the year 1759 ended, Amherst decided that four companies of rangers would remain in service until the spring. These would perform scouting duties at Britain's newly won fortresses. Major Rogers' and Captain Johnson's companies were at Crown Point with a detachment sent to Number Four. Captain Waite was sent to Fort Brewerton at the west end of Lake Onieda. Captain Moses Hazen's company was posted to Quebec. All other companies were disbanded, but the officers were kept on full pay until Amherst decided how many companies he would need for the spring campaigns. On 24 November 1759, the rangers of the disbanded companies were mustered out.[5]

The 100 Toes Expedition – 25 December 1759

The year ended badly for the rangers. On Christmas day, while Rogers was away at Albany sorting out his financial claims, a British captain led a group of one hundred grumbling regulars and rangers from Crown Point to Ticonderoga to bring back new clothing. This became known as the "100 Toes Expedition." Instead of wearing moccasins and socks to reduce the chance of frostbite, they were directed to march in regulation shoes. All with shoes suffered frostbite. Upon their return, the surgeon at Crown Point went to work cutting off toes and the number amputated totaled more than a hundred. The result of this foolish error was that nearly a quarter of the two companies at Crown Point were incapacitated.[6] The press reported the incident.

> New York Jan 28. By several persons who come to town last week from Albany, we learn that all was quiet and well at the several fortresses of Niagara, Crown-Point, & c. That several of the soldiers who were out on command there were very much frost bitten in the late extreme cold weather.[7]

As the new year of 1760 dawned Rogers struggled to sort out his financial records following the raid.[8] He had gone into debt financing his rangers' weapons and supplies. He was now seeking reimbursement from the Crown. Although some ranger companies had been disbanded, a low level of recruiting continued in order to replace losses that occurred during the raid and also to prepare for the campaigns of the following spring. Newspaper articles spurred interest in the rangers and there was no lack of recruits. Some were no more than boys. This led to one of the saddest incidents of the war.

Rogers was in Albany in late January finishing his financial paperwork and had gathered sixteen recruits. He would move north to Crown Point. By early February he was at Fort Ticonderoga and joined a caravan of sixteen provision-ladened sutler sleighs bound for Crown Point. In Rogers' sleigh he had his recruits and a large amount of cash to pay troops. Rogers' sleigh went ahead of the sutlers for what he expected to be an uneventful ten mile journey to Crown Point.[9]

Meanwhile, in February, 1760 after an unsuccessful raid on British shipping at Fort Ticonderoga, Jean-Baptist Levrault de Langis (Langy), Rogers' deadly adversary after the Saint Francis raid, decided to set up ambush at Five Point near Lake Champlain and snare any British forces that wandered into his trap. He had a force of seventy troops that included Indians and Canadians. This was a long shot, but he hit pay dirt. On 12 February, Rogers was half way to Crown Point when the French spotted the convoy and attacked. Langy recognized

Rogers in the lead and concentrated fire on Rogers' sleigh from ambush killing the horses. The sutlers turned tail and rushed back to Fort Ticonderoga leaving Rogers trapped and immobile. For some reason the recruits had not been issued muskets that were stored in a trunk in the sleigh. There was no time to break these out and as they were overrun the recruits fought with knives and tomahawks. It was a slaughter. Five rangers were killed and four were captured before Rogers broke out with the survivors and returned to Fort Ticonderoga.

The press reported the incident.

> BOSTON Feb. 25. Friday last an express returned here from Albany, by him we are informed that last Thursday as Maj. Rogers with a party of his men and a number of Slays, with provisions and stores, were going from Ticonderoga to Crown Point, they were fired upon by a party of about 150 French and Indians, and 3 of his rangers killed, and 9 taken prisoner; several sleys were also taken by the enemy, and 2 or 3 horses killed, but, all the drivers escap'd: Maj. Rogers himself narrowly escap'd being either kill'd or taken, but was so lucky as to be in first sley, which the enemy let quietly pass by them, in hopes thereby to have secured the rest.[10]

All of the money was lost to Langy. The funds included Rogers' own money.[11] Langy returned to Montreal with the money and prisoners. This was the last time that Rogers would face his nemesis. Langy was later drowned after falling through the ice in the Saint Lawrence: an inglorious end to a skilled warrior.[12]

While Britain's ally, Prussia had several defeats in Europe, the British victory in America at Quebec prompted France to attempt an effort to reverse their fortunes in the New World. The French decided to reinforce their forces in North America and on 10 April 1760 a flotilla left Bordeaux and arrived in the Gulf of Saint Lawrence in mid-May. The size of the force was underwhelming and totaled 400 troops, five transports and one frigate. The problem for the French was that this token was more than matched by British relief force that also arrived in May 1760.[13]

> . . . in the middle of May he [Amherst] received the alarming word that Murray had been besieged at Quebec, had been defeated on the Heights of Abraham, and doubted whether he could hold the fortress. It was clear that the great victory gained by Wolfe during the preceding year was insecure, as long as the French held the country at large. Both Amherst and the Government in England were stunned at this unexpected turn of affairs. Horace Walpole was annoyed and disapproving. "Who the deuce," he wrote, "was thinking of Quebec. America was like a book one has read and done with, but here we are on a sudden reading our book backwards."
>
> The General's inventive mind conceived the notion of relieving pressure on Quebec by a pretended attack on Montreal. To accomplish this he ordered Major Rogers with three hundred rangers to slip up Lake Champlain, get past the head of the Lake if he could, and destroy the powder magazines at Chambles about thirty miles south of Montreal. Rogers was to keep away from any general engagement in order that the French might not see the small number of men involved. "This may alarm the Enemy & may force some of their troops away from Quebec," Amherst noted in his journal. "Tis all I can do till I get more Troops here to the advance garrisons." Meanwhile he sent relief forces to Quebec from Louisbourg.[14]

Amherst created four new ranger companies on 1 March 1760 to prepare for the British advance on the French stronghold at Montreal. Spring would find optimism among the British that final victory in the New World was near. There was some bumping, grinding and unhappiness among the ranger officers since there were not enough billets to accommodate all officers. John Stark graciously gave up his claim to command a company and left the rangers.[15] Recruiting efforts intensified to bring in people between 16 and 30 to fill the new companies.

By May, the ranger companies were up to strength and ready for action. Action would soon follow.

On 25 May 1760, Amherst issued his orders to Rogers: a ranger force of 300 troops was to destroy the villages of St. John's, Chambly and Wigwam Martinique. The purpose of this raid was to draw troops away from Levis at Quebec. This was a key mission for the rangers since provincial troops were slow to reach Amherst and he lacked the forces to move against Levis. This raid was the only help that Amherst could give to Murray.[16]

Rogers would lead 250 men against St. John's and Chambly while Lieutenant Robert Holmes would lead 50 men to destroy Wigwam Martinique. Rogers sailed to Missisquoi Bay and on 3 June he dropped off Lieutenant Holmes and his party. Rogers then returned to Lake Champlain where his whaleboats landed with 213 troops on the night of 4 June at King's Bay. He had been seen and a force of over 300 was marching against him. He deployed his troops to meet the attack.

> When his scouts relayed the probable point of attack the Rangers and Light Infantry held an ideal battle site on the Pointe au Fer peninsula on the shore of present-day King's Bay. On Rogers' left was the bay with his whaleboats drawn up on the shore. On his right was a bog which Rogers dispatched Ensign Farrington and seventy Rangers through, by the edge of present Griffith Bay, to fall upon their rear. The maneuver had been well timed, for Rogers was informed of the approach of his attackers by his scouts who relayed intelligence right up to the time of the attack. Although the numerical odds were 3 to 2 in favor of the French force, still, Rogers skillfully minimized this factor by the above alertness, and the following elements of surprise. The 300 or more French, Canadians and Indians were well led by the famed Partisans, LaForce and Longville. The primeval forests retained their natural hues as Rogers' Rangers in their green uniforms blended with Nature's garb. So much so, in fact, that the French were not aware of them until an advance party

walked into Rogers' line and were attacked. This happened at 11:30 A. M., and the main body began their attack "with their usual intrepidity and yelling," which was returned with like spirit by Rogers' men.

Rogers had to engage La Force's 300 men with approximately 144 Rangers and Light Infantry, until Farrington, with the other 70, had time to make his way through the swamp and fall upon the French rear. Consequently Rogers had his hands full, and the battle was nip and tuck for several hot moments. A number of Indians took cover behind some of Rogers' whaleboats and he threw a contingent behind the remaining boats. An amusing interlude followed: When the Indians could not reload as fast as the Rangers they started throwing stones, which aroused the competitive spirit of the Rangers, who shouted that they would equalize the weapons and also fight with stones. The Rangers proved to be peers in their speed and accuracy with the stones as well as reloading and firing muskets, for the Indians were so accurately pelted with these primitive missiles that they abandoned the boats with howls. At the same time Farrington fell upon the French rear, on the way they destroyed a number of Indians in the swamp, who were being exhorted by their medicine-man. As soon as Farrington began his attack, Rogers "pushed them in front, which broke them immediately." The French Grenadiers broke first, the others followed, retreating in a westerly direction away from Farrington and Rogers. Rogers pursued them with the bulk of his force for about a mile until they entered a thick cedar swamp and split up into small parties and escaped with all of their wounded. It started to rain again very hard, and Rogers immediately gathered his force together at the whaleboats and crossed to Isle La Mote, where he encamped, buried his dead, and sent the wounded back to Crown Point on one of the sloops.

The wounded were attended by the English surgeon, James Jameson. Thanks to the negligence of his superior, Surgeon-General Napier, who dispatched him from Albany without bandages and instruments, many of the wounded died on the voyage to Crown Point, in spite of the heroic efforts of Surgeon Jameson to improvise for them on Isle la Motte before they sailed. Captain Grant and other officers generously offered their linen shirts and

Jameson dressed the wounds without applying the non-existent medicines. As a consequence, Captain Johnson, who was badly wounded in three places, died before he reached Crown Point. The Corps lost a valuable officer due to the criminal neglect of Napier in not furnishing Jameson with a medicine chest. The enormity of Napier's folly cannot be over-emphasized.

Rogers' losses, besides Captain Noah Johnson, were 16 Rangers killed, and 8 wounded; Ensign John Wood of the 17th Infantry was killed in the first fire and two of his men were wounded. French losses were at least 32 killed, among them a noted Mohawk interpreter; and 19 wounded, including both the Commanders. La Force was mortally wounded in the chest, while Longville suffered a slighter wound. Rogers Rangers gathered more than 34 fine firelock muskets, and 3 Indian scalps. They would have gathered more of the latter for the bounty, but the French Indians had beat them to it, and scalped their own brethren before retreating.[17]

While Rogers had scored a clear victory over the French, the Holmes attack was a debacle. After he was dropped off at Missisquoi Bay by Rogers for his attack, Holmes followed the wrong river and did not get to Wigwam Martinique. Instead he found roaming bands of Indian hunters and abandoned his mission because he had been warned by Rogers not to take any unnecessary risks. Holmes had failed to accomplish his mission and found his way back to Rogers. Rogers then returned to Crown Point. Meanwhile, Levis abandoned his siege of Quebec. Thanks to continuing raids by the rangers, the French thought that the entire British army was advancing from Crown Point. Also, help from France would arrive too little and too late.[18] The newspapers reported the May raids.

> Boston June 30th
> ... Our Advices from Albany that since the Skirmish of Major Rogers mentioned in our last, he has been to a Place called St. Peter (Between Nut Island and Montreal) and burnt about 16 or

20 Houses, being all in the Village, and brought off 35 Men Prisoners, leaving the Women and Children behind.[19]

July and August of 1760 were consumed in the preparation for the attack on Montreal that it was hoped would end the war. Amherst's plan was to crush Montreal in the jaws of attacks from three directions. General Haviland would move north from Crown Point, Murray would attack from Quebec and Amherst would move down the Saint Lawrence from Oswego. The forces arrayed against the French were staggering. Eleven thousand troops were led by Amherst. Haviland had over three thousand and Murray had 3,800 regulars. The problem for the French was that they could not determine which thrust to parry first and any one of the three was powerful enough to be a fatal blow.[20] With Canadian militia melting away and their Indian allies deserting them, en masse, the French prepared to surrender Montreal on 6 September 1760. The next morning, Governor Vaudreuil presented Amherst with no less than fifty articles that would govern the capitulation of Canada to the British. Amherst agreed to most of the terms but insisted that the French troops would lay down their arms and return to France and those Canadians who elected to remain would be welcome to do so: as British citizens. Several other terms were also declined.[21] With that, Vaudreuil signed and in the words of historian Frances Parkman "half a continent had changed hands at the scratch of a pen."[22] It appeared that the Seven Years' War was over and had been won by the British, but not quite.

While the rangers were fighting the Abenaki and General James Murray was freezing in Quebec, George Washington was enjoying the life of a country gentleman. He had quit the army in December 1758 and would not serve again until the War of Independence. No doubt Washington read with interest the press stories of the rangers' exploits. Washington had not been idle following Braddock's Defeat in 1755 and continued to serve until he resigned in 1758.

Lt. Governor Dinwiddie rewarded Washington in 1755 with a commission as "Colonel of the Virginia Regiment and Commander in Chief of all forces now raised in the defense of His Majesty's Colony" and gave him the task of defending Virginia's frontier. The Virginia Regiment was the first full-time American military unit in the colonies (as opposed to part-time militias and the British regular units). Washington was ordered to "act defensively or offensively" as he thought best. While Washington happily accepted the commission, the coveted redcoat of a British officer as well as the accompanying pay continued to elude him. Dinwiddie as well pressed in vain for the British military to incorporate the Virginia Regiment into its ranks.[23]

In command of a thousand soldiers, Washington was a disciplinarian who emphasized training. He led his men in brutal campaigns against the Indians in the west; in 10 months his regiment fought 20 battles, and lost a third of its men. Washington's strenuous efforts meant that Virginia's frontier population suffered less than that of other colonies; Ellis concludes "it was his only unqualified success" in the war.[24]

In 1758 Washington participated in the Forbes Expedition to capture Fort Duquesne. He was embarrassed by a friendly fire episode in which his unit and another British unit thought the other was the French enemy and opened fire, with 14 dead and 26 wounded in the mishap. Washington was not involved in any other major fighting on the expedition, and the British scored a major strategic victory, gaining control of the Ohio Valley, when the French abandoned the fort. Following the expedition, he retired from his Virginia Regiment commission in December 1758. Washington did not return to military life until the outbreak of the revolution in 1775.[25]

4. Closing In

> It is recommended to the soldiers as well as the officers, not to mind the waves of the lake; but when the surf is high to stick to their oars, and the men at helm to keep the boat quartering on the waves, and briskly follow, then no mischief will happen by any storm whatever.[1]
>
> *Robert Rogers*

The fall of Montreal led to a new mission for the rangers. Amherst needed to explore the western frontier and defeat any of the French and their Indian allies who might oppose the British conquest of North America. Some of the western French commanders and their Indian allies, the British-hating Ottawa, would not be swayed by the British victory in the east. No British force had moved west of Fort Pitt since Braddock's defeat in 1755. What was needed was a fast-moving strike force that could move quickly to find, defeat and disarm the French in the Great Lakes basin. This was a perfect mission for the rangers. Rogers got the job.[2]

Fort Detroit Surrenders to Robert Rogers – 29 November 1760

On 13 September 1760, one year to the day after he had left Crown Point for Saint Francis, Rogers and 200 rangers pushed off from the Montreal wharf in 15 whaleboats. They would be moving south on the Saint Lawrence River through Lake Erie to Detroit. They made good time as the winter weather approached. Amherst had ordered Rogers to make contact with General Monckton at Fort Pitt before continuing south to Detroit. They reached Fort Pitt on 17 October. The press reported Rogers' arrival.

Philadelphia Nov. 13

On the 16th ult. Major Rogers, and Captain Brehem, an Engineer, arrived at Pittsburgh, in 33 Days from Montreal with Dispatches from General Monckton; and on the 18th in the morning the Major and the Engineer returned from Presque Isle, with a Detachment of the Royal Americans Commanded by Capt. Donald Campbell, who are to join a Body of Rogers' Rangers on Lake Erie, and to proceed to take possession of the French Forts at Detroit, and Michilimackinac; these, with all their Dependencies being particularly mention'd in the capitulation of Canada.[3]

Pontiac, or "Ponteach" (1712?-1769) (Wikipedia)

They spread the word along the way of the British victory, the fall of Montreal and New France, and the British conditions for the French surrender. By this time of year, storm surges on Lake Erie were enormous reaching heights of twenty-two feet. Several boats were damaged and the expedition stopped to make repairs. They continued and at Sandusky met with the dreaded Ottawas. They asked that Rogers wait until their chief Pontiac arrived. Pontiac wanted to meet Rogers, so the rangers waited for the chief that would one day become one of the most famous of the Indian chiefs. Pontiac arrived and in Rogers' words "He puts on an air of majesty and princely grandeur." Pontiac was described by Indian agent, Croghan, as "a shrewd, sensible Indian of few words, and commands more respect amongst these nations than any Indian I ever saw."[4] Pontiac wanted to know what his purpose was and why Rogers had not requested permission to pass through his land. Rogers explained that they were on their way to contact the French and let them know of the French defeat. His purpose was to "remove the French out of this country, who had been an obstacle in our way to mutual peace and commerce."[5] Pontiac and Rogers exchanged gifts and Rogers was allowed to proceed. Pontiac also provided him with an escort. On 25 November, Rogers reached the mouth of the Detroit River and met with the French commandant, Captain Francois-Marie Picote de Belestre. Rogers provided Belestre with a copy of Vaudreuil's letter and the terms of capitulation. Following discussions, the French laid down their arms and surrendered on 29 November 1760 at Detroit. The accomplishments were large. In a journey that lasted over three months, Rogers had traveled hundreds of miles through bad weather to the northwestern frontier. He had secured the surrender of the French without firing a shot and had made peace with the tribes, most notably the Ottawa and in particular Chief Pontiac.

> A nearly unimaginable swath of the continent had changed hands, the largest international transfer of land in history. When the peace was formalized in February 1763, the British Empire would swell larger than that of imperial Rome, most of its vast gains in the New World, where it now reached from the Atlantic west to the Mississippi River and from Hudson Bay south to the Gulf of Mexico.[6]

Rogers reached Fort Pitt on 13 January 1761 and informed General Monckton of the details of his trip. The rangers had traveled 1,600 miles in four months, more than

Lewis and Clark would travel a generation later.[7] The press welcomed the return of the rangers when they arrived in Philadelphia.

> PHILADELPHIA Feb. 12. On Monday last the brave Major Rogers, with Captain Breme, arrived here from his long and fatiguing March to Detroit, where he was sent by His Excellency General Amherst, in order to take Possession of the French Forts there; and from whence he was to have proceeded to Michillmackinac, 360 Miles beyond it, to bring off the French Soldiers that were in Posts at that Place (as mentioned in former Paper) But that he could not accomplish on account of the Ice, so was obliged to return after having got 200 Miles of it. The Major met with no Opposition, the People laying down their Arms, to the Capitulation of Canada, and seemed in general, well satisfied with being under an English Government. At Detroit he found betwixt Four and Five Hundred Men Capable of bearing Arms; 'tis a fine level rich Country, where before the war, there was a great deal of Wheat raised, Plenty of Cattle and the Inhabitants lived very comfortably; tho' they have not done so of late, most of the cattle being killed, and their fields not cultivated as usual. As soon as the Arrival of this Gentleman was known, the People here, to testify their Sense of his distinguish Merit, immediately ordered the Bell to be rung and shewed the other Marks of Respect. Yesterday he set off for New York.[8]

Rogers met with a grateful Amherst upon his return and was rewarded with a British regular army commission as captain. He would command an independent company. This was a prize sought by other colonials including Washington, but only Rogers achieved this goal.[9] He would now embark on the final act of the Seven Years' War in the New World: the pacification of the Cherokees in South Carolina. Before that, he had more important things to attend to.

Elizabeth Browne

Elizabeth Browne Rogers (1741-1813) (Wikipedia)

In May 1761 Rogers visited Portsmouth, New Hampshire after Amherst gave him a 30-day furlough. Portsmouth was an expanding town of 4,000; not nearly as large as Boston with its 15,000, but Portsmouth was home to some of the most famous families in the colonies: the Chases, Jeffreys, Rindges and Moffats. Trade had brought great wealth to Portsmouth.[10] By June 1761 Robert Rogers was nearly thirty years old and had been at war since his teen years. The brutal campaigns were taking their toll and it was time to think of other things. Rogers' financial difficulties followed him to Portsmouth. William Aiken and several other ex-rangers filed actions of attachment in Portsmouth for money owed and damages. There was at least one counter-suit and legal actions continued without result that year. In the words of Amherst. The colonials seemed possessed with "the disease of lawsuits."[11]

Rogers was, perhaps, the colony's most famous son and was greeted by many as he strolled the streets. Rogers' fellow Masons hosted a party for him at the Earl of Halifax Tavern. Among those present was Arthur Browne, chaplain of the Saint John's Masonic Lodge and the rector at the Anglican Queen's Chapel. After meeting and discussion, Rogers promised to attend Browne's Sunday service. At the service, Rogers noticed a beautiful nineteen year old lady with long brown hair. It was Arthur Browne's oldest daughter, Betsy.

> Love letters followed.
> Whenever I Set down to write to you Love and grief beyond degree together with pure gratitude and warm affection which I have for you my Dearest Betsy Invites from my Eyes a Shower. I often bid my passions all begon and call fro thoughtless Rest but my fanceys Meet you a thousand times Every day.[12]
>
> **Robert Rogers**

Rogers' campaign to win Betsy's hand was successful. They were wed on 30 June 1761, the date he was scheduled to ship out to South Carolina for the Cherokee War.[13]

The Cherokee War

The Rogers' expedition west to Fort Pitt and Detroit followed an earlier battle fought by General John Forbes and George Washington in 1758. In April 1758 Washington got word that Forbes had been given the mission to return to Fort Duquesne (later called Fort Pitt), the site of General Braddock's defeat three years earlier. Forbes' mission was to seize Fort Duquesne and Washington believed that he was best qualified for this task and asked his fellow survivor of the Braddock defeat, Thomas Gage, to pen a letter of introduction to Forbes. This was done and Washington volunteered his services in a letter to Forbes.

> I mean not, Sir, as one who has favors to ask of him – on the contrary, having entirely laid aside all hopes of preferment in the military line (and being induced at present to serve this campaign from abstract motives, purely laudable), I only wish to be distinguished in some measure from the general run of provincial Officers, as I understand there will be a motley herd of us. This, I flatter myself, can hardly be deemed an unreasonable request, when it is considered, that I have been much longer in the Service than any provincial officer in America.[14]
>
> ***George Washington***

Both Forbes and his second in command, Henry Bouquet, welcomed Washington to the campaign. They wished to avoid Braddock's mistakes and what better advisor could they have than Washington? Washington would command one of the three brigades moving on Fort Duquesne. He was the only colonial officer commanding a brigade. Relations did not stay cozy very long. Washington suggested that they follow Braddock's route to Fort Duquesne. Washington's reason was that it would maintain Virginia's claim to the Ohio country. It was the obvious route since it was an Indian trail that had been cut as Braddock's road and the Indians knew the best route to travel. He was overruled by Forbes. The problem was that the Royal Engineers had planned a more northern route that was thirty miles shorter and this route would avoid the Shenandoah Valley of Virginia.[15] Washington appealed to the governor of Virginia, Francis Fauquier which did no good. The new route would avoid Virginia and Washington was convinced that the new campaign was doomed. The colonial contempt for British regulars took hold of Washington and his words and conduct following the decision approached that of insubordination. Nevertheless, he prepared his Virginia Regiment for the campaign with diligence. To improve Washington's chance of success, the Virginia assembly doubled the size of Washington's force to two thousand men. He was determined that his regiment would be the best. He trained and equipped his troops like Rogers' Rangers. It is not known if he used Rogers' Rangers as a template or had a copy of the Rogers' Ranging Rules, but he closely followed both. Washington's troops were tutored in Indian-style warfare.[16]

William Shirley (1694-1771) (Wikipedia)

. . . "Indians," he claimed, "are the only match for Indians." This was less a statement of racial or ethnic enlightenment than a practical assessment that ten Indians were worth more than one hundred Virginia soldiers in a forest fight. He strongly supported the attempt to recruit Catawba and then Cherokee warriors from the Carolinas and gave orders to his troops "to be cautious what they speak before them: as all of them understand English, and ought not to be affronted." Despite his best efforts, the Indian populations of the region remained resolutely pro-French and the decisive factor in making his mission a wholly defensive holding action, which eventually took the shape of multiple forts or stockades strung out on the west side of the Blue Ridge and garrisoned by detachments of his Virginia "blues."

They were called that because of their distinctive uniforms, which Washington designed himself: "Every officer of the Virginia Regiment is, as soon as possible, to provide himself with uniform Dress, which is to be of fine Broad Cloth: The Coat Blue, faced and cuffed with Scarlet, and Trimmed with Silver: The Waistcoat Scarlet, with a plain Silver Lace, if to be had-the Breeches to be Blue, and every one to provide himself with a silver-laced Hat, of a Fashionable size." The officers' uniforms were but the outward manifestation of Washington's larger goal, which was to make the Virginia Regiment a truly special unit, "the first in Arms, of any Troops on the Continent, in the present War." They were to look sharper and drill with greater precision than any group of British regulars, and they were to master the mobile tactics of "bushfighting" with Indian-like proficiency. Within a year Washington believed he had created just such an elite force, which, because it was constantly engaged in combat operations patrolling the Virginia frontier, had a battle-tested edge no other colonial or British troops could match.

His pride in them was both professional and personal. "If it shou'd be said," he wrote Dinwiddie, "that the Troops of Virginia are Irregulars, and cannot expect more notice than other Provincials, I must beg leave to differ, and observe in turn, that we want nothing but Commissions from His Majesty to make us as regular a Corps as any upon the Continent." He had come to regard himself as superior to anyone, British or American, in conducting this kind of guerrilla war, and it rankled him that neither he nor his troops were paid at the same rate as British regulars. "We cannot conceive," he complained to Dinwiddie in what turned out to be prophetic language, "that because we are Americans, we shou'd therefore be deprived of the Benefits Common to British Subjects." His protest on this score was more personal than ideological; that is, it derived less from any political convictions about colonial rights than from his own disappointment that neither he nor his regiment were sufficiently appreciated. In the spring of 1756 he traveled all the way to Boston, his first trip to the northern colonies, to plead his case for equal pay and higher rank as a British officer to William Shirley, then acting commander for North America, who listened attentively but did nothing. He was a serious young man who took himself and his Virginia Regiment seriously, and expected others to do the same. He also managed to combine a broad-gauged grasp of his mission, in all its inherent frustrations, with a meticulous attention to detail. He drafted literally thousands of orders that all began "You are hereby ordered to . . . " and then proceeded, in language more incisive and grammatically cogent than his earlier writing, to focus tightly on a specific assignment: If you come upon a massacred settlement, harvest the corn crop before moving on; when constructing stockades, clear the surrounding trees and brush beyond musket range (a lesson he had learned from Fort Necessity); when a ranger in the regiment is killed in action, continue his salary for twenty-eight days to pay for his coffin; if ambushed in a clearing, rush toward the tree line from which the shots came while the enemy is reloading [These were similar to Rogers' Orders and were, perhaps, copied during Washington's trip, north]. Officers were held to a higher standard of deportment, to include controlling their wives: "There are continual complaints to me of the misbehavior of your wife," he apprised one captain. "If she is not immediately sent from the camp . . . I shall take care to drive her out myself, and suspend you." The old adage applied: if God were in the details, Colonel Washington would have been there to greet Him upon arrival.[17]

Forbes and Bouquet fully supported Washington. They had no wish to repeat the Braddock disaster.

First, they agreed to retain a large detachment of Cherokees as scouts, which Washington insisted were "the only Troops fit to Cope with Indians on such Ground." Second, they adopted the ranger uniforms of enlisted men in the Virginia Regiment instead of the traditional redcoats of the British army. Forbes called it "Indian dress," adding that "wee must comply and learn the Art of Warr, from Enemy Indians, or anything else who have seen the Country and Warr carried on in it." In effect, Forbes was acknowledging that the Virginia Regiment was the professional model and the British regulars the rank amateurs in this kind of campaign. Third, Forbes and Bouquet agreed to train their lead units in the forest-fighting tactics Washington had developed. If ambushed, the troops should "in an Instant, be thrown into an Order of Battle in the Woods," meaning they should advance in two groups to the tree line and flank the enemy on the left and right while the Indian scouts circled to the rear. Finally, the Virginia Regiment would be included in the vanguard, since, as Washington put it, "from long Intimacy, and scouting in these Woods, my Men are as well acquainted with all the Passes and difficulties as any Troops that will be employed."[18]

Skirmishes in September led to significant casualties when General Grant offered to lead a force of six hundred men quickly forward to assault the fort. Forbes agreed and the result was a pitched battle before the fort that caused Grant to lose almost three hundred men killed or captured and the British effort failed. After that a siege settled down until 12 November 1758 when Washington encountered French skirmishers outside of the fort and in the engagement that followed, Washington's troops mistakenly fired on each other. Washington's regiment sustained heavy casualties, most from the "friendly fire" incident. Casualties could have been higher, but Washington stepped between the two factions knocking muskets down with his sword. Later, after the War of Independence, Washington would claim that his life had been "in as much jeopardy as it had ever been before or since"[19] French prisoners taken after the fight revealed that Fort Duquesne was in a sorry state of repair and ripe for the taking.

> Of the sorry state of the fort's defenses, Jean-Daniel Dumas, who had held the field against Braddock's advance, wrote that Fort Duquesne was "fit only to dishonor the officer who would

be entrusted with its defense." . . . that officer was Francois-Marie le Marchand de Lignery and even he couldn't be certain of the exact number of troops under his command because of the free flow of Canadian militia and Indian allies into and out of his gates. Estimates ranged from 1,000 to more than 2,000, but some of these were no doubt strung along the Allegheny supply line from Presque Isle.[20]

Washington notified Forbes who ordered an immediate attack on the fort. Washington complied and found a smoking ruin when he entered the fort. The French knew that they were vastly outnumbered and had no food or help on the way. They abandoned Fort Duquesne.

> According to an eyewitness account in the *Pennsylvania Gazette,* the following evening "a heavy firing was heard from thence [Fort Duquesne]." It "continued first for about an hour, then ceased for some time, and began again, and lasted half an hour; and that afterwards a rumbling noise was also heard, like that of great guns at a distance." No one was quite sure what to make of it at the time, but an investigation the next day revealed the source of the huge explosion. As an express messenger to the *New York Gazette* reported: "Monsieurs did not stay for the approach of our army, but blew up the fort, spiked their cannon, threw them into the river, and made the best of their way off; carrying with them everything that was valuable, except the spot of ground where the fort stood."
>
> Indeed, Commandant Lignery had followed his orders and blown up the principal works of Fort Duquesne rather than let them fall into British hands. He and his remaining garrison of about 400 men dispersed, a few going down the Ohio toward the Illinois country and the others withdrawing up the Allegheny to Venango and Presque Isle. "After much fatigue and labor," wrote another British participant, "we have at last brought the artillery to this place, and found the French had left us nothing to do, having on the 24th instant blown up their magazines, and burned their fort to the ground."
>
> There were grisly scenes to be encountered. The unburied bodies of Grant's fallen troops littered the ground for three miles to within 100 yards of the fort. By one account, the heads

of a number of brave Highlanders were placed on "a long row of stakes that the Indians had erected along their well-beaten path to the fort . . . and underneath these were hung their Scottish kilts."

As Forbes and his troops assembled at the forks of the Ohio and hurriedly began work on a small stockade to accommodate a winter garrison, a number of Ohio Indians, who only a few weeks before had been on the other side, gathered to confer with the general. His subordinates assured them that it would be a small facility, intended to reestablish trade. Afterward, the *Pennsylvania Gazette* reported "that the French, by being obliged to abandon Fort Duquesne, have lost a vast tract of country, and the various tribes of Indians inhabiting it, seem, in a certain manner, reconciled to his Majesty's protection and government."[21]

While Forbes was at work at the forks of the Ohio, Washington returned to Virginia and left the army a month later. A small force of Pennsylvanians was left behind at what was now called Fort Pitt while Forbes returned to Philadelphia in January, 1759. He enjoyed a brief period of notoriety as the victor at Fort Duquesne before he died a few weeks later at age fifty-one from a "wasting disease."

Nearly seven hundred Cherokees in South Carolina were recruited and arrived in Pennsylvania in mid-May 1758. The problem was that the slow pace of road building left them with little to do and they drifted away to their southern homeland.[22] This was part of the problem that Rogers would have to deal with when Amherst sent him south to pacify the Cherokees.

While France and Great Britain focused most attention on the north and western frontier, the conflict extended south to New Orleans and into Alabama and the Carolinas. In November 1758 Governor William Lyttelton of South Carolina wrote to William Pitt who was then Secretary of State suggesting an attack against French settlements on the Alabama and Mississippi rivers beginning with Fort Toulouse near what is now Wetumpka, Alabama. Lyttleton would induce the Cherokees and other tribes to join the campaign. Nothing came of his Fort Toulouse proposal since attention was focused elsewhere, but it demonstrated that Lyttelton was an activist who had no problem with going to war.

When some of the Cherokees were returning from the Forbes campaign they were mistakenly killed by South Carolina militiamen. Others found that whites had encroached on their hunting grounds. The Cherokees and the other tribes settled in towns clustered along the Georgia/Carolina frontier. Attakullakulla was the Cherokee leader. They were called the "civilized tribes"[23] because they settled and farmed as the colonials did. Hence their improved lands were coveted by the whites. The tribes favored the British over the French during the war but this would change.

Friction between the Cherokees and white settlers continued and Attakullakulla tried to mediate but when Cherokees attempted to negotiate with Lyttelton, he seized some of them as hostages demanding that the Cherokees hand over the person responsible for the recent death of a white settler. When this did not happen, Lyttelton marched the militia to Fort Prince George along with the hapless hostages; however, an outbreak of smallpox sent the militia fleeing back to Charleston. This left Fort Prince George in a vulnerable position. Vengeful Cherokees were at the gates, relatives of the hostages demanded their release and the commandant was sitting on three tons of linens, muskets and ammunition that were promised to the Cherokees but withheld by Lyttelton. At this point Lyttelton took off for Jamica where he had been appointed governor and left the mess that he had created to his successor, William Bull.

On 16 February 1760 the Cherokees lured the commandant out of Fort Prince William under the guise of a parley and murdered him. In the attack that followed the fort held and the hostages were executed. This set off the war that spread across the Carolina frontier. Bull appealed to Amherst for help and British regulars were sent in. The British moved to relieve Fort Prince William destroying Cherokee villages along the way. From there, the British planned to push further to Fort Loudoun but were ambushed along the way losing a hundred troops and most of their pack animals. At this point they gave up the fight and returned to Charleston.

At Fort Loudoun 200 militiamen commanded by Captain Paul Demere had a problem. They were isolated, surrounded, starving, and ready to desert. Since Virginia was closer to Fort Loudoun than Charleston, South Carolina he asked Virginia to send help. Virginia troops started to march but before they could arrive Captain Demere surrendered to the Cherokees on 8 August 1760. The terms of the surrender allowed Demere, his troops and their families to be escorted to Fort Prince Edward.

> Three days later Cherokee warriors rose from the forest and killed more than two dozen soldiers, reserving special retaliation for the leader, Paul Demere, captain of a South Carolina independent company, who was scalped alive, beaten with clubs, and forced to dance, then had his arms and legs chopped off. As incensed braves stuffed his mouth full of dirt, reported one eyewitness, they taunted: "You English want land, we will give it to you."
>
> Amherst had decided that Rogers would replace Demere and informed Lieutenant Colonel James Grant, commanding the 1761 punitive campaign, that Rogers would join him once he had settled his accounts, "which will not take him up long," although on that front Amherst and Rogers alike were sadly in error.[24]

Rogers would be delayed many months in settling his accounts While he was tied up, the war continued. While

Rogers was not present for this campaign his rangers were, most notably, Captain Manley Williams, who was killed in a skirmish with the Cherokees on 27 June 1760.[25]

British regulars landed at Charleston on 6 January 1761. General Grant's force of 2,800 troops reached Fort Prince George in May. Amherst's orders were "to chastise the Cherokees [and] reduce them to the absolute necessity of suing for peace." So Grant moved north from Fort Prince George. The Cherokees lay in ambush but were routed by Francis Marion's company of rangers. Marion who later earned the title of the "Swamp Fox," during the War of Independence sustained heavy casualties but cleared the way for Grant who proceeded to destroy fifteen Cherokee villages and their crops along the way. The Cherokee sued for peace and peace talks to end the two-year war began between Grant and Attakullakulla in August 1761. The treaty was signed in Charlestown in December 1761. Cherokee boundaries were pushed further west.[26] Rogers arrived in Charleston on 21 August 1761 with eighteen rangers.[27] While he had missed the Cherokee War, he probably witnessed the peace negotiations. He spent months in South Carolina recruiting before returning north. He had added to his debts while in South Carolina and debt collectors followed him to Portsmouth. South Carolina merchants Smith and Nutt claimed £23 that he owed them and while this was partially paid, the New Hampshire Supreme Court confirmed all of the 1761 made judgments against him in Portsmouth.[28] His finances continued to spiral out of control and he needed a government position that would get him out of debt. For this he would need the help of Amherst and others and he had a plan.

While most of the fighting between France and Great Britain in North America ended in 1760, it continued elsewhere and it was not until the Treaty of Paris on 10 February 1763 that the war in North America ended while the Treaty of Hubertusburg ended the war in Europe five days later on 15 February 1763. The Seven Years' War made major changes to the economic, political, governmental and social relations between the European principals, Great Britain, France, and Spain. France lost nearly all of New France to Great Britain and ceded Louisiana to Spain. France and Great Britain suffered major financial impacts that would grow into major issues for both nations in the years that followed. For the soldiers in the New World that had been minor players in the French and Indian War such as Washington, Rogers, John Stark, Francis Marion, Israel Putnam, Pontiac, Thomas Gage and many others: they would be found in major leadership roles in the conflicts that followed.

5. The Uneasy Peace

Legacy of the War

Britain's triumph in the Great War for Empire contained the seeds of the American Revolution. England emerged from the war with an expanded empire and a staggering national debt, much of it resulting from the struggle in North America. Britain wanted to administer its new empire with maximum efficiency, which in part meant enforcing the Navigation Acts, a series of laws designed to regulate colonial trade for the mother country's benefit. Americans had consistently violated laws through smuggling and bribery. Strict enforcement would help alleviate England's financial distress but would crimp the colonial economy.[1]

Pontiac's War Begins – 7 May 1763

Following the travel of Robert Rogers to the wilderness in 1760-1761 where he met Chief Pontiac, the frontier remained peaceful for a short time. The British victory over the French meant new ownership in North America and the Indians became dissatisfied with the trading practices of the British. Jeffery Amherst, the architect of Indian policy, cut back on the provisions previously provided by the French, especially gunpowder and ammunition needed by the Indians for hunting. Amherst viewed the provisions as bribes to keep the Indians peaceful and indeed, they were. Following the war, British colonists moved into Indian territory in increasing numbers and by 1761, Indian leaders were calling for an effort to eject the British settlers and attempt to revive an Indian and French alliance. Pontiac entered the world stage on 27 April 1763 when he called a council of Indian nations near Fort Detroit to discuss a surprise attack on Fort Detroit.

> It is important for us, my brothers, that we exterminate from our lands this nation which seeks only to destroy us. You see as well as I that we can no longer supply our needs, as we have done from our brothers, the French. . . . Therefore, my brothers, we must all swear their destruction and wait no longer. Nothing prevents us; they are few in numbers, and we can accomplish it.[2]
> ***Chief Pontiac***

Pontiac was an Odawa[3] chief who was born between 1712 and 1725, perhaps near the Detroit or Maumee rivers. Little is known of his early life but by the time Robert Rogers visited him in 1760, he was chief of the Ottawas. His visit with Rogers had a lasting effect on his reputation. Rogers' visit to London in 1765 was the first of several. In London after the French and Indian War, Rogers wrote a play about Pontiac entitled *Ponteach: or Savages of America*. It helped make Pontiac famous and historian Richard White claims that the play made Pontiac the most famous Indian of the eighteenth century. Perhaps too famous since whites concluded that he was chief of all of the Indian nations which he was not. As a consequence whites tried to deal with Pontiac as a representative of all nations which created jealousy and confusion among the other tribes.

It was known as Pontiac's War and it started on 7 May 1763 when Pontiac and three hundred followers attempted to take Fort Detroit with a surprise attack. It failed and he laid siege to the fort. Although he was joined by nine hundred warriors from other tribes, his efforts were unsuccessful and he withdrew to Illinois Country. His attacks signaled a general uprising by Indians throughout the Ohio valley. Widespread attacks against British and colonial forts and villages followed, but the French were spared.

Amherst sent reinforcements under Captain James Dalyell of the 1st Foot, his aide-de-camp, with orders that he gather any forces that he could and relieve Niagara and Fort Detroit. Robert Rogers joined the campaign under Dalyell and by early July 1763, Rogers had enlisted twenty-nine men to join his rangers that now numbered thirty-seven men. Dalyell had over two hundred.[4] On 31 July, the British forces moved forward to relieve the siege of Fort Detroit attempting to make a surprise attack on Pontiac's encampment. Pontiac was ready and waiting, possibly alerted by French settlers, and defeated the British at Parent's Creek two miles (3 km) east of the fort. However, he did not accomplish the destruction of this British force which would have greatly demoralized the British and dissuaded more British efforts to break the Indian siege of Fort Detroit. The creek, or run, was said to have run red with the blood of the 20 dead and 34 wounded British soldiers and was henceforth known as Bloody Run. Indian losses were said to be five killed and eleven wounded. Major William Eyre reported in a letter to General Thomas Gage "Major Rogers was particularly active in covering the retreat."[5] The attack's commander, Captain James Dalyell, was one of those killed. After learning of Dalyell's death, General Jeffrey Amherst offered a £200 bounty to anyone who would kill Pontiac.

Eventually the Ohio Valley was pacified by the British and an effort was made to end the war. On 25 July 1766 Pontiac met with the British Superintendent of Indian Affairs, Sir William Johnson at Fort Ontario in Oswego, New York. This meeting formally ended hostilities. What followed was an increase in the white presence in the Ohio Valley that insured British supremacy in the region.

Pontiac's fame and power increased during the uprising and by 1766 he was acting arrogantly with the other tribal leaders and they ousted him. On 10 May 1768, he wrote to British officials to explain that he was no longer chief of his people. Pontiac was murdered on 20 April 1769 near the French village of Cahokia. A Peoria warrior was avenging his uncle who was badly wounded by Pontiac. The closing lines of a play that Robert Rogers' wrote, *Ponteach: or Savages of America* are his tribute to Pontiac.

And though I fly, 'tis on the Wings of Hope. Yes, I will hence where there's no British Foe, And wait a Respite from this Storm of Woe; Beget more Sons, fresh Troops collect and arm, And other Schemes of future Greatness form; Britons may boast, the Gods may have the Will, Ponteach I am, and shall be Ponteach still.[6]

Chief Pontiac

Pontiac's War ended Jeffrey Amherst's career in America. He was called home and called to account for his conduct of Pontiac's War. Amherst had many enemies on both sides of the Atlantic and the conflict had seen many bloody losses by the British. It was a brutal era with thousands of British men, women and children butchered by the Indians, but it was an atrocity of the British that is remembered today: biological warfare. The smoking gun in this case was correspondence between Amherst and Colonel Henry Bouquet. In July 1763 Amherst wrote to Bouquet "that he had heard that smallpox had broken out at Fort Pitt and wondered whether the disease could not be spread to good advantage." [7] Bouquet replied.

> I will try to inoculate [sic] the bastards by means of Blankets that may fall in their hands, taking care however not to get the disease myself. As it is pity to expose good men against them, I wish we could make use of the Spaniard's Method, and hunt them with English Dogs.[8]

Henry Bouquet

Small pox laden blankets and other items were distributed to the Indians. It is not clear what impact this had on the tribes, but one outbreak of small pox was reported among the Delaware and Shawnee. The event is remembered today at Amherst College. Because of Jeffrey Amherst's role in biological warfare against the Indians, today's students wanted to do some name changing as seen, below. They had to settle for less.

AMHERST COLLEGE
The Board of Trustees
January 26, 2016

Dear Member of the Amherst College Community,

During the past several months President Biddy Martin and the members of the Board of Trustees have had scores (all right, hundreds) of communications from alumni, students, and others about the matter of Lord Jeffery Amherst. The communications reflect and embody many points of view. A lot of them begin with something like the following: "I know there are far more important issues facing the College, but...." . . .

The mascot question arose anew in this context, starting some while ago and intensifying over the past year and a half. Certain basic facts are broadly familiar. The town of Amherst was named after Lord Jeffery, and the College was named after the town. Lord Jeffery had no connection with the College and died a generation before its founding. Lord Jeff was adopted unofficially by students as a mascot roughly a century ago. The College itself has never officially adopted Lord Jeff as a mascot—or adopted anyone or anything else as a mascot, for that matter. *Those who dislike the symbolism of Lord Jeff have various reasons for their view, but a central one has always been his suggestion, in wartime correspondence, that smallpox be used against Native Americans. Nothing may have come of his proposal, defenders counter; they add, for context, that harsh tactics were employed by both sides in the conflict. Thinking about these events leads immediately into gnarly debates about how we understand history, about the very nature of war, about the weight we give to words and actions, and about who has standing to render moral judgments.* [Italics added by author] . . .

Lord Jeff as a mascot may be unofficial, but the College, when its own resources are involved, can decide not to employ this reference in its official communications, its messaging, and its symbolism (including in the name of the Inn, the only place on the campus where the Lord Jeffery name officially appears). The Board of Trustees supports such an approach, and it will be College policy. The Inn's new name will reflect its deep connections with Amherst College and the town of Amherst. Beyond that, people will do as they will: the College has no business interfering with free expression, whether spoken or written or, for that matter, sung. Period. We hope and anticipate that understanding and respect will run in all directions. ***To those who argue that stepping back from Lord Jeff as an unofficial mascot takes us down some sort of slippery slope that calls into question the name of the town or the College, the board would respond that you can find slippery slopes anywhere you look, that real life isn't a philosophy class or court of law, and that people long ago figured out the common-sense way to deal with slippery slopes: just draw the line. Amherst College will always be the name of the school.* . . .**

We can and will achieve this ambition. We will be proud to have done so. And we will be better for it in countless ways.

Sincerely,

Murphy
Chair, Board of Trustees[9]

Jeffery Amherst was replaced by Major General Thomas Gage, the shallow underachiever.[10] This was the same Gage who would oppose Washington during the War of Independence. Gage was also a bitter enemy of Robert Rogers.

Thomas Gage (1721-1787) (Library of Congress)

Rogers spent weeks at Detroit before returning east. Bloody Run was his last Indian engagement. In months that followed, Rogers spent time in New York City, Boston and Portsmouth attempting to recoup his financial losses incurred in supporting the war effort as well as defending himself against law suits for loans not repaid. This went on for months that turned into years. When he visited New York City in January 1765 he was arrested for an outstanding debt and held until soldiers sympathetic to his plight broke into the jail and freed him. Finally in March 1765, he set sail for London leaving Betsy behind in Portsmouth. He hoped to secure support for an expedition to find the Northwest Passage or failing that, obtain a captaincy in a regiment.[11] He would accomplish other things on his visit to London. His arrival in London was noted by the *Public Advertiser* on 3 August 1765.

> The gallant Major Rogers is lately arrived from America to solicit some Preferment from the Ministry. This Gentleman was the first Person in America who raised a Body of Troops at his own Expence, and headed them against the Indians who were in the Service of Our Enemies – His Regard for the Welfare of his Country however, utterly exhausted his private Fortune; and he now has the Rank of a Major, with the half-pay of a Captain, while several Gentlemen, who were employed under him as Subaltern Officers, are advanced to be Lieutenant Colonels, and are in a fair Way of rising to the first of our Military Honours and Emoluments.[12]

Rogers was impressed with London's size and wealth. It had arisen from the Great Fire of 1666 as a new metropolis and financial center, but in many ways the London that greeted Rogers was little better than the hostile frontier in America. Raw sewage ran through the streets and the Thames served not only as the source of drinking water but also for dumping all sorts of nasty things such as dead creatures, sewage, and the products of slaughter houses and manufacturing. Use of coal for fuel throughout the city kept inhabitants in an eternal haze that also polluted the drinking water and ravaged the townspeople with lung diseases. Diseases such as typhus and typhoid fever flourished and many died young before their time. One of those who would succumb to typhus was Charles Townshend, a former first Lord of the Admiralty.

Charles Townshend (1725-1767) (Creative Commons)

Two years before his death Townshend became enamored with Rogers, having read the newspaper accounts of Rogers. Rogers' cause was helped by the publication of his *Journals and a Concise Account of North America.* These were published in the fall of 1765 at the same time that his proposal to find the Northwest Passage was under consideration by the Board of Trade.

> The Rout Major Rogers proposes to take, is from the Great Lakes towards the Head of the Mississippi, and from thence to the River called by the Indians Ouragon, which flows into a Bay that projects North-Eastwardly into the Country from the Pacific Ocean, and there to Explore the said Bay and its Outletts, and also the Western Margin of the Continent to such a Northern Latitude as shall be thought necessary.[13]

Charles Townshend supported Rogers' proposal that was read before the Lords of Trade on 6 September 1765. The Rogers' proposal seemed sound and Board President, the Earl of Dartmouth, wrote the King supporting the proposal. George III in turn forwarded the Rogers' proposal to the Committee of the Privy Council, his advisors. There was a problem with all of this: the cost would be high. The cost estimate included among other items an exploring force of 228 troops. At this time Britain was under a staggering debt of 150,000,000 lbs caused by the Seven Years' War. To help pay the national debt the Stamp Act was inflicted on the Colonies and opposition to it was growing. This was the first direct tax on the colonies by the British Parliament that included no representatives of the colonies. The effective date of the act was 1 November 1765 and it had been discussed in government and coffee houses on both sides of the Atlantic long before its effective date. Battle lines had been drawn and this and other acts would eventually lead to the War of Independence. The impact on Rogers was that there would be no funds available for his expedition to find the Northwest Passage.[14]

The Search for the Western Sea[15]

The Northwest Passage is a sea route connecting the northern Atlantic and Pacific Oceans. In the 21st Century, global warming provides a year-round sea route through the Arctic without the need for ice-breakers. Until 2009 Arctic pack ice prevented marine shipping throughout most of the year. Since then, the Arctic sea route provides passage for ships too large to pass through the Panama Canal and shortens the sea route by weeks for all shipments from Northern Europe to destinations in the Pacific such as China. As of 2016, the largest ship to navigate the Northwest Passage was the cruise liner *Crystal Serenity* of gross tonnage 69,000. It started on 10 August 2016 sailing from Vancouver British Columbia with 1,500 passengers to New York City arriving twenty-eight days later.[16]

Before global warming and the Panama Canal (opened in 1914) ships sailed from Europe to the far east through the southern tip of the new world through what is called the Strait of Magellan, a natural passage between the Atlantic and Pacific Oceans. This route is plagued by the unpredictability of winds and currents and the narrowness of the passage. A water passage across North America would cut months off of the voyage to the Far East. Many attempts were made to find such a passage but all failed. Finally, the British Parliament took action.

> The Discovery of North-West Passage Act 1744 (18 Geo. II, c.17) was an Act of Parliament of Great Britain passed in 1745 and repealed in 1818. It offered a public reward for the successful discovery of a Northwest Passage from the Atlantic to the Pacific. The preamble to the Act stated the expected economic benefits of the discovery of the passage, and that it would be "a great encouragement to adventurers" to offer a prize. The allocated sum was 20,000*l*, to be paid to the owners of the first ships to successfully make such a passage. The Act established a group of commissioners to determine the validity of any claims, and

restricted the scope of the Act to only apply to British subjects. It further required all British subjects to provide help and assistance to the explorers when required.[17]

No progress was made in discovering the Northwest Passage following the Act of 1744 until it was repealed in 1818. Following Rogers unsuccessful bid, he had an audience with the King on 16 October. George III was sympathetic to Rogers' financial problems and had followed items in the press and had read his proposal. The King approved several measures that helped Rogers. Rogers would receive £500 as reimbursement for his expenses. He would also receive a major's full pay and a captaincy in the Royal Americans. Most important, he was given command of Fort Michilimackinac. While these measures did not solve his many financial problems, they helped. A prompt settlement of his military-related debts was also promised. Rogers took advantage of his visit with the king to present George III with copies of his new books, *Journals of Major Robert Rogers* and *A Concise Account of North America*. Rogers was not only a prolific writer, but also had an understanding of the value of public relations.

George III, King of Great Britain (1738-1820) (Library of Congress)

Rogers' fame exceeded that of Benjamin Franklin and Washington in Europe.[18] When he departed London to return to the Colonies he left behind a revised proposal for the Northwest Passage expedition. It was a far less costly plan. Charles Townshend promised to submit the proposal after Rogers departed.

Fort Michilimackinac Restored (Wikipedia)

Fort Michilimackinac was a fort and trading post at the Straits of Mackinac. It was built on the northern tip of the lower peninsula of the present-day state of Michigan around 1715. It was located along the Straits that connect Lake Huron and Lake Michigan. Present-day Mackinaw City developed around the site of the fort. Rogers arrived in New York on 6 January 1766 eager to assume command of his new post, Fort Michilimackinac. While Rogers and Elizabeth prepared for their trip to Fort Michilimackinac, a very interesting person sought a meeting with Rogers.

Jonathan Carver (1710-1780) (Library of Congress)

Jonathan Carver was born in Weymouth, Massachusetts in 1710. He was twenty-one years senior to Rogers and had his own vision of an expedition to find the Northwest Passage.

> Records show that Carver was enrolled in a Massachusetts militia unit raised at the town of Deerfield on the frontier in 1755, although he may have served in such a unit even earlier. He was at

Fort William Henry on Lake George with a combined British and British American force in 1757 when it was captured by French and Indian forces under General Louis Joseph Montcalm, and where, despite Montcalm's orders, many of the captured soldiers were massacred. Carver himself was being led off into the woods by two Indians to what he presumed would be his death when they released him to pursue a British officer in full uniform, apparently a more tempting victim. Carver escaped with minor wounds.

He served as a second lieutenant in a militia battalion the following year. By 1763, when the French conceded defeat and forfeited their North American territories to the British, Carver had risen to the rank of captain and was commanding a company of militia troops.[19]

His resume was as impressive as Rogers'. He was an explorer, surveyor, map maker and talented writer. He hardly looked the part. By the time of his meeting with Rogers in 1766, he was middle-aged and unlikely to be able to lead any expedition. The two should have been competitors for a Northwest Passage expedition, but Rogers had a proposal pending approval in London for an expedition and Carver did not.[20] While Rogers and Betsy were planning their move to Fort Michilimackinac, Rogers and Carver met. Earlier expeditions by others had shown that a Northwest Passage via the great lakes did not exist and Rogers was certain that a waterway north and west of the Great Lakes would lead to the Pacific. The current reward for finding the Northwest Passage was £20,000 and both Rogers and Carver were eager to collect. Rogers needed money. Promises that Rogers had received in London for reimbursement of war expenses were now in the hands of Gage who was determined to whittle down or dismiss Rogers' claims. Rogers agreed to support Carver's expedition and enlisted the help of James Tute, a former member of Rogers' Rangers.

In May 1766, Rogers, Betsy, and their entourage sailed up the Hudson. Rogers would meet with Sir William Johnson, the Superintendant of Indian Affairs, at his estate on the

Mohawk River called Johnson Hall. Johnson would have much to say about Rogers' activities when he assumed his post at Fort Michilimackinac. There was bad blood between the two that stemmed from the recent war and an attempt by Rogers to get a land grant in an area that Johnson considered his domain.[21] It also rankled Johnson that Rogers had been selected to command at Fort Michilimackinac without his approval. Gage was also an enemy of Rogers since he was miffed by a Crown appointment without his knowledge. Further, he was directed by London to reward Rogers for his wartime service and reopen the matter of Rogers' army accounts. A report of the balance due to Rogers was to be sent to London.[22] An infuriated Gage wrote to Johnson.

> He is wild, vain, of little understanding, and of as little Principle, but withal has a share of Cunning, No Modesty or veracity and sticks at Nothing. Be So good to Send me your Advice in what manner he may be best tied up by Instructions and prevent [sic] doing Mischief and imposing upon you.[23]
>
> *Thomas Gage*

When Rogers arrived to visit Johnson, he had already established as enemies two of the most powerful men in North America, a fact he would later regret. The post at Fort Michilimackinac was one of enormous power. In January Johnson wrote to Gage that Rogers "will have it in his power To confine the Trade in a great degree to himself & Friends."[24] Both Johnson and Gage were well aware of Rogers' spending habits and intended to curb Rogers' tendency to run up bills. There was great potential for this since Rogers had been instructed to provide gifts and supplies to the Indians in order to keep them friendly. The meeting was more or less cordial and Rogers received his instructions from Johnson on 3 June 1766.

> Rogers' role would be to keep the peace, to acquaint the Indians at Michilimackinac that as long as they "continue to behave as Friends and Men who regard their

Engagements . . . they may be assured of Johnson's] Friendship & Good Offices, and that His Majesty will not permit any of his Subjects to wrong them." He was to "avoid giving any umbrage to the Indians, and... prevent any quarrels from arising between them & the Soldiers or Traders." He was to report offenders to Johnson, and cultivate the "Confidence & Esteem of the Indians."[25]

Prior to his departure from Johnson's estate, a letter had been sent to Rogers by Joseph Hopkins. Hopkins was a Marylander and former colonial officer who had switched sides and now served the French. Hopkins had a checkered past that mixed good soldiering with skaldugery. He had served with Rogers and had commanded a ranger company raised in 1762 for service at Fort Detroit. His bad conduct surfaced in a letter from his superior, Major Gladwin to General Gage. Rogers was one of many who endorsed the Gladwin letter. In doing so, he insured that he had earned Hopkins undying hostility.

> Sir:
> As Captain Hopkins has been Accused by Lieutenant Cuyler of Ungentleman like Behaviour, in selling Rum etc. at a Profit and Overcharging the Men of his Company for Necessary's furnished by him-The Officers of the Garrison whose Names, are Under-mentioned do therefore refuse *to* do duty with him till such times as he Clears his Character.[26]
>
> ***Robert Rogers***

Hopkins somehow escaped court-martial and when the siege was lifted at Fort Detroit he traveled to London to seek reward for his service. When this was refused, he threw his lot in with the French and soon found himself on the island of St. Domingo in the service of France. Since he knew that Rogers, like most colonial officers, received poor treatment from the British, he ventured a letter to Rogers in the hope of luring Rogers into a conspiracy against the British.

As I promised, you were remembered in my Conversations with

the Minister of the King I now Serve... I cannot think of persuading or enticing you on, until there shall be a Certainty fixed for you, or such of our Acquaintance as will follow my Example, you know the injustices we have suffered particularly yourself, nor is it in the power of England to recompence you for the disgraces you underwent for having Served them too faithfully.[27]

Joseph Hopkins

The letter to Rogers was one of several sent to colonial officers in the hope of luring them to join the French. The Stamp Act was generating bad feelings among the colonials toward Britain and turning a colonial against the mother country could do nothing but improve the fortunes of France in the New World. It was a very clever plot. If the letter reached its mark and the colonial joined against the French, it was a win and others might join the recipient. If the letter was intercepted, it could discredit a loyal colonial in the eyes of the British. In the case of Rogers, it appears that it was intended to be intercepted. The letter to Rogers arrived aboard a French vessel with the letter marked "From Maryland." It was on thin paper easily read by holding it to the light. A group of suspicious letters to colonial officers was seized and sent to Gage who examined them. After reading the letter to Rogers he resealed it and sent it to Johnson with instructions that it be given to Rogers.

I am likewise to beg of you, for very particular Reasons, which I can't now mention, that you will give the strongest Orders to your Interpreters and Commissarys to watch Major Roger's Transactions with the Indians and that they send you Information if he holds any bad Conversation with them ... I hope no such thing will happen, if it does, it will be chiefly at the Detroit, particularly with Pondiac, Tho' if he begins there, he will no doubt do the same at Missilimakinak. Your People should keep their Instructions secret and not divulge what you write them on this Subject.[28]

Thomas Gage

By the time the letter arrived at Johnson Hall on 10 June 1766, Rogers and Betsy were already on their way to Fort Michilimackinac. Johnson read the letter through the thin tissue and forwarded it to Rogers. Johnson and Gage were both delighted. The trap had been set.

The Carver Expedition Begins – 3 September 1766

Rogers and Betsy arrived at Fort Michilimackinac on 10 August 1766. Shortly after his arrival he started planning for an expedition to find the Northwest Passage. The £20,000 offered by the Crown was much on his mind. He later wrote.

> Immediately after my arrival at Michilimackinac I Received a Letter from Doctor John Campbell (whom I desired might be appointed Agent for those Discoveries) directing me to proceed Immediately in the manner I have done, telling me in the Strongest Terms, that nothing could Recommend me more to his Majesty and his ministers than those Discoveries; I also received a Letter from Mr. Townshend recommending these Discoveries, with various Letters from Sundry Gentlemen in England to the same effect.[29]
>
> ***Robert Rogers***

Carver and Tute arrived before September 1st and it was agreed that Tute would command the expedition and Carver would be "Draftsman to the Detachment." Rogers' duties as commander of Fort Michilimackinac prevented him from commanding the expedition. Rogers granted a commission to Carver to explore and agreed to pay him eight shillings a day until discharged. Carver was simply an employee of Rogers.[30]

> Carver and Rogers did not know each other well, although it is possible that they had met during the period of their military service. Carver certainly knew of Rogers' well-publicized achievements in the war. Upon learning that this famous frontiersman had requested officials of the Crown in London to authorize an expedition into the interior, he had offered his services. Although Carver was already fifty-six years old and

only a self-taught map maker, he had, as he told Rogers, "studiously endeavoured to inform [himself] in every science necessary for a compleet draughts man." He had journeyed extensively through New England and nearby parts of Canada and had drawn maps of the region. In need of a map maker to chart his expedition, Rogers took Carver on not expressly to find a Northwest Passage, but merely "to explore the interior and unknown Tracts of the Continent of America at the back of Your Majesty's Colonies, and to Inspect the same and make Observations, Surveys and Draughts thereof." It is possible that Carver did not at first know that Rogers had far greater aspirations than that.[31]

Carver arrived at Michilimackinac on August 28, 1766, and formally received his commission from "Robert Rogers Esqr. Agent to the Western Indians and Governor Commandant of His Majesty's Garrison." He was directed to "set out from this post immediently." With the help of previously drawn maps, mostly the work of French explorers and believed to be of limited reliability, he was to proceed through Lake Michigan to Green Bay and then, by way of the Fox and Wisconsin rivers to the Mississippi, along which he was to ascend as far as the Falls of St. Anthony, at the site of present-day Minneapolis. That was expected to be the farthest extent of his journey before winter set in. He was to make "an exact plan of the countery by the way marking down all Indian towns with their numbers, as also to take survaies of the diffrant posts, lakes, and rivers as also the mountains."

Carver was to winter in the area, and in the spring he was to dispatch a written report to Rogers at Michilmackinac by one of the traders who regularly traversed the region. Instructions for him to continue farther westward might be sent to him. If he received none, he was to return to the fort by way of the Illinois and St. Joseph rivers to Lake Michigan and then along the lake's eastern shore, mapping the area and keeping detailed records of all he saw.[32]

Carver would leave two weeks in advance of Tute.[33] Rogers' proposal read by George III provided that the search for the Northwest Passage would go to the "head of the Mississippi" (Lake Itasca in Minnesota) and thence west to the

Pacific.[34]   Carver pushed off from Fort Michilimackinac on 3 September followed by Tute two weeks later. The entire expedition was a far less than the 200 man force originally proposed to the King. Tute kept a journal of his journey.

> Left Michilimackinac in a bark canoe Sept 17, at 6 a.m. Saw Chief Mamickquoine at Little Ottawa village on Little Detroit Island on Amanistick River, about 30 leagues from Michilimackinac. Gave Chief a little rum and enticed him to come to Michilimackinac in the spring to see his father (Rogers). Visited Chief Otter of a Menominies village on Manomemacon River; then Fort La Raye, 18 leagues WSW of above River and one mile up River du Renard on N shore. Next visited Chief Econeme, or the Horse's village of Minomines a half mile up this River. Visited a village of Puentes; the village of Sackin, of Washebones; village of Otagamies; then determined to winter on River du Dard on west side of Mississippi, 12 leagues below Ouaconsang. Built their house when Trader Bruce came down and persuaded Tute to go and winter on a River called Ione. Tute set off Nov 30, on foot with Bruce. A canoe with portion of party's provision preceding them the day before. . . . Expedition left La Hun on May 21, 1767, in two canoes up the Mississippi. Eighth day arrived at the Chippewa River; decided to skirt Sioux country by proceeding up this river. Visited village on Lake Ottawa, staying six days. Ran out of provisions at end of Lake Superior and sent a canoe off to meet the French canoes from Michilimackinac, which returned the sixth day with a small replenishment. Gave a stand of Colors to Chief of the carrying-place (Chippewa Indians). After consultation found they did not have the necessary provisions to continue and agreed to return to Michilimackinac, arriving Aug 29, 1767.[35]
>
> ***James Tute***

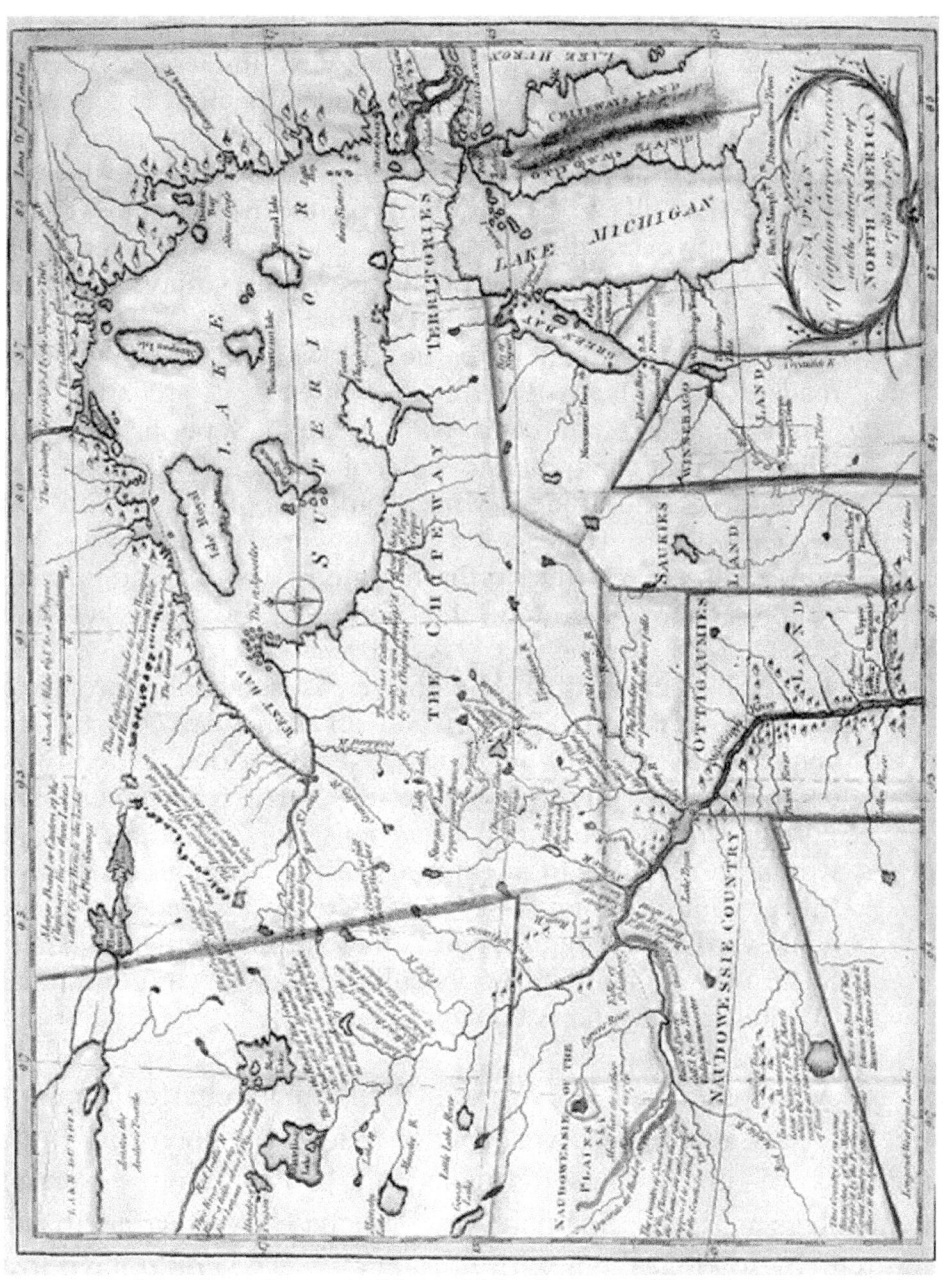

Jonathan Carver's Map of His Journey (Creative Commons)

Carver's plan was to continue up the St. Pierre to its headwaters, where, according to Indian report, a short portage would bring him to the head-waters of another river flowing westward to the Pacific. The route was a delightfully simple one, on paper, and it is unfortunate that Carver found no opportunity of testing it. While at Michilimackinac he had obtained from Mr. Rogers, the officer in charge, a scanty supply of goods to use as presents to the Indians in his proposed journey, and a further supply was to be sent on to him at the Falls of St. Anthony on the Mississippi. These goods, however, did not arrive, and he was reluctantly compelled to abandon the St. Pierre route, so inviting in its simplicity.

Being disappointed here, he determined to try another road. Returning to Prairie du Chien, he ascended the Mississippi and made his way to Lake Superior, through what was practically unknown territory, hoping at the Grand Portage to find traders who would supply him with the needed goods. If he could have secured these, it was his purpose to attempt the northern route by way of Rainy Lake, Lake of the Woods, and Lake Winnipeg. From the latter he expected to ascend the Assiniboine to its head-waters, which, like those of the St. Pierre, he believed approached the westward-flowing river; and crossing over to this convenient stream, he anticipated no serious difficulty in completing his journey to the Pacific. The traders at Grand Portage unfortunately had no goods to spare, and as it would be madness to attempt a journey through unknown tribes without them, Carver reluctantly turned his steps homeward, paddling around the north shore of Lake Superior, and studying its peculiarities with a good deal of intelligence and accuracy.[36]

Along the way Carver was mapping uncharted country up the Mississippi. Carver found that by dispensing huge amounts of gifts, they dissuaded the tribes from aligning themselves with the Spanish and French. Carver wrote in his journal "by loading them with presents . . . we should have lost two if not more very valuable [Indian] nations."[37] The success of Carver and Tute in aligning the tribes with Britain carried with it a very large cost. Trinkets and supplies for the Indians were paid for with drafts that Rogers would redeem at Fort Michilimackinac.

They reached Grand Portage on Lake Superior hoping that Rogers had sent supplies for him. No supplies were found but a note from Rogers had been left chiding Carver for his expenditures. Carver returned to Fort Michilimackinac in a rage against Rogers. The Carver expedition had produced maps and journals that added to the knowledge of Britain's new territory, but his exploration did not extend far beyond the Mississippi before it ended.[38] The waters that he followed had been used by French traders and explorers so there was nothing new, but his maps provided far greater accuracy. When he arrived at Fort Michilimackinac on 29 August 1767, he was in for a shock. The Crown had disavowed the Rogers' commission on the basis that Rogers did not have the authority to send Carver on his expedition, hence no funds would be paid. In spite of the support and efforts of Charles Townshend in London, Rogers' proposal for an expedition to find the Northwest Passage was never approved. Carver was outraged. He had spent two years of his life traveling, exploring and mapping. He had acted in good faith believing he had been legitimately hired by the Crown. Now he would get nothing. He would sail for London to plead his case. He left his wife, Abigail, in the colonies and left for Britain in 1769. He would never see Abigail again. Carver would spend the last eleven years of his life in London petitioning for what he believed was a fair reward for his work. He would start a second family (poor Abigail) and would write his book, *Travels Through the Interior Parts of North America in the Years 1766, 1767, and 1768*. The book is his greatest contribution to history. Published in 1778, two years before his death, it was widely read. Since Carver was the first English-speaking explorer to venture into the region of the upper Mississippi, his book fired the imagination of others. He was the first to use the term "Oregon" and guessed at what became known as the Continental Divide. The Lewis and Clark's

Expedition nearly forty years later would confirm much of what was contained in Carver's *Travels*. He published other works including his journals. Throughout his works, he failed to mention that he was a hired agent of Robert Rogers. Before he died in 1780 he received two separate grants from the Crown, but not the £20,000 offered for finding the Northwest Passage.[39]

Treason

Another surprise awaited Carver when he arrived at Fort Michilimackinac. Robert Rogers was under suspicion of plotting treason against Great Britain and was arrested on 6 December 1767. In the spring of 1768 Rogers and Carver would travel together to Fort Detroit: Rogers in irons in the brig and above him Carver was working on his journal. Rogers' journey from prestige to irons is a story of an unforgiving bureaucracy. When he took command of Fort Michilimackinac he met with the merchants and traders whose spokesman read a letter.

> It gives us a particular Satisfaction, that you are appointed our Governor, more especially at a Time that many of the Indian Nations, almost worn out with repeated Solicitations for Traders, are on the Eve of Discontent; but our Hopes from you, Sir, to reconcile Matters, and put the Trade upon a proper Footing, are very sanguine. You have already distinguished yourself in a military, and have now a fair Opportunity of doing it in a civil Capacity. Your Activity, and the many eminent Services you rendered your Country in the Course of the last war, and the reputation you have by that means gained amongst the Indians, will add Weight to your Councils, and re-establish the national credit, through the most extensive and remotest Part of his Majesty's Dominions.[40]

Most criticisms were aimed at Captain William Howard, Rogers' predecessor who was at this time packing his things to leave. Howard set goods prices too high and the Indians were going elsewhere to trade their pelts. Accusations were leveled against Howard and Johnson that they were profiting from this, but it is not clear how they made their profits. The solution would be to allow traders to take lower priced goods to the Indians and winter with them. The problem was that many of the traders were French and could not to be trusted so only a few British traders were allowed to winter with the Indians. In violation of instructions given to him, Rogers put things right by issuing passes that allowed French traders to winter with the Indians. Daniel Claus a Johnson employee wrote to Sir William Johnson.

> By the last account from Michilimackinac, Major Rogers was arrived there, and immediately without hesitation, gave a general permit to all Traders to go wintering, for which he is vastly liked and applauded here. The Traders that came from there told me also that his behavior towards the Indians was liked and approved of by them, as well as the people of the place.[41]
>
> ***Daniel Claus***

Rogers had been very successful in dealing with the tribes. In the summer of 1767 he held a grand council at Fort Michilimackinac. He gathered the chiefs[42] on 15 June congratulating them on their efforts to keep the peace.

> He thanked those among them who had kept the peace over the winter, and gave a belt to the Chippewa leader called the Grand Sable. The Chippewas' old enemies the Sioux, Winnebagoes and other western Indians "whom they had struck and wounded," he said, were also "coming to this Fort to visit their Father." Rogers hoped that the Sable's people "would behave peacefully towards them and be of a temper when they arrived to bury all enmity & settle all past differences."[43]

At the end of the council, Rogers distributed a generous amount of presents to those in attendance and this assured the alliance of the tribes with Great Britain. At this time a new face appeared at Fort Michilimackinac. Benjamin Roberts was Johnson's newly appointed commissary for Fort

Michilimackinac. Johnson later described him as "a Man [who] has no money & few friends . . . carried with him a heavy load of personal and professional baggage."[44] Rogers was not thrilled by this new addition to Fort Michilimackinac. Roberts could not accomplish anything that Rogers was not already doing and Rogers wrote to a Montreal merchant on 18 July "There is a Commissary for Indian affairs Just Arrived at the Garrison, *viz* Mr. Roberts greatly to my astonishment as he is not Appointed by the Crown only a warrant from Sir William Johnson."[45]

Roberts was in fact Johnson's spy and played the role. Rogers had been ordered by Gage to stop drawing drafts in May, a fact that Roberts was happy to remind Rogers. Rogers continued to draw drafts since he was committed to holding the council. The amount for the council gifts exceeded £4,000. Large Indian expenses were common. Edward Cole who ran Johnson's Illinois commissary ran up a bill of over £10,000 in one year and the expenses were paid.[46] Gage told Johnson that none of the bills should be paid since they were charged "soly [sic] by his own authority . . . contrary to the orders and Instructions given him by you as well as me."[47] Another motive for the failure to pay was the suspicion shared by Johnson and Gage that the money was somehow related to a Rogers' conspiracy to betray British possessions to the French.[48] For quite some time, Rogers had considered ways to rid himself of both Johnson and Gage. He was pushing to turn Fort Michilimackinac "& its dependencies" into a separate province. There was support for this scheme in Montreal and Quebec since these towns directly benefited from the trade at Fort Michilimackinac.[49] Johnson and Gage were now the deadly enemies of Robert Rogers.

By now, Rogers was deeply in debt to local merchants who had provided him with supplies for the Carver expedition. Johnson and Gage were not inclined to provide Rogers with any relief and many of his drafts were not honored. He had also borrowed funds from his personal Secretary, Nathaniel Potter. When Potter and Rogers quarreled in late July, probably about money, it came to blows and Potter was sent running back to his quarters. Potter's health had never been good and he decided to apply for leave to go back home. In mid–August he visited Benjamin Robert's to apply for leave. While with Roberts he volunteered surprising information that was sent to Johnson.

> Major Rogers wanted to engage him in some bad Affairs, and had Villainous designs in his head, that he Major Rogers was in Correspondence with Captain Hopkins in the French Service, and Potter related the Substance of the Letter ... which he alledged Major Rogers had shewn him... that Major Rogers had told him, Potter, he intended in the Spring sending a Party into Lake Superior, and another by La Baye [Green Bay] . . . and to join these Parties in order to go down by the Mississipi to New Orleans.[50]

The entire account sounds concocted and made no sense. Why would Rogers leave his post and sail down the Mississippi to New Orleans? He could cut a deal with French agents that were always nearby. Since the contents of the Hopkins note were known to Roberts, he and Potter may have come up with the accusation sent to Johnson. Roberts had already told Johnson that Potter was of bad character and as information dribbled out, Potter's motive became clear. Potter told Henry Bostwick who owned the house where Potter resided that "he had a method of getting all of the money that Rogers owed him."[51] Roberts now offered Potter a deal: if he would swear something against Rogers, Johnson or his deputy would get him paid the money owed him. The deposition that Potter produced included the information regarding the Hopkins letter and added new allegations unrelated to treason. It seems that on 20 August 1767 forty small kegs of rum were smuggled out of Roberts' warehouse and hidden on a small nearby island. When Roberts found out he sent men to retrieve the stolen rum. These were challenged by Rogers' men who claimed that the rum was taken to pay them the wages that were owed since Rogers had no money. Roberts was quick to report this to Johnson with the comment that "New scenes of Villainy open every Day."[52] Roberts next wrote a statement for Captain Frederick Spiesmaker, an officer of the garrison.

> I impeach Robert Rogers Esqr. Commandant of Michilimackinac for holding Secret Correspondence with the Enimies of Great Britain, & forming Conspiracies, I desire you in your Allgiance to Seize his person & papers amongst which you will find Sufficient proof ... I have now discharged my Duty."[53]
>
> ***Benjamin Roberts***

On 29 September 1767, Daniel Potter gave his formal statement to William Hay, Chief Justice at Montreal. He reiterated all the accusations previously provided and added that if Rogers' proposal for Fort Michilimackinac as a separate province was not approved, he, Rogers, would desert to the French and "stir up the Indians against the English."[54] On the 19th of October Gage issued an order that Rogers should be arrested as a traitor to King and Country. He would be sent to Fort Detroit or Montreal for trial.[55] It appeared that the bureaucracy had achieved its revenge on Rogers.

Court-martial – 20 October 1768

Guy Carleton (1724-1808) (Library of Congress)

General Guy Carleton,[56] commander of the Northern District of America in Montreal, considered the charges against Robert Rogers. He wrote to Lord Sherburne in London a fair comment on the whole affair.

"It must be acknowledged that Mr. Potter bears but a very bad Character," he wrote the Earl of Shelburne, "and may be actuated by views of self-interest and motives of revenge; unhappy it is for Major Rogers that his character does not stand in so fair a light as to permit a neglect of Potter's information." To Gage, Carleton wondered why Rogers, if truly guilty of Potter's accusations, would have quarreled with him and then "let him quietly slip through his Fingers."[57]

Guy Carleton

On 6 December 1767 Robert Rogers was arrested for treason and held at Fort Michilimackinac with Betsy while evidence was collected. For months Rogers was confined and Betsy brought food to him. The two dreamed that he would be released or rescued from his confinement. Their conversations were overheard and rumors started that Rogers would attempt an escape. Joseph-Louis Ainsse, a Frenchman with close ties to the Indians was sent to question Rogers and concluded that there was no truth to the rumor; however, when questioned by Captain Spiesmaker he reversed his opinion concluding that a rescue by Indians might be planned. The myth got out of hand with theories that Captain Hopkins was waiting with four battalions of French troops to aid in the escape. The result of this was that information was developed for possible use at the Rogers trail and security was increased. Rogers was put in chains in solitary confinement.[58]

The Rogers affair received media attention with frequent articles informing the public of items of interest.

"The Wife of Major ROGERS came to Town last Wednesday Evening," noted *The Boston Evening-Post* of Monday, August 22, 1768. "It is said by some that the Major is innocent of the Crimes he is charged with." Elizabeth had stopped earlier in Newport to obtain depositions against Nathaniel Potter; now in Boston she was seeking "a Certificate also of Mr Potters Character from the Clergy," as Robert had requested of her.[59]

He was not well treated and it was not until August 1768 that Rogers finally arrived at Montreal for the trial. On 20 October 1768, the court-martial of Robert Rogers convened. The court consisted of ten captains, one major, and two lieutenant colonels. All were British army officers. Rogers had counsel, but under procedures in place at that time, he would conduct his own defense questioning witnesses. The articles of accusation that had been filed against Robert Rogers were read.

> *First,* for having traitorously designed to desert to the French after "plundering the Traders and others of His Majesty's Subjects ... and Stirring up the Indians against His Majesty and His Government." *Second,* "for holding a Correspondence with His Majesty's Enemies." *Third,* for "Disobedience of his Orders and Instructions during his Command at Michilimackinac in having undertaken expensive Schemes and projects, and lavished away money amongst the Savages." The latter were seen as being "Conformable to the Council given in a Letter to him by an Officer in the French Service and formerly a Captain in His Majesty's Army."[60]

Benjamin Roberts was the first prosecution witness and he testified that Johnson had showed him the Hopkins letter and that Potter had told him of the Rogers plot to join the French. Roberts denied that he had promised Potter a reward for his affidavit against Rogers. Captain Spiesmaker stated that he had no notice of Rogers' bad conduct or mismanagement until the arrival of Benjamin Roberts. Others testified that Rogers planned to desert to Captain Hopkins with the help of members of his garrison (not identified). The Hopkins letter was read to the court and was; in fact the prosecution's only exhibit supporting the accusation of seditious correspondence. The prosecution alleged that the Carver/Tute expedition was an effort to connive with the Indians and the French to hand over the frontier to France. The persecution's case was followed by the defense.

Rogers opened with a summary of his plan to find the Northwest Passage which had turned out to be a very costly endeavor. He told the court that Gage's charge that he was a traitor to king and country was not in the Articles of Accusation. On the first charge, traitorous designs, He reminded all of Potters' bad character and noted that he had not had the opportunity to cross-examine Potter. He denied that he had ever answered the Hopkins letter. In answer to the second charge of stirring up the Indians he replied that all proceedings had been in public with records sent forward to Johnson and Gage. The third charge of lavishing away money among the savages was answered by the fact that the expense report was examined and approved by officers of the garrison. Witnesses for Rogers attested to his excellent character as well as the necessity of large expenditures and gifts to maintain Indians loyalty to the crown.

Two days before the trial ended the *New York Gazette* predicted.

> I dare say he will be very honorably acquitted. In the Course of the Trial, it appeared, the Prosecution was formed from the utmost Prejudice and Malice, and entirely ill-grounded; and tho' it is allowed that from his Indifference and Carelessness, upon some Occasion, his Conduct was such, as gave Room for some trifling Suspicion; yet the Punishment, and most unheard of Treatment he met with in his Confinement, was enough for one of the greatest Malefactors to have met with.[61]

The last witness was called on 31 October 1768 and later in the day the court rendered its verdict.

> *The Court* having taken into Consideration the Articles of Accusation preferred against Major Robert Rogers, together with the Evidence in Support of the Charge, as well as what the Prisoner had to offer in his Defence, *Is of Opinion,* that Major Robert Rogers *is not Guilty* of any one of the Articles laid to His Charge; and therefore doth acquit him of the same.[62]

On 5 January 1769, Gage forwarded the record of proceedings of the Rogers trial to Secretary of War Barrington indicating his intention to release Rogers to the confines of Montreal. It was not until February that the Gage order to release Rogers arrived in Montreal and it was during this period that Betsy gave birth to their first child, Arthur Rogers.

Finally on 1 March 1769 Gage received a ruling from Charles Gould, Deputy Judge-Advocate of England who stated after listing the charges.

> His Majesty is pleased to approve the Opinion of the Court of Acquitting said Major Robert Rogers of each of the said Articles of Charge and to Order that he be released from the Confinement; at the same time it appears to His Majesty, that there was great reason to suspect the said Major Rogers entertaining an improper and dangerous correspondence, which suspicion the Account afterwards given of his meditating an Escape tending to confirm.[63]
> ***Charles Gould***

The result was that while Rogers had been acquitted of all charges, Gage refused to reinstate him in command at Fort Michilimackinac and he would not be paid for his service there.[64]

The backdrop to this entire affair was civil unrest in the colonies. The Stamp Act was followed by several other acts that became known as the Intolerable Acts. Discontent with Great Britain was growing. Mid-October 1768 found Gage on his way to Boston to deal with increasing unrest. Two British regiments had been sent from Halifax to reinforce the garrison and Gage believed that he was facing an actual state of rebellion.[65] The colonists had read the accounts of the Rogers' court-martial and were sympathetic to his cause.

By now, Rogers was pursued by creditors and out of a job. He decided to return to London to seek redress and said his goodbyes to Betsy and Arthur. His good friend and ally, Charles Townshend had died so he would be without support in his endeavors.

Return to London

There was a multiplicity of motives to lure Rogers upon his second journey to England. His most powerful friends were there, as his most powerful enemies were in America. His financial affairs at home lay in utter ruin, and by the expedient of a quick passage he might escape his debtors until they could instruct London agents to continue harrying him. To the public he was still favourably known across the water; while in his own country, although he had his eager partisans in Canada, where many were induced to believe that he had been spitefully wronged by the tools of Johnson, a general ill-savour attached to his name. Finally, his angry resentment against the commander-in-chief and the superintendent of Indian affairs made it a daily humiliation to remain longer upon a continent in which they were in power.

His three direct purposes at the seat of empire were to work some malice against the party of Johnson; to obtain a fresh appointment in some part of King George's wide dominions; and somehow, by obtaining payment for his losses at Mackinac and elsewhere, to find his way through all the mazes of his indebtedness to solvency. His liabilities totalled thirteen thousand pounds, and to keep himself from falling into a debtor's prison was his immediate care.[66]

Robert Rogers arrived in London in early September, 1769. His first action was an attempt to obtain his pay for time spent in his command of Fort Michilimackinac. Before action could be taken on this he was thrown into debtor's prison by an impatient creditor. It was a short stay and he was soon rescued by an unnamed benefactor who paid off the creditor and the pay for command at Fort Michilimackinac was soon awarded. London was alive with gossip about his problems and efforts to obtain funds.[67]

Rogers seemed to be enjoying some success in his many expense claims submitted to the Crown, but his creditors were still after him. The specter of Debtors' Prison still hung over his head. The people of London were with him and the London Evening Post related a strange incident on 1 October 1771.

Tuesday last, about two o'clock, after Major Rogers had passed through Dartford, the post-chaise man who drove him told him a highwayman hovered around the chaise. As soon as the fellow came to the Major, he seized him by the hand and pulled him into the chaise. The highwayman answers the description in an advertisement of Sir John Fielding's. The Major carried him to the Mayor of Gravesend, and after an explanation there, sent him to the Rotation-house in Bow-street.[68]

During his time in London he continued his efforts to obtain approval for a Northwest Passage expedition. He had developed a new route that he thought was more promising. Jonathan Carver had forgiven Rogers when he found out that Rogers had received assurances from London for the Carver expedition in 1766. The fact that London authorities reneged was not the fault of Rogers. Carver sought to join Rogers in a new expedition. Rogers requested support from Royal Society of London and Benjamin Franklin. In spite of all this effort, Rogers' new expedition was not approved. On 16 October 1772 Robert Rogers was committed to Fleet Debtors' Prison. Creditors claimed a debt of over £1,800, a relatively small sum, but Rogers had no money.[69]

Rogers remained in debtors' prison for nearly two years but in 1774 bankruptcy laws were enacted in Great Britain and Rogers petitioned for release by complying with their provisions. On 4 August 1774 Rogers was released from debtors' prison. Under the new law he was allowed to keep forty shillings, wearing apparel and working tools. All other assets were forfeit. Rogers was forty-three and his health as not good. His years in prison had taken their toll.

He petitioned for a return to his retired status and his pension. These were granted and allowed him to remain in London to submit additional petitions. His claims were denied and no action was taken on his new plan to seek the Northwest Passage. The growing troubles in the colonies killed any interest in the Northwest Passage. Robert Rogers would return to the colonies and on 4 June 1775, he set sail for America on the *Baltimore*. He was returning to a boiling cauldron.[70]

6. War of Independence and After
Washington

Martha Dandridge Custis Washington (1731-1802) (Library of Congress)

While Robert Rogers was languishing in a London debtors' prison, George Washington was enjoying the aristocratic life style of a country gentleman living at Mount Vernon in Virginia. His life featured fox hunting, billiards, races, and cockfights. His marriage to the wealthy widow, Martha Dandridge Custis on 6 January 1759 brought with it considerable property and social standing.

He increased his land holdings when he applied for land bounties promised to those who had volunteered to serve in the French and Indian War. He received title to 23,200 acres near the Ohio River in what is now West Virginia. Washington also doubled the size of his Mount Vernon estate to 6,500 acres by buying up land and increased the slave population to over 100. He was a successful planter and raised tobacco, wheat and other commodities. His operations included flour milling, horse breeding and a distillery that produced 1,000 gallons of whiskey a month. At the time of his death his distillery produced more whiskey than any other in the United States. His restored distillery was reopened in 2016. As a leader of the social elite in Virginia he held frequent parties. Before his increased wealth and social status, as a respected military leader of the recent war, he was elected to the Virginia provincial legislature representing Frederick County in the House of Burgesses for seven years beginning in 1758.

Washington's leading military and political role in the War of Independence began in 1767 when he voiced opposition to the 1765 Stamp Act. This and the Townsend Acts that followed in 1767 caused widespread protests in the colonies. In May 1769 Washington introduced a resolution drafted by his friend George Mason that called for a boycott of British goods until the acts were repealed. Although the Townsend Acts were repealed, other acts followed. The Intolerable Acts of 1774 were viewed by Washington as "an invasion of our Rights and

Privileges."[1] He told a friend "I think the Parliament of Great Britain has no more right to put their hands in my pocket without consent than I have to put my hands in yours for money."[2] Washington was gradually taking a leading role in the opposition to Great Britain's acts. In July 1774 he chaired the meeting that adopted the "Fairfax Resolution." This called for the convening of a Continental Congress and other actions to oppose Great Britain. He was selected as Virginia's delegate to the First Continental Congress. War with Great Britain started in April 1775 when the Battles of Lexington and Concord were fought near Boston. At the Second Continental Congress the Continental Army was created on 14 June 1775. Washington was in a unique position. He had commanded troops during the French and Indian War, had prestige, bearing, charisma, and was widely known as a strong Patriot. Perhaps most important, he represented the largest colony, Virginia, in a war that was largely a New England conflict. There was a need to unify the North and the South. What better way than to select a southerner to command the combined forces of the colonies? When John Adams of Massachusetts nominated Washington to command the Continental Army, the Continental Congress approved the appointment. On 23 August 1775 Great Britain issued a Royal proclamation that branded American Patriots as traitors. Patriot leaders faced confiscation of their property and would be hanged. Washington was now a traitor to the Crown and had much to lose.

The Chameleon

Was Robert Rogers a traitor to the Patriot cause? Rogers' fans then and now defend his actions arguing that he was forced to join the British because the Patriots rejected his applications. Even John Stark, Rogers' old comrade, the hero of the Battle of Bennington in the War of Independence, supported this view in his memoirs published years later.[3] Washington thought Rogers a spy. Historians tend to assign Robert Rogers into one of three categories. He was for sale to the highest bidder and would go with the best offer because he was trapped by debt; he was seeking to join the Patriot cause because of loyalty to his countrymen; or he was loyal to the Crown and was a spy. It may be that Rogers had decided to join the British in their fight against the Colonials. In March 1775 he was negotiating with Lord Dartmouth requesting command of a British regiment. On 19 April 1775 the "Shot heard round the World" had been fired at Lexington and Concord. It was now a shooting war in the colonies. He received no reply from Lord Dartmouth and left for American three months later on 4 June 1775.[4]

A Rabble in Arms

After fighting bad weather and a hurricane, the *Baltimore* arrived in America after a two month voyage from Britain. Robert Rogers made his way to Williamsburg, the capital of Virginia. It was early August 1775 and Rogers carried news from London. The Crown planned to distribute £40,000 "among the Canadian Indians to induce them to fall upon the Colonies."[5] Major John Campbell, Quebec's new Indian Department Superintendent, would be in charge of the operation. Further, Rogers claimed that his old enemy from the Saint Francis Raid, Father Roubaud, would be the chief advisor for the scheme. How much Roubaud was involved is not clear but the fact was that he had left the Jesuit order, married, and switched his allegiance from France to Great Britain. Roubaud was now a spy and advisor to the British.[6]

At this time in his life Rogers' years in prison had taken their toll on his health and his years in London pubs had turned him into an alcoholic. John Adams said at the time that one third of the people are Loyalist, one third are Patriot and a third don't give a damn. Most thought that Rogers fell into the last category. He had been away from the colonies for too long and while still famous and quoted in the press, he was old news. The business of his treason trial and association with the British in pursuit of the Northwest Passage left fellow citizens to wonder whose side he was on. His focus remained on the Northwest Passage and reuniting with Betsy and his son whom he had not seen in six years, but first he would visit Philadelphia, the hub of resistance to the British.

Rogers arrived in Philadelphia in the third week of September 1775. The Second Continental Congress had reconvened nine days earlier. He had friends in high places. Israel Putnam, his former ranger, was now one of four major generals serving under George Washington. Rogers also had enemies in high places. General Gage's troops had been decimated at Bunker Hill and were besieged in Boston. Rogers appeared to be warming to the Patriot cause. Massachusetts delegate John Adams (Future U. S. President) recorded in his diary.

> The famous Partisan Major Rogers came to our Lodgings to make us a Visit. He has been in Prison – discharged by some insolvent or bankrupt Act. He thinks we shall have hot Work, next Spring. He told me an old half Pay Officer, such as himself, would sell well next Spring. And when he went away, he said to S. A. [Sam Adams] and me, if you want me, next Spring for any Service, you know where I am, send for me. I am to be sold. – He says the Scotch Men at home, say damn that Adams and Cushing. We must have their Heads, &c.[7]
>
> *John Adams*

Rogers told Adams that he wanted to return to his family in Portsmouth. At this point he was destitute and still possessed by the notion of finding the Northwest Passage. He shared is thoughts with Richard Whitworth, at the end of September. Whitworth was a Member of Parliament and supporter of the search for the Northwest Passage.

I am exceedingly chagrin'd at my present Situation and the more so on Account of our intended Expedition for the discovery of the North West passage, as the present times will not permit it to be carried on unless affairs were Settled between the Mother Country and her Colonies. For in the present Situation of affairs every man wou'd be made prisoners.[8]

Robert Rogers

The Pennsylvania Committee of Public Safety had taken notice of Rogers and ordered his arrest the day after his meeting with John Adams. He was to appear before the board for questioning. His status as a half-pay retired British officer placed him under suspicion. Rogers' case was considered by the Continental Congress and the Committee was directed to discharge Rogers on the condition that he sign his parole that he would not take up arms against the inhabitants of America in the present controversy. Rogers immediately did this promising:

> . . . on the Honour of a Soldier and a Gentleman, that I will not bear Arms against the American United Colonies in any manner whatever during the present contest between them and Great Britain, and that I will not in that time attempt to give intelligence to General Gage, the British Ministry, or any person or persons of any Matters relative to America.[9]

Robert Rogers

In Britain a significant portion of the population favored the colonials and wanted an end to the war being waged by the British army. The London press often seemed to favor the Patriot cause. While Rogers was in Philadelphia the London press reported.

> The late Duke of Newcastle scrupled not to acknowledge Colonel Washington and Major Rogers "two of the bravest and most experienced Officers in the King's Service" – The Colonel is now in his own Service; and if he could fight so courageously for his

King, there is no Doubt of his displaying a redoubled valour for himself.[10]

More extraordinary accounts followed in the press. In early October the London press announced that Robert Rogers had joined the Patriot cause.

> A letter lately received from Philadelphia says, "The renowned Major Rogers is arrived at this place from England. As soon as his arrival was known, he was joined by a number of men who belonged to Rogers's rangers in the late war. The Major immediately marched into the interior parts of the country, where he was joined by an incredible number of Indians, who, with their leader (Rogers), has joined the provincial army. The rangers wear a cap like the English light horse, round which is this motto, ROGERS AND FREEDOM.[11]

The fiction went beyond belief. On 16 October the press in London published the following articles.

> London... A gentleman just arrived from America has given the following advice: That he saw Major Rogers not far from Virginia, in full march, with colours flying, at the head of a great body of Indians, in support of the Americans; that the Major offered to make the above gentleman an officer in his army; that the Major had been appointed by the continental congress Commander in Chief of the Indians; that the inhabitants of Philadelphia have subscribed £1000, which have been given to Major Rogers; that the Major's regimentals are green, faced with red, trimmed with silver lace; round the collar of his coat is worked in silver, FREEDOM TO AMERICA; and that the two Indian nations of Creeks and Choctaws have both joined the Major's army.[12]

Another account soon followed.

> The Major, (who is a native of Ireland), at about fourteen years of age, embarked for America; where he employed the chief of his time in hunting . . . When he arrived to years of maturity, he married the daughter of Mr. Brown, a clergyman, of Rhode-Island; by whom he had two sons, who are both living... On his arrival at Philadelphia, he was

received with the utmost applause by all ranks of people, and is now at the head of a numerous Indian army.[13]

The source of the fiction is unknown. It may be that Rogers was acting as his own press agent feeding stories to the London press. Stories like these could land him a position as a senior officer in the Continental Army or get him hanged. At this time, Rogers' true intentions regarding the war were unknown perhaps even to himself. He was still relatively young, forty-four years of age and in spite of prison's impact on his health and alcohol, the press accurately described him as "strong, robust and [a] bold man; deliberate, of few words, generous to a fault, and desperate when roused."[14]

The last comment was relevant to Rogers' situation. He was destitute. His mind was focused on senior rank in the British Army. If that failed, his retired half-pay was insufficient to live on. He could be persuaded to switch sides if offered a commission as a senior officer in the Continental Army. Benjamin Franklin had signed a certificate for Rogers that he needed to travel in the colonies. He decided to stop in New York City on his way home to Portsmouth. Enroute to New York City he lost ". . . at or near the stage or ferry house at Amboy a black leather pocket with steel clasps [containing] Amongst other papers of consequence . . . the copy of my Parole with the committee's permission of my going to New Hampshire or where else I had occasion.[15] He reported this fact to the Patriot Committee of Public Safety upon his arrival in New York City and was allowed freedom of the city until his documents were either found or he received replacements from Philadelphia. Rogers wrote to Benjamin Franklin on the 29th of September explaining his plight and asking for the issue of new documents. While in the city he wrote to General Gage on 30 September 1775. Gage was still trapped in Boston by Washington's troops and artillery. After apologizing for past differences, Rogers asked Gage to allow him to reenter military service.[16] Rogers had little stomach for fighting his countrymen and if allowed reentry into the British Army he hoped for a posting elsewhere in the empire. It was now clear that Rogers was courting both sides and would go with the first that offered him employment. His desperate financial situation seemed to drive his actions.

He like many others hoped that the conflict would be peacefully ended and the colonies would return to British rule. This would also allow an expedition to find the Northwest Passage, something impossible in the current environment. He wrote to his friend Richard Whitworth explaining that "the present Contest between Great Britain and America" made it impossible to even consider launching a Northwest Passage expedition.[17] While in the city he visited New York's Chief Justice William Smith who wrote.

> . . . he [Rogers] hoped to pacify his Creditors by a Composition in Lands & save a Farm or two for his own Subsistence in Cumberland or Gloucester [in New York province]. His pockets were then pennyless, & I advised & reproved him from meer Motives of Charity to a Prodigal, who had once served his Country with Credit & had beggard his Family. I knew this Man well during the last War. He was raised by General Shirley & commanded the Rangers. He got a Company in the Army & then gamed himself into Poverty.[18]
>
> *William Smith*

William Tryon (1729-1788) (Wikipedia)

Next Rogers visited the Royal Governor, William Tryon. Tryon was ill and sick of being intimidated by the Patriots. He wanted to return to Britain and had little time for anything, but took the time to listen to Rogers' sad story. He took the time because he wanted to find out what was going on in Philadelphia. It seemed the same as in New York. What other intelligence information Rogers related to Tryon was not recorded. People did not want independence and if the Parliament would cease taxing the colonies, the war could be ended. Tryon rummaged and found a few old land grants signing these over to Rogers forgiving the fees.[19] For Rogers this was a windfall. He could sign some over to his creditors and keep some land for himself to start a new life.

Rogers received the second copy of his parole from Philadelphia and departed New York City on 10 October 1775. He traveled north to inspect land grants and visit his brother, James who resided near what is now Windham, Vermont. James was doing quite well. He had received a 23,000 acre land grant to establish a township and was now prosperous. Rogers stayed a few days with his brother and departed. His next stop was at Dartmouth College built in 1769 by Eleazar Wheelock to educate Native Americans including those from Saint Francis. He chatted with Wheelock offering him assistance in obtaining land, an offer that Wheelock declined. After Rogers departed Wheelock wrote to Washington.

> On the 13th ultimo the Famous Major Rogers came to My House, from a Tavern in the neighborhood where he called for Refreshment. I had never before seen him. He was in but an ordinary Habit, for one of his Character. He treated me with great Respect; said he came from London in July, and had spent twenty Days with the Congress in Philadelphia, and I forget how many at New York; had been offered & urged to take a Commission in favor of the Colonies, but, as he was now on half-pay from the Crown, he thought proper not to accept it; that he had fought two Battles in Algiers under the Dey; that he was now on a Design to take care of some Large Grants of Land made to him.[20]
>
> *Eleazar Wheelock*

The bit about Algiers was pure fiction, perhaps stated to mask the fact that Rogers was in debtors' prison at that time. Wheelock was suspicious of Rogers, a fact not lost on

Washington. Wheelock would later append his report to Washington. On December 1, nineteen days after Rogers' visit two soldiers returning from Montreal informed Wheelock that they had been told by a captured French officer "that Major Rogers was second in command under General Carleton; and that he had lately been in Indian Habit through our Encampment at St. John's and had given a plan of them to the General [Carleton]; and suppose he made his escape with the Indians which were at St. John's."[21]

Rogers departed Dartmouth for home in Portsmouth. It was hardly a warm homecoming after six years and four months. He spent a few days bonding with his son Arthur and made the usual promises to Betsy about impending wealth. She had heard it all before. He said his goodbyes to Betsy and Arthur and headed for Boston in December 1775.

William Howe (1729-1814)(Library of Congress)

On 26 September 1775, Gage handed over command of British forces in America to General William Howe. Gage was recalled in disgrace to London. Under his command, 325 British regulars had been killed and nearly 1200 were wounded since 19 April, the Battles of Lexington and Concord. Worse, Washington still had the British bottled up in Boston. The "Rabble in Arms"[22] was now a match for British regulars. Even Gage admitted "the Rebels are not the despicable Rabble too many had supposed to be."[23] The Rogers letter to Gage arrived in Boston after Gage had departed for London. Howe replied to Rogers and informed William Legge, Lord Dartmouth, Secretary of State for the Colonies . . . [24] William Howe had fought at Quebec and appreciated the value Rogers could bring to the British army. Howe's late brother George Augustus was a champion of Robert Rogers. George Augustus Howe was considered to be the "best officer in the British army." He clearly understood the value of rangers and unconventional warfare. Unfortunately, George Augustus Howe was killed in the disastrous British loss to the French at the Battle of Carillon in 1759. Lord George Germain, Dartmouth's successor wrote to Howe "The King . . . approves your attention to Major Rogers, of whose firmness and fidelity we have received further testimony from Governor Tryon, and there is no doubt you will find the means of making him useful."[25] It was evident that the British did not want Rogers on the other side and would do what was necessary to recruit him. Rogers, on the other hand, had as his top priority the Northwest Passage expedition that would be possible if the war was ended. The Northwest Passage was not on the British agenda. As Rogers traveled to Boston in December 1775 the city was under siege by the Patriots.

The city had been under siege since the Battle of Bunker Hill[26] fought on 17 June 1775. Several former Rogers' Rangers fought for the Patriots. John Stark, a ranger captain who had served under Rogers, was now a colonel and a Patriot hero of the battle. Stark would achieve greater fame as the Continental Army commander at the Battle of Bennington. At Bunker Hill, Stark held the line at the Mystic River beach and stacked up ninety-six British dead in front of his wall before the British broke off. They would not attack Stark's wall again.

Daniel Barnes was now a captain commanding a company in Colonel Jonathan Ward's regiment. Jonathan Brigham was in Barnes' company and related what he saw during the battle years later in an interview during his pension application.

> On the seventeenth June, 1775, declarant [Jonathan Brigham] was engaged in the battle at Bunker's Hill. The firing on the part of the British commenced at an early hour in the morning from their ships and batteries. But the engagement did not become general until a little after noon, when their forces crossed Charles River and attempted to dislodge the Americans from the redoubt which they had erected the preceding night. The battle was severe and the British repulsed at every charge until, for want of ammunition, the Americans were compelled to retire. The awful solemnities of that day are still deeply impressed upon declarant's mind, and the scenes of carnage and death and the inconceivable grandeur of the immense volume of flames illuminating the battlefield from the burning of Charlestown appear as vivid as if the events of yesterday.[27]
>
> *Jonathan Brigham*

The British Attack on Bunker Hill (Library of Congress)

Soon after starting his fifty mile journey to Boston, Rogers met Caleb Stark, the son of John Stark. They traveled together to Boston. Decades later Caleb's son recorded his father's recollections.

> After traveling a few miles he was joined by another horseman. The stranger was a tall, well-formed, fine looking person, wearing the undress uniform of a British officer. He inquired politely of our young adventurer who he was, and where he was going; and upon being informed that he was proceeding to the camp at Medford, to join his father, Colonel Stark, the stranger said: "You are, then, the son of my old comrade. Your father and I were fellow-soldiers for more than five years. I am travelling in the same direction, and we will keep company." The stranger was the celebrated Major Robert Rogers, of " French war" notoriety. As they journeyed on, the major insisted on defraying all the road expenses, and toward

evening took his leave, transmitting to his old associate in arms, Colonel Stark, a message, soliciting an interview at a tavern in Medford.[28]

Caleb Stark

Stark and Rogers met at Medford Tavern. Rogers stated that he was still undecided about which side he would join. Stark was very clear. Nothing could induce him to join the British and he thought that no peaceful resolution of the conflict was possible. Stark stated "I have taken up arms in her defence, and God willing, I will never lay them down until she has become a free and independent nation."[29] Next Rogers wrote to Washington.

> I do sincerely intend Your Excellency for a continuance of the permission for me to go unmolested where my private Business may take me as it will take some Months from this for me to settle with all my Creditors – I have leave to retire in my Halfpay, & never expect to be call'd into the Service again. I love North America, it is my native Country, & that of my Family, and I intend to spend the Evening of my days in it. I should be glad to pay you my respects personally, but hear that its prudent to first write you this Letter, I shall wait at this place for your Excellency's command.[30]

Robert Rogers

Washington suspected that Robert Rogers was a British spy. He had received Wheelock's report of his meeting with Rogers. Wheelock had appended a remarkable note to his report.

> On December 1, nineteen days after Rogers' visit, two soldiers returning from Montreal informed Wheelock that they had been told by a captured French officer "that Major Rogers was second in command under General Carleton; and that he had lately been in Indian Habit through our Encampment at St. John's, and had given a plan of them to the General; and suppose he made his escape with the Indians, which were at St. John's."[31]

Eleazar Wheelock

The note appears to be no more than an unsupported rumor but Washington ordered General John Sullivan to interrogate Rogers at the Patriot encampment at Winter Hill overlooking Boston. Sullivan did as ordered and reported back to Washington.

John Sullivan (1740-1795) (Wikipedia)

Sullivan took down Rogers' recital of his travels since leaving New York in early October. "He says every thing in Mr. Wheelock's Letter Except that of his coming down from

Canada," and being an officer in Carleton's army, was correct. Why had Rogers come down to the American camp where "he had no Business"? Rogers replied that he needed a permit signed by Washington to avoid "being Suspected and Treated as a person unfriendly to us," wrote Sullivan.[32]

Rogers continued his journey next stopping at Albany to patch up his financial situation. There he met with General Philip Schuler, American Commander of the Northern Department. He was not aware that Washington had written to Schuler directing him to interrogate Rogers especially about Wheelock's note of activities in Canada.[33] Schuler met with Rogers and wrote to Washington stating that the Wheelock intelligence was false and Washington acknowledged that Schuler was probably correct, ". . . but being much suspected of unfriendly views to this country [Rogers] Conduct should be attended to with some Degree of Vigilance and Circumspection."[34] Next, Rogers left Albany on 5 January 1776 for New York City to meet with Governor Tryon. He had documentation that he had collected to support his land grant applications. The situation had vastly changed since Rogers' visit in mid-October. The Patriots had tightened their grip on the city. Fearing for his life, Tryon left the city and now resided on board the British commercial ship *Duchess of Gordon* anchored in the bay. It was there that Rogers presented his land Grant Claims to Governor Tryon. On the 8th of February he met with General Sir Henry Clinton who promised Rogers that he would recommend him to the commander-in-chief. Rogers agreed to accept a British army post anywhere but not in North America unless he could "get rid of the oath" he had sworn for his parole. Clinton made the following entry in his journal.

> [Told] Major Rogers that if he chose to join me, I did believe that his services would be such as would induce me to recommend him to gov't & the commander in chief [He] said if he could get rid of the oath he would I told him he was the best

judge how it was tender'd to him & if he was reconciled to coming I should be glad to receive him but no positive conditions.[35]

Henry Clinton

Rogers was prepared to side with the British if the conditions were right. His original hope that peace would be restored and the colonies would return to Britain making pursuit of a Northwest Passage possible was no longer a possibility. The Pennsylvania Journal reported.

> "'Tis gone!'Tis past! The grave hath parted us – and death, in the persons of the slain, hath cut the thread of life between Britain and America." As for Tories, "we will make peace with you as enemies, but we will never reunite with you as friends."[36]

It was expected that Washington and his army would abandon Boston and move to New York City. Rumors flooded the city that General Howe would follow to seize New York City. A frenzy of preparation was in progress to defend against a British occupation. Patriot General William Alexander, Lord Stirling took command of New York City and prepared for the British invasion.

William Alexander (Lord Stirling) (1726-1783) (Library of Congress)

At first Stirling allowed boats to row out to Tryon's ship with mail and goods but when reports of subversive activities by Tryon circulated, the free flow was limited. In a colossal case of bad timing, Rogers wrote to Stirling on 22 March 1776 shortly after Tryon's subversive activities became know. Rogers asked permission to send two men to Tryon with a packet of land surveys. An angry Stirling not only denied his request but "banished him out of [the city] & cut off his Access to the Govr."[37] The possibility of land grants evaporated. Rogers was running out of options. He decided to go to Philadelphia where his parole was still good for reasons not clear. Perhaps he still wanted to pursue a commission in the Continental Army. In Philadelphia he found no employment and the prospect of Debtor's prison prompted him to return to Portsmouth and Betsy. The homecoming in Portsmouth was not a happy event. Apparently the symptoms of an old case of syphilis or a new case flared and Betsy banished him from the bedroom. This was the last time that Rogers would see Betsy and Arthur. His proven infidelity would become the basis of a divorce sought by Betsy two years later.[38]

Rogers continued to pursue a position in the Continental Army and asked a trader, John Langdon to pen letters of introduction to New Hampshire delegates, Josiah Bartlett and William Whipple. Langdon was also a loyal Patriot and delegate. With some misgivings, Landon wrote to Bartlett on 3 June 1776.

> This will be handed you by Major Rogers who has been here for short time, in which I've had frequent Interviews with him and opportunity of Conversing fully in matters, find him well inclined and ready to Serve his Country in this grand Struggle - and I wish his military abilities might be imployed for us, shall be much pleased if you'll speak to him on the Subject, and if anything should turn up for his Advantage, and the real Service of the United Colonies, I've no doubt you'll do everything in your power to Serve him and the Country.[39]
>
> *John Langdon*

The Plot to Kill George Washington

At this time, events were rapidly unfolding in New York City. Washington and his army arrived in the city on 13 April and one of his primary concerns was Tory spies that infested the city. On 10 June 1776 an intensive search for Loyalists started and they were hunted down. Tar and feathering became the order of the day and not a few were murdered by the mob. During this mini-reign of terror an anti-Patriot plot was uncovered that involved assassination attempts on Washington, Putnam and General Nathaniel Greene. News of the plot broke when Isaac Ketchum, a loyalist, was arrested for counterfeiting. He fingered two men (also arrested for counterfeiting) as being part of the plot: Thomas Hickey and Michael Lynch. Alarm was raised because Hickey was a member of Washington's personal guard. Others were arrested. A gunsmith named Gilbert Forbes confessed that he had been paid off by David Matthews, the Mayor of New York. Matthews in turn admitted that Tryon had "put a bundle of paper money into his hands" for the purchase of rifles and muskets.[40]

> The entire conspiracy had the unintended effect of rallying support for Washington, whose life had been in jeopardy. But he didn't want to exaggerate the plot, which might have been demoralizing. In reporting it to John Hancock, he said it had been concocted by the guilty parties "for aiding the King's troops upon their arrival. No regular plan seems to have been digested, but several persons have been enlisted and sworn to join them." He also believed that 200 to 250 Loyalist conspirators were hiding in the Long Island woods and swamps; he had boats patrol the Narrows at night to intercept anyone trying to flee to British-controlled Staten Island.
>
> Mayor Mathews and several others were packed off to Connecticut to serve jail time- a lenient sentence for a treasonous plot-and either escaped or were let go without a trial. Washington decided to make an example of Hickey and ordered every brigade to witness his hanging at eleven A.M. on June 28, 1776. The gallows were erected in a field near the Bowery, and twenty

thousand spectators-virtually the entire New York population-turned out to watch. Hickey waived his right to a chaplain, calling them 'cutthroats;' and managed to hold back tears until the hangmen actually looped the noose around his neck.[41]

The press reported the execution.

NORWICH July 1. Last Friday about 12 o'clock was executed at New-York (after being tried and condemned by a Court-Martial) John------ [Hickey], an Irishman, who was concerned in a wicked and unnatural Conspiracy against the Lives of General Washington and a number of the Inhabitants of the United Colonies: He formerly belonged in the Ministerial Army, but deserted from that, and listed in the Continental Service as one of the General's Life-Guard. It is said the General conversed with him after he had got to the place of Execution, and offered to repreave him if he would discover his Confederates, but the stubborn Fellow refused to give away any names. He was about 27 Years of Age, he did not appear to be the least dawnted when he arrived at the Gallows.[42]

The conspiracy included many actions. The King's Bridge at the northern end of Manhattan Island would be cut down, powder magazines would be blown up, and the city would be set on fire. All of this was intended to support the arrival of Lord Howe that was expected soon. Although few of these ambitious plans got beyond the conjecture stage, some actions were executed. Recruiting was accomplished; arms were obtained and distributed to New York Tories; and an attempt was made to poison Washington which failed. With the death of Hickey, Washington seemed content to consider the affair ended and used the Hickey execution to warn others who might be tempted to betray the American army.

It is thought that Governor Tryon was financing the conspiracy, but his involvement is unproven. His papers published in 1981 provide no clues. The Tryon papers from 2 November 1775 through 7 July 1776 are missing.[43] This may be because he fled the city to the British vessel during this period.

What is known is that "The Governor [Tryon] had combed through the files and had taken with him to the *Duchess of Gordon* as many of the official papers as he had thought he might need."[44] Either the papers were lost or he may have destroyed them because they were incriminating. As a result, documentation about anything that went on between Rogers and Tryon has been lost. Tryon's papers continue on 8 July with a relevant letter between two Patriots.

> Joseph Hewes
> To Samuel Johnston
> Philadelphia, 8th July 1776
> A hellish plot has lately been discovered at New York to Murder Genl. Washington and some other Officers of the first rank, blow up the Magazine & spike up the Cannon, the persons employed [stricken] had it in charge & have actually enlisted a number of men for the King's Army, it was to have been put in execution on the first arrival of the Army from Halifax, one of Genl. Washington's guards has been put to death for being concerned in it, the Mayor of the City and some others are confined, I believe many of them are guilty, [stricken] it has been said the matter has been traced up to Govr. Tryon.
>
> I enclose you a Resolve of Congress which please to forward to your Council of Safety, I also enclose a letter to Mr. Burke, if you can do anything for the Gentlemen who subscribe it, I hope you will do it, they are my friends and friends of America. I sent you a Commission of this kind some time ago, you have not mentioned it in any of your letters. I will trespass no longer on your patience, Remember me to your Family and Connections and be assured I am with Affection and Regard.[45]
>
> ***Joseph Hewes***

The names were stricken but probably included Robert Rogers because Rogers' meetings with Tryon were remembered by members of the Committee to Detect Conspiracies. At this time Rogers was bound for New York City to collect money from someone who owed him. It has never been proven that he was involved in the plot and intended to collect money from

Tryon. Upon his arrival he was arrested by American soldiers on 26 June 1776.

On 1 July 1776, three days after submitting his draft of the "Declaration of the thirteen united States of America" to Congress, Thomas Jefferson wrote to a friend William Fleming "The famous Major Rogers is in custody on violent suspicion of being concerned in the conspiracy"[46] By the end of June, George Washington and other generals had interrogated Robert Rogers. This was the first time Washington and Rogers had met. Both had much in common. Both were born in the colonies, both were veterans of the French and Indian War, both were Freemasons, they were the same age and were both over six feet tall, something unusual in that age. There were vast differences; however. Rogers was born in poverty and would do anything for money as seen by his counterfeiting activities years earlier. Washington was born into wealth and increased it. Most important, Washington was an honorable man and Rogers had demonstrated that he was not. Rogers told Washington that he had been arrested while on his way to Philadelphia on business with Congress. This was clearly a lie since he was picked up far from any direct route to Philadelphia and was headed to New York City to collect money owed him and to obtain his land grants.[47] Washington wrote to Congress reminding the members about Rogers' bad reputation and his status as a British officer on half-pay. He then summarized what Rogers had related to him. Washington seemed predisposed to be lenient with his fellow Freemason, but he urgently wanted to warn Congress about the man.

> In his defense Rogers insisted that the Business ... he has with Congress, is a secret offer of his services, to the end that in case it should be rejected, he might have his way left open to an employment in the East Indies to which he is assigned and in that case he flatters himself he will obtain leave of Congress to go to Great Britain.[48]
>
> *George Washington*

Washington sent Rogers under guard to Philadelphia with the letters on his person when he was arrested. These proved nothing but Washington thought that "from their Tenour calculated to recommend him to Congress."[49] Rogers was imprisoned upon his arrival in Philadelphia. From his cell he was pushing to get an application before Congress and on 1 July he attempted to get William Whipple, the New Hampshire delegate to visit him since he had "come on important business with Congress."[50] Whipple wrote to Langdon.

> [Rogers] has made no application to Congress & if he shod I think him a man of too infamous a Carrecter to be imploy'd in the Cause of Vertue, as I have not seen the letter its impossible for me to know the subject of it but I must confess it will give me great pain if it proves to be a recommendation for undoubtedly Rogers has shewn it, & you may rely on it that General Washington has not apprehended him without sufficient Grounds.[51]
>
> *William Whipple*

Other members of Congress were convinced that Rogers was a part of the plot. Delegate John Penn (North Carolina) wrote to Samuel Johnson.

> Philada. June 28th. 1776
> Dear Sir:
> I arrived here several days ago in good health & found Mr. Hewes well. I am truly sorry to inform you that our affairs are in a bad situation in Canada. I fear by the time you receive this our army will have left that Country. Unfortunately for us the small pox has gone through our Troops there, which has in some measure occasioned our misfortunes. I expect we shall be able to make a stand at the lakes. General Burgoin with a very considerable force arrived in Canada some time ago. He lately made Prisoners Brigad General Thompson and several other officers tho' we had but few men killed or taken at the time. A dangerous plot has lately been discovered at New York. The design was to blow up the Magazine and kill General Washington, a large number are under confinement some of note. Governor Tryon is at the bottom, several of the

General's Guard were bribed, it seems when the whole is made known we shall be much surprised. The famous Rogers that was so active last war is one of the number & now confined.

The first day of July will be made remarcable; then the question relative to I will be ajitated and there is no doubt but a total seperation from Britain will take place. This Province is for it; indeed so are all except Maryland & her people are coming over fast, I shall be much obliged to you to give the inclosed letters passes and when you have an opportunity to let me know what is doing in the busie world your way.

I am with great respect, Dear Sir, Your mo. Obt. Servt.
John Penn
[P.S.] Please to give my Complts. To your Lady & Miss Peggy. J. P.][52]

Congress had more important matters to consider. On the 4th of July 1776, the Declaration of Independence was adopted by Congress and any hope of reunion with Great Britain was forever lost as was a Northwest Passage expedition.

Delegate Josiah Bartlett (New Hampshire) in his letter to William Whipple (New Hampshire) noted that while confined, Rogers asked permission to leave the country. Rogers had been caught and now wanted to escape America. His request was denied, but if he would not be released by legal means, other methods would be used.

Philadelphia 9th July 1776
Sir:
Your highly Esteem'd favor of the 18 Ulto inclosing Instructions to join with the other Colonies in Declaring these United Colonies Free & Independent States, came very Seasonably to hand. As we were so happy as to agree in sentiment with our Constituents gave us the greater Pleasure to Concur with the Delegates of the other Colonies in the inclos'd Declaration, which was yesterday published in form in this City and is to be Publish'd at the Head of the Army at New-York next Thursday.

> A plan of Confederation is now forming, which when finished will be transmited to each Colony for their aprobation.
>
> Major Rogers (whose Conduct it seems was Suspicious) was take up some time since by order of General Washington and sent under Guard to this City. He Requested leave to go to England by way of the West Indies but Congress not thinking it proper, have directed him to be sent to New Hampshire to be dispos'd of as the Authority there shall think Best.
>
> We have the Honour to be, with Great Respect, Your Most obt Serts. Josiah Bartlett[53]

Congress ordered that Rogers be returned to New Hampshire "to be Dispos'd of as that Government shall judge best."[54] On 10 July 1776 Rhode Island delegate William Ellery wrote to his brother "Major Rogers who was under Guard here made his Escape last Evening. He may do Mischief, if he should not be taken."[55] Rogers was being held. No charges were leveled against him and no trial was set. He may have escaped because he knew that more damning evidence could be assembled against him or, more likely, he had given up his efforts to join the Patriot cause. His scruples about fighting his fellow Americans and violating his parole instantly disappeared when he escaped.

Robert Rogers headed for New York City after his escape. Lord Howe had landed there at the end of June 1776 and the Continental Army withdrew to Long Island. Robert Rogers joined the British army at Staten Island and was commissioned as a lieutenant colonel. The British were well aware of his duplicity, lying and other character flaws made clear to the Patriots, but they respected his ability to command troops and his courage in battle. Howe gave him the job of raising a battalion of rangers and wrote to Lord Germain on 6 August 1776. "Major Rogers, having escaped to us from Philadelphia, is empowered to raise a battalion of rangers, which, I hope may be useful in the course of the campaign."[56]

It is evident that Rogers decided to join the British in their war against the Americans before he left Britain in June 1775. He was waiting for his British army commission from Lord Dartmouth at that time, but it is also clear that he was for sale to the highest bidder as seen in his repeated efforts to obtain a commission in the American army after he arrived in America.

Washington thought that Rogers was a spy for the British and this is probably true.[57] The fact that Rogers was a retired British officer in half-pay status made most Americans suspicious of him and his interactions with the British seem to confirm this. When Rogers visited Tryon he provided information about the Americans in Philadelphia and received land grants and probably money as well. Based upon that, the label of spy would certainly apply. One curious aspect of Washington's view of Rogers is his concern about Rogers in the battles that followed in late 1776. Washington frequently wanted information about Rogers' location. This is very odd since Rogers composed only a small fraction of the British forces arrayed against the Continental Army. Washington's interest was caused by Rogers' knowledge of the Americans, their leaders and the fact that Rogers' leadership ability and courage under fire was far superior to most of his British army peers. Washington considered him to be a dangerous foe capable of doing far more damage than the size of his force would indicate. Washington summarized his view: " . . . Rogers is an Active instrument in the Enemy's hands, and his conduct has peculiar claims to our notice."[58]

The Queen's American Rangers

Rogers set about recruiting for the Queen's Rangers. The ranger unit was named to honor Charlotte of Mecklenburg-Strelitz, consort of George III. For starters, he had the residue of Queen's Loyal Virginia Regiment, a unit badly defeated by the

Americans at the Battle of Great Bridge several months earlier. To that base he could add British volunteers and Loyalist refugees streaming into British held territory. By 21 August Rogers had ten companies, but the battalion was under strength.

Battle of Long Island, 27 August 1776

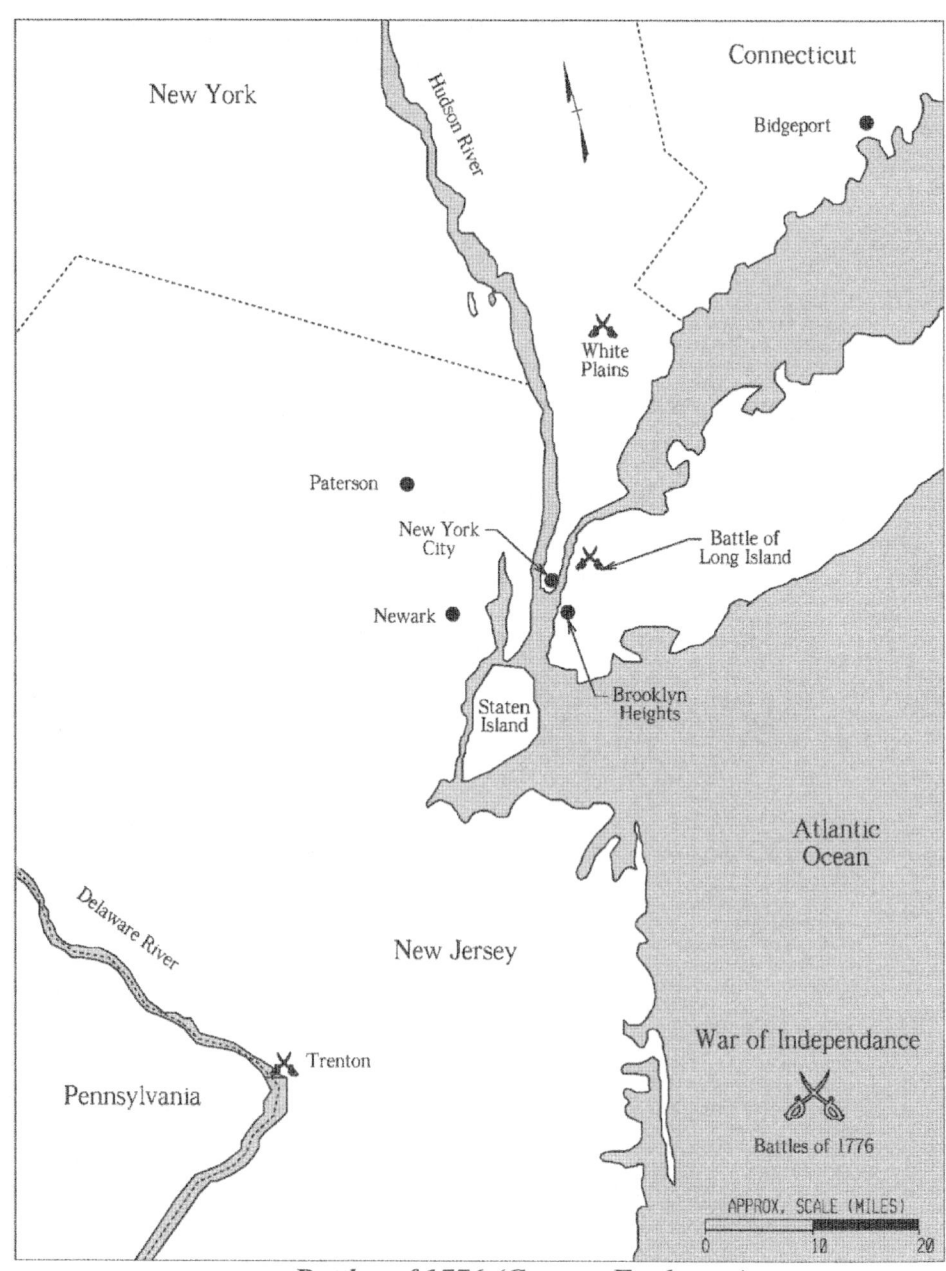

Battles of 1776 (Connor Eggleston)

The British army was bottled up in Boston for months before Lord William Howe decided to break out and move to Halifax, Nova Scotia to await reinforcements from Britain. Richard Howe, William's brother, commanded the fleet. Viscount Richard Howe had gained a reputation for his talent in amphibious operations during the war with the French, experience of great value during the current war. The British fleet departed Boston with the troops on 17 March 1776. At Halifax Lord Howe rearmed and planned to move to New York and seize the city. The British needed a victory since a stalemate would be humiliating and expensive to maintain. The British settled on a plan to seize New York City, attempt to gain the allegiance of the rebels, mobilize the Loyalists, and establish New York City as a base from which they could raid sea ports and eventually defeat the American Army. The royal navy could move troops faster than Washington could move his army on land. Most important, Howe wanted to cut off New England from the other colonies and he thought that he could do that by controlling the Hudson River.

While Howe waited for reinforcements in Halifax, Washington was dealing with his own problems. Washington's goal was to wear down the British and keep his army intact at all costs. He had moved to New York City in April after Howe left Boston.[59] In a very short time Washington had 3,000 troops that were moved to Brooklyn in early May since it seemed unlikely that they could hold New York City, itself for long.

> New York was a poor defensive position for the American forces, especially considering the overwhelming strength of the Royal Navy. Lord Howe had a fleet of over 400 ships at his disposal, with 30 ships of the line (major warships mounting more than sixty guns). The Americans could mount no resistance at all to this fleet (privateers disrupting the shipping of British supplies was the only naval effort made at the time). Indeed, the Continental Navy did not get its first ship of the line until near the end of the war. In 1776, New York City occupied the bottom tip of Manhattan, or

York Island. The North or Hudson River divided Manhattan from New Jersey to the west, while the East River separated it from Long Island to the south and east. At the northern tip of Manhattan, two bridges connected it with Westchester County. Manhattan, vulnerable to being cut off by an amphibious force moving up either the Hudson or East Rivers, was a difficult enough position to hold. The situation was made even worse by the fact that the city was overlooked by high ground (the Columbia Heights, commonly referred to as the Brooklyn Heights) on Long Island, making it also necessary to hold this land if New York City was to remain tenable and passage through the East River was to be contested. In turn, the works on the Brooklyn Heights needed to be protected against a possible landward assault, so a chain of fortifications, linked by entrenchments, was established across the neck of the Brooklyn Peninsula.[60]

Washington knew that he could do little to prevent the British occupation of Staten Island unless the Staten Island militia would fight so he issued a stirring proclamation.

> The time is now near at hand which must probably determine whether Americans are to be freemen or slaves; whether their houses and farms are to be pillaged and destroyed, and they consigned to a state of wretchedness, from which no human efforts will probably deliver them. The fate of unborn millions will now depend, (under God) on the courage and conduct of this army. Our cruel and unrelenting enemy leaves us no choice but a brave resistance or the most abject submission. This is all we can expect. We have, therefore, to resolve to conquer or die. Our Country's honor calls upon us for a vigorous and manly exertion; and if we now shamefully fail, we shall become infamous to the whole world. Let us, therefore, rely upon the goodness of the cause and the aid of the Supreme Being (in whose hands victory is) to encourage and animate us to great and noble action.
>
> The eyes of all our countrymen are now upon us; and we shall have their blessings and praises if happy we are in being the instrument of saving them from the tyranny meditated against them. Let us therefore animate and encourage each other, and show the whole world that freemen contending for liberty on their own ground is superior to any slavish mercenaries on earth.

> The General recommends to the Officers great coolness in time of action, and to the soldiers a strict attention and obedience, with a becoming firmness and spirit.[61]
>
> *George Washington*

Washington's stirring proclamation did little to influence reality. The Staten Island militia was outnumbered twenty to one and Howe landed there virtually unopposed on 2 July 1776. Six miles away, Washington's troops watched the forest of enemy ship masts off Staten Island from New York City.[62]

Forts were constructed near Brooklyn Heights which towered over the East River. Washington guessed that the British would land troops on the southern end of Manhattan while British troops on Long Island would move to attack Brooklyn Heights. Howe asked Washington to surrender the city and this reported in the press.

> NEWBURY-PORT July 12. It was yesterday currently reported in Boston and this town, that after the New-York last Thursday's paper was printed, the Regulars made a second attempt to land some of their men, in which they met with a second repulse, and the loss of between 3 and four hundred men, 70 of which were killed, the rest taken prisoners, it is also said about 40 of our men, were killed and wounded.
>
> We hear from New-York, that Gen. Howe sent a flag of truce in the king's name to demand possession of that city. And that his Excellency General Washington very politely refused to comply with his request.[63]

Washington thought that an attack on Long Island would be a diversion with the main attack on Manhattan. Washington divided his force leaving half on Manhattan and waited for the British attack.

> By mid-August fresh contingents of British ships had converged on New York, rounding out an expeditionary force of 32,000 troops, including 8,000 Hessian mercenaries, and revealing the magnitude of the threat to the Continental Army. Making a

major statement about the peril of the American revolt, the Crown had enlisted seventy warships, a full half of the Royal Navy, to deliver an overwhelming blow against the Americans. It decided to gamble all on a military solution to a conflict that was, at bottom, one of principle and that depended ultimately on recovering the lost trust of the former colonists.

A subdued Washington knew the stage was set for a major confrontation. "An attack is now therefore to be expected," he wrote, "which will probably decide the fate of America." His army of only 10,500 men, 3,000 of them ailing, was sadly outnumbered and outgunned. Even though he tried to put on a brave face, he approached the impending confrontation with dread. "When I compare" the British Army "with that which we have to oppose them, I cannot help feeling very anxious apprehensions," he confided to Brigadier General William Livingston. As more militiamen streamed into New York, Washington's army expanded to 23,000 soldiers, but many were callow youths grabbed from shops and farms who would soon confront a highly professional military force. Washington's pronouncements acquired a darker tinge, as if he intuited the many deaths that lay ahead."We must resolve to conquer or die," he intoned in general orders."With this resolution and the blessing of heaven, victory and success certainly will attend us."

The night of August 21, almost the eve of battle, witnessed an electrical storm of such portentous grandeur that it might have been conjured up by Shakespeare. Major Albert Benedict, posted on the elevated portion of Long Island known as Brooklyn Heights, which towered over the East River and housed the main American fortification, left this graphic description of the celestial pyrotechnics whizzing through the sky, "In a few minutes the entire heavens became black as ink, and from horizon to horizon the whole empyrean was ablaze with lightning ... The lightning fell in masses and sheets of fire to earth, and seemed to strike incessantly and on every side."

The Howe brothers postponed an invasion to give the Hessian troops a week to recuperate from their transatlantic journey and to see if their feeble peace overtures bore fruit. Baffled by the delay, Washington found "something exceedingly mysterious in the conduct" of these brothers, who spouted catchphrases of peace amid a huge military buildup The paramount question was whether the enemy would land on Manhattan or on Long Island, prompting Washington to hedge his bets by dividing his forces. This strategy, if seemingly prudent, ran the grave risk of having British ships storm up the East River, snapping links between the army's two wings. To avert this possibility, Washington sank wrecks in the channels of Upper New York Bay-one could see masts of submerged ships poking up from the water - and seeded the East River with spiked obstacles to thwart vessels.[64]

To the citizens of New York City he issued a warning published by the Newspapers.

> Commander in chief for the army of the United States of North America.
> Whereas a bombardment and an attack upon the city of New York by a cruel and inveterate enemy, may be hourly expected. And as there are great numbers of women, children and infirmed persons, yet remaining in the city, whose continuance will rather be prejudicial than advantagous to the army, and their persons exposed to great danger and hatred: I do therefore, recommend it to all such persons, as they value their own safety and preservation, to remove with all expedition, out of the said town at this critical period, trusting that with the blessing of heaven, upon the American Army they may soon return to it in perfect security. And I do enjoin and require all the Officers and soldiers in the Army, under my command to forward and assist such persons in their compliance with the recommendations.
> Given under my hand, at Head Quarters, New York, August 17, 1776.[65]
>
> *George Washington*

At 0510 hours on 22 August 1776 the British landed an advanced guard of 4,000 troops on Long Island. By noon the British had 15,000 troops and 40 artillery pieces on the shore. Washington was wrong. The main British effort would be against Long Island. By 26 August the British were ready to attack. A night attack was staged and the British moved out

2100 hours under the command of General Henry Clinton. Washington planned to block the passes leading to Brooklyn Heights and inflict heavy casualties on the British but one of the passes through the Gowanus Heights was left unguarded. Ten thousand British troops marched through the pass that night and this enabled them to get behind the American blocking positions.

Robert Rogers was busy on Staten Island recruiting troops for his Queen's American Ranger Battalion. By the time of the battle he had formed ten companies, but they were under strength. Rogers led his battalion across the East River and the Queen's American Rangers were across by the 27th.

On the morning of 27 August Clinton signaled a fierce frontal attack on the blocking positions while they were simultaneously attacked from the east. The Queen's American Rangers apparently were attached to one of the attacking British regiments, but little is known of their participation in the battle.

The Americans soon found the enemy in their rear and many scrambled to fall back to Brooklyn Heights.[66] In some cases, units attempted to stop the British in order to allow others to escape to Brooklyn Heights. It turned into a slaughter as American units were surrounded and annihilated. The brutality of the Hessians was notorious. They executed any Americans who attempted to surrender.[67]

Clinton and Howe held back a final assault on Brooklyn Heights for fear of heavy casualties seen at Bunker (Breed's) Hill in Boston. What followed was two days of rain and fog that delayed any further attacks. This may have saved Washington's army. At 1600 hours on 29 August Washington held a council of war and decided to withdraw his army across the East River to New York City. This was a risky move since the British fleet was standing in the East River between Long Island and the city. A night withdrawal of Washington's forces was accomplished under conditions of heavy fog without loss. By the morning of 30 August, 9,500 American troops were in New York City.[68] That same morning Washington's troops surprised one of Rogers' recruiting sessions in Westchester. The leader, William Lounsberry was killed and fourteen recruits were captured.[69] Newspapers reported details of the battle on Long Island.

> PHILADELPHIA Sept. 5. Extract of a letter from New-York, dated Sept. 1, 1776.
> "Last Monday, morning we went over to Long Island, and about midnight we were alarmed by the return of some of the scouting parties who advised us that the English were in motion, and coming up the island with several field pieces. It was generally thought not to be the main body, but only a detachment, with a view to possess themselves of some advantageous heights. Upon which near three thousand men were ordered out, consisting chiefly of the Pennsylvania and the Maryland troops, to attack them on their march. About sunrise we came up with a very large body of them. The Delaware and Maryland battalions made one party, Col. Atlee, with his battalion a little before us, had taken post in an orchard and behind a barn, and on the approach of the enemy he gave them a very severe fire, which he bravely kept up for a considerable time, until they were near surrounding him, when he retreated to the woods."[70]

Joseph Plumb Martin was a Continental soldier from Connecticut who was present at the battle. He was fifteen years old at the time of the battle and would later write a book about his experiences in the War of Independence.[71] Initially, Martin was stationed in New York City but his unit was ordered across the East River to reinforce Washington's army on Long Island. Joseph Plumb Martin tells the story from a private soldier's viewpoint something seldom found in accounts of battles. His dry sense of humor maintains reader interest for example, " . . . we continued some days, keeping up the old system of starving."[72] After raiding the wine cellar of General Israel Putnam, he escaped back to his unit with his mates. Putnam, a former member of Rogers' Rangers, threatened to hang him and the others with him.

I remained in New – York two or three months, in which time several things occurred, but so trifling that I shall not mention them; when sometime in the latter part of the month of August, I was ordered upon a fatigue party; we had scarcely reached the grand parade, when I saw our sergeant-major directing his course up Broadway, towards us, in rather an unusual step for him; he soon arrived and informed us, and then the commanding officer of the party, that he had orders to take off all belonging to our regiment and march us to our quarters, as the regiment was ordered to Long Island, the British having landed in force there. Although this was not unexpected to me, yet it gave me rather a disagreeable feeling, as I was pretty well assured I should have to snuff a little gunpowder. However, I kept my cogitations to myself, went to my quarters, packed up my clothes, and got myself in readiness for the expedition as soon as possible. I then went to the top of the house where I had a full view of that part of the Island. I distinctly saw the smoke of the field artillery, but the distance and the unfavourableness of the wind prevented my hearing their report, at least but faintly. The horrors of battle then presented themselves to my mind in all their hideousness. I must come to it now, thought I, - well, I will endeavour to do my duty as well as I am able and leave the event with Providence. We were soon ordered to our regimental parade, from which, as soon as the regiment was formed, we were marched off for the ferry. At the lower end of the street were placed several casks of sea-bread, made, I believe, of canel and peas-meal, nearly hard enough for musket flints; the casks were unheaded and each man was allowed to take as many as he could, as he marched by. As my good luck would have it, there was a momentary halt made; I improved the opportunity thus offered me, as every good soldier should upon all important occasions, to get as many of the biscuit as I possibly could; no one said anything to me, and I filled my bosom, and took as many as I could hold in my hand, a dozen or more in all, and when we arrived at the ferry-stairs I stowed them away in my knapsack. We quickly embarked on board the boats; as each boat started, three cheers were given by those on board, which was returned by the numerous spectators who thronged the wharves; they all wished us good luck, apparently; although it was with most of them, perhaps, nothing more than ceremony. We soon landed at Brooklyn, upon the Island, marched up the ascent from the ferry, to the plain. We now began to meet the wounded men, another sight I was unacquainted with, some with broken arms, some with broken legs, and some with broken heads. The sight of these a little daunted me, and made me think of home, but the sight and thought vanished together. We marched a short distance, when we halted to refresh ourselves. Whether we had any other victuals besides the hard bread I do not remember, but I remember my gnawing at them; they were hard enough to break the teeth of a rat. One of the soldiers complaining of thirst to his officer; look at that man, said he, pointing to me, he is not thirsty, I will warrant it. I felt a little elevated to be stiled a man. While resting here, which was not more than twenty minutes or half an hour, the Americans and British were warmly engaged within sight of us. What were the feelings of most or all the young soldiers at this time, I know not, but I know what were mine;-but let mine or theirs be what they might, I saw a Lieutenant who appeared to have feelings not very enviable; whether he was actuated by fear or the canteen I cannot determine now; I thought it fear at the time; for he ran round among the men of his company, sniveling and blubbering, praying each one if he had aught against him, or if he had injured any one that they would forgive him, declaring at the same time that he, from his heart, forgave them if they had offended him, and I gave him full credit for his assertion; for had he been at the gallows with a halter about his neck, he could not have shown more fear or penitence. A fine soldier you are, I ought, a fine officer, an exemplary man for young soldiers! I would have then suffered anything short of death rather than have made such an exhibition of myself; but, as the poet says,

"Fear does things so like a witch,
'Tis hard to distinguish which is which."

The officers of the new levies wore cockades of different

colours to distinguish them from the standing forces, as they were called; the field officers wore red, captains white, and the subaltern officers green. While we were resting here our Lieutenant-Colonel and Major, (our Colonel not being with us,) took their cockades from their hats; being asked the reason, the Lieutenant-Colonel replied, that he was willing to risk his life in the cause of his country, but was unwilling to stand a particular mark for the enemy to fire at. He was a fine officer and a brave soldier.

We were soon called upon to fall in and proceed. We had not gone far, about half a mile, when I heard one in the rear ask another where his musket was; I looked round and saw one of the soldiers stemming off without his gun, having left it where we last halted; he was inspecting his side as if undetermined whether he had it or not, he then fell out of the ranks to go in search of it: one of the company, who had brought it on (wishing to see how far he would go before he missed it) gave it to him. The reader will naturally enough conclude that he was a brave soldier. Well, he was a brave fellow for all this accident, and received two severe wounds, by musket balls, while fearlessly fighting for his country at the battle of White Plains. So true is the proverb, "A singed cat may make a good mouser." Stranger things may happen.

We overtook a small party of the artillery here, dragging a heavy twelve pounder upon a field carriage, sinking half way to the naves in the sandy soil. They plead hard for some of us to assist them to get on their piece; our officers, however, paid no attention to their en- treaties, but pressed forward towards a creek, where a large party of Americans and British were engaged. By the time we arrived, the enemy had driven our men into the creek, or rather mill-pond, (the tide being up,) where such as could swim got across; those that could not swim, and could not procure anything to buoy them up, sunk. The British having several fieldpieces stationed by a brick house, were pouring the cannister and grape upon the Americans like a shower of hail; they would doubtless have done them much more damage than they did, but for the twelve pounder mentioned above; the men having gotten it within sufficient distance to reach them, and opening a fire upon them, soon obliged them to shift their quarters. There as in this action a regiment of Maryland troops, (volunteers,) all young gentlemen. When they came out of the water and mud to us, looking like water rats, it was a truly pitiful sight. Many of them were killed in the pond, and more were drowned. Some of us went into the water after the fall of the tide, and took out a number of corpses and a great many arms that were sunk in the pond and creek.

Our regiment lay on the ground we then occupied the following night; the next day in the afternoon, we had a considerable tight scratch with about an equal number of the British, which began rather unexpectedly, and a little whimsically. A few of our men, (I mean of our regiment,) went over the creek upon business that usually employed us, that is, in search of something to eat. There was a field of Indian corn at a short distance from the creek, with several cocks of hay about half way from the creek to the cornfield; the men purposed to get some of the corn, or any thing else that was eatable. When they got up with the haycocks, they were fired upon by about an equal number of the British, from the cornfield; our people took to the hay, and the others to the fence, where they exchanged a number of shots at each other, neither side inclining to give back. A number, say forty or fifty more of our men, went over and drove the British from the fence; they were by this time reinforced in their turn, and drove us back. The two parties kept thus alternately reinforcing until we had the most of our regiment in the action. After the officers came to command, the English were soon routed from the place, but we dare not follow them for fear of falling into some snare, as the whole British army was in the vicinity of us; I do not recollect that we had any one killed outright, but we had several severely wounded, and some, I believe, mortally.

Our regiment was alone, no other troops being near where we were lying; we were upon a rising ground, covered with a young growth of trees; we felled a fence of trees around us to prevent the approach of the enemies' horse. We lay there a day longer, in the latter part of the afternoon there fell a very heavy shower of rain which wet us all to the skin, and much damaged our ammunition; about sunset, when the shower had passed over, we were ordered to parade and discharge our pieces, we attempted to fire by platoons for improvement, but we made blundering work of it; it was more like a running fire, than firing by divisions: however, we got our muskets as empty as our stomachs, and with half the trouble, nor was it half the trouble to have reloaded them, for we had wherewithal to do that, but not so with our stomachs.

Just at dusk, I, with one or two others of our company, went off to a barn, about half a mile distant, with intent to get some straw to lodge upon, the ground and leaves being drenched in water, and we as wet as they; it was quite dark in the barn, and while I was fumbling about the floor someone called to me from the top of the mow, inquiring where I was from; I told him. He asked me if we had not had an engagement there, (having heard us discharging our guns,) I told him we had and a severe one too; he asked if many were killed;-told him that I 'saw none killed, nor any very badly wounded. I then heard several others, as it appeared, speaking on the mow. Poor fellows, they had better have been at their posts, than skulking in a barn on account of a little wet, for I have not the least doubt but that the British had possession of their mortal parts before the noon of the next day.

I could not find any straw, but I found some wheat in the sheaf, standing by the side of the floor; I took a sheaf or two and returned as fast as I could to the regiment. When I arrived the men were all paraded to march off the ground; I left my wheat, seized my musket and fell into the ranks. We were strictly enjoined not to speak, or even cough, while on the march. All orders were given from officer to officer, and communicated to the men in whispers. What such secrecy could mean we could not divine. We marched off in the same way that we had come on to the island, forming various conjectures among ourselves as to our destination. Some were of opinion that we were to endeavour to get on the flank, or in the rear of the enemy. Others, that we were going up the East river, to attack them in that quarter; but none, it seems, knew the right of the matter. We marched on, however, until we arrived at the ferry, where we immediately embarked on board the batteau, and were conveyed safely to New York, where we were landed about three o'clock in the morning, nothing against our inclinations.

The next day the British showed themselves to be in possession of our works upon the island, by firing upon some of our boats, passing to and from Governor's Island. Our regiment was employed, during this day, in throwing up a sort of breastwork, at their alarm post upon the wharves, (facing the enemy,) composed of spars and logs, and filling the space between with the materials of which the wharves were composed, - old broken junk bottles, flint stones, &c. which, had a cannon ball passed through, would have chanced to kill five men where the ball would one. But the enemy did not see fit to molest us.[73]

Joseph Plumb Martin

He later closed by saying that he located some of the wine lifted from General Putnam's cellar and finished the job.

Nathan Hale

It had been just two months since the signing of the Declaration of Independence and both sides were desperately seeking to increase their strength for the war. Rogers was dropped off by the brig, *Halifax* near Flushing, New York between 16-18 September 1776. Rogers passed Nathan Hale, a young school teacher, on the road and became interested in the young man. He suspected that Hale was a Patriot and up to no good. He wanted to learn more about Hale and befriended him. Rogers was quite well known in the region, but Hale had not heard of him. Rogers played the role of an avid Patriot and invited Hale to dine with him at a nearby Tory-owned tavern. The two had a grand time and both were soon drunk. In reply to Rogers' stream of questions, Hale confided his mission to Rogers explaining that he had been sent by General Washington to spy on the British. Although he was an officer in Washington's army, Hale was in civilian clothes and if captured he would be executed as a spy. Consider Tiffany, a Tory shopkeeper provided an account of the encounter.

> [Rogers] detected several American officers, that were sent to Long Island as spies, especially Captain Hale, who was improved in disguise, to find whether the Long Island inhabitants were friends to America or not. Colonel Rogers having for some days,

observed Captain Hale, and suspected that he was an enemy in disguise; and to convince himself, Rogers thought of trying the same method, he quickly altered his own habit, with which he Made Capt Hale a visit at his quarters, where the Colonel fell into some discourse concerning the war, intimating the trouble of his mind, in his being detained on an island, where the inhabitants sided with the Britains against the American Colonies, intimating withal, that he himself was upon the business of spying out the inclination of the people and motion of the British troops. This intrigue, not being suspected by the Capt, made him believe that he had found a good friend, and one that could be trusted with the secrecy of the business he was engaged in; and after the Colonel's drinking a health to the Congress: informs Rogers of the business and intent. The Colonel, finding out the truth of the matter, invited Captain Hale to dine with him the next day at his quarters, unto which he agreed. The time being come, Capt Hale repaired to the place agreed on, where he met his pretended friend, with three or four men of the same stamp, and after being refreshed, began the same conversation as hath been already mentioned. But in the height of their conversation, a company of soldiers surrounded the house, and by orders from the commander, seized Capt Hale in an instant. But denying his name, and the business he came upon, he was ordered to New York.[74]

Consider Tiffany

They took him to General Howe's quarters in New York City where he was interrogated by Howe and others. Hale readily told them everything he knew and pleaded for his life without avail. Howe handed him over to the Provost Marshal, a horrible man named William Cunningham. Cunningham enjoyed the torture and hanging of Patriots and in a twist of fate, he himself would be hanged years later in London for forgery. Cunningham treated Hale badly and hanged him on 22 September 1776. Hale had a mole on his neck and his death proved the old-wives' tale that a man with a mole on his neck would hang. A Chinese proverb said that the mole meant a short life. Nathan Hale was twenty-one years old at the time he died.[75] British Lieutenant Frederick Mackenzie was stationed in

New York City at the time and paid a final tribute to Hale in his diary.

> A person named Nathaniel Hales, a Lieutenant in the Rebel Army, and a native of Connecticut, was apprehended as a Spy . . . upon Long Island; and having this day made a full and free confession to the Commander in Chief of his being employed by Mr. Washington in that capacity, he was hanged at 11 o'clock in front of the Park of Artillery. He was about 24 [sic] years of age, and had been educated at the College of Newhaven in Connecticut. He behaved with great composure and resolution, saying, he thought it the duty of every good Officer, to obey any orders given him by his Commander-in-Chief; and desired the Spectators to be at all times prepared to meet death in whatever shape it might appear.[76]
> ***Lieutenant Frederick Mackenzie***

The quote attributed to Hale "I only regret that I have but one life to lose for my country." appears to be a myth.

Nathan Hale (1755-1776) (Creative Commons)

By October Rogers' Queen's American Rangers was nearly at full strength and numbered 400 troops. Among those joining was Captain John Shepherd, a Rogers' Ranger from the French and Indian War. It was at this time that Howe decided to defeat Washington by encircling his army.

Battle of White Plains, 28 October 1776

After his defeat on Long Island, Washington escaped to Manhattan with his army of 9,000 on the night of 29-30 October 1776. Howe's attempt to trap Washington with an encircling movement failed when his landing at Pell's Point had to be aborted due to American resistance on 18 October. Howe than established his camp seven miles from the lightly defended American supply depot at White Plains. Washington continued to move north from New York City with part of Howe's army in pursuit. When Washington realized that Howe was near White Plains and could capture his supplies, he ordered his army to assemble at White Plains while Howe was moving slowly toward that village.

General Stirling led Washington's advance when he received word that the Queen's American Rangers had seized the town of Mamaroneck near White Plains. Stirling ordered Colonel John Haslet's Delaware Regiment to attack Rogers and his rangers. Haslet reached Rogers camp at 0400, 22 October and surprised the rangers killing some and capturing others. As dawn approached Rogers rallied his rangers and they moved up a slope to the summit where they poured down fire on the Delaware Regiment. In the bitter fighting that ensued, Haslet was forced back and withdrew from Mamaroneck. Haslet had lost four dead, fifteen wounded, and a few captured. Rogers lost twenty dead, nine wounded and thirty-six were taken prisoner. Rogers left to raid the village of Bedford and took no further part in the Battle of White Plains. Haslet described Rogers "On the first fire, he [Rogers] skulked off in the dark . . . the late worthless Major."[77]

Johann Rall (1726-1776) (Wikipedia)

On 22 October Washington established his headquarters just north of White Plains and ordered two lines of trenches to be dug on raised ground overlooking a plain that the British troops would cross. On the morning of 28 October 1776, Howe marched his troops against the American trenches at White Plains. The British vastly outnumbered Washington's army of 9,000. Howe moved forward with Clinton's troops on the right and the Hessians under Colonel Johann Rall the left. Rall struck the American line first but was driven off. This stopped the entire British line that regrouped and then attacked. The American line broke and Washington ordered a withdrawal that was successfully executed.

Joseph Plumb Martin was in the battle and recorded what he saw.

>Sometime in October, the British landed at Frogg's neck, or point, and by their motions seemed to threaten to cut off our retreat to York Island [Manhattan]. We were thereupon ordered to leave the Island. We crossed King's bridge and directed our course toward the White Plains. We saw parties of the enemy foraging in the country, but they were generally too alert for us. We encamped on the heights called Valentine's hill, where we continued some days, keeping up the old system of starving. A sheep's head which I begged of the butchers, who were killing some for the "gentleman officers," was all the provisions I had for two or three days.
>
>While lying here, I one day rambled into the woods and fields, in order, if possible, to procure something to satisfy the cravings of nature. I found and ate a considerable quantity of chestnuts, which are, as Bloomfield says of his acorns, "Hot thirsty food," which was, I suppose, the cause of our Doctor's blunder, as I shall relate directly. I returned to camp just at sunset, and met our orderly sergeant, who immediately warned me to prepare for a two day's command. What is termed going on command, is what is generally called going on a scouting party, or something similar. I told the sergeant I was sick and could not go; he said I must go to the Doctor, and if he said I was unfit for duty, he must excuse me. I saw our Surgeon's mate close by, endeavouring to cook his supper, blowing the fire and scratching his eyes. We both stepped up to him, and he felt my pulse, at the same time very demurely shutting his eyes, while I was laughing in his face. After a minute's consultation with his medical talisman, he very gravely told the sergeant, that I was unfit for duty, having a high fever upon me. I was as well as he was; all the medicine I needed was a bellyful of victuals. The sergeant turned to go off for another man, when I told him that I would go, for I meant to go; I only felt a little cross, and did not

know how, just then, to vent my spleen in any other way. I had much rather go on such an expedition than stay in camp; as I stood some chance while in the country to get something to eat. But I admired the Doctor's skill; although, perhaps not more extraordinary than that of many others of the "faculty."

We marched from Valentine's hill for the White Plains, in the night. There were but three of our men present. We had our cooking utensils, (at that time the most useless things in the army,) to carry in our hands. They were made of cast iron and consequently heavy. I was so beat out before morning, with hunger and fatigue, that I could hardly move one foot before the other. I told my messmates that I *could* not carry our kettle any further; they said they *would* not carry it any further; of what use was it? They had nothing to cook and did not want anything to cook with. We were sitting down on the ascent of a hill when this discourse happened. We got up to proceed, when I took up the kettle, which held nearly a common pail full, I could not carry it; my arms were almost dislocated; I sat it down in the road, and one of the others gave it a shove with his foot, and it rolled down against the fence, and that was the last I ever saw of it. When we got through the night's march we found our mess was not the only one that was rid of their iron bondage.

We arrived at the White Plains just at dawn of day, tired and faint-encamped on the plains a few days and then removed to the hills in the rear of the plains. Nothing remarkable transpired, while lying here, for some time. One day, after roll-call, one of my messmates with me, set off upon a little jaunt into the country to get some sauce of some kind or other. We soon came to a field of English turnips; but the owner was there, and we could not get any of them without paying for them in some way or other. We soon agreed with the man to pull and cut off the tops of the turnips at the halves, until we got as many as we needed. After the good man had set us to work, and chatted with us a few minutes, he went off and left us. After he was gone, and we had pulled and cut as many as we wanted, we packed them up and decamped, leaving the owner of the turnips to pull his share himself.

When we arrived at the camp, the troops were all parading. Upon inquiry, we found that the British were advancing upon us. We flung our turnip plunder into the tent-packed up our things, which was easily done, for we had but a trifle to pack, and fell into the ranks. Before we were ready to march, the battle had begun. Our regiment then marched off, crossed a considerable stream of water which crosses the plain, and formed behind a stone wall in company with several other regiments, and waited the approach of the enemy. They were not far distant; at least, that part of them with which we were quickly after engaged. They were constructing a sort of bridge to convey their artillery, &c. across the before mentioned stream. They however soon made their appearance in our neighbourhood. There was in our front, about ten rods distant, an orchard of apple trees. The ground on which the orchard stood was lower than the ground that we occupied, but was level from our post to the verge of the orchard, when it fell off so abruptly that we could not see the lower parts of the trees. A party of Hessian troops, and some English, soon took possession of this ground: they would advance so far as just to show themselves above the rising ground, fire, and fall back and reload their muskets. Our chance upon them was, as soon as they showed themselves above the level ground, or when they fired, to aim at the flashes of their guns-their position was as advantagious to them as a breastwork. We were engaged in this manner for some time, when finding ourselves flanked and in danger of being surrounded, we were compelled to make a hasty retreat from the stone wall. We lost, comparatively speaking, very few at the fence: but when forced to retreat, we lost, in killed and wounded, a considerable number. One man who belonged to our company, when we marched from the parade, said, "Now I am going out to the field to be killed;" and he said more than once afterwards, that he should be killed; and he was- he was shot dead on the field. I never saw a man so prepossessed with the idea of any mishap as he was. We fell back a little distance and made a stand: detached parties engaging in almost every direction. We did not come in contact with the enemy again that day, and just at night we fell back to our encampment.

In the course of the afternoon the British took possession of a hill on the right of our encampment, which had in the early part of the day been occupied by some of the New-York troops. This hill overlooked the one upon which we were, and was not more than half or three fourths of a mile distant.

The enemy had several pieces of field artillery upon this hill, and, as might be expected, entertained us with their music all the evening. We entrenched ourselves where we now lay, expecting another attack. But the British were very civil, and indeed they generally were, after they had received a check from Brother Jonathan [an emblem representing New England similar to the caricature Uncle Sam], for any of their rude actions; they seldom repeated them, at least, not till the affair that caused the reprimand, had ceased in some measure to be remembered.

During the night we remained in our new made trenches, the ground of which was in many parts springy; in that part where I happened to be stationed, the water, before morning, was nearly over shoes, which caused many of us to take violent colds, by being exposed upon the wet ground after a profuse perspiration. I was one who felt the effects of it, and was the next day sent back to the baggage to get well again, if I could, for it was left to my own exertions to do it, and no other assistance was afforded me. I was not alone in misery; there were a number in the same circumstances. When I arrived at the baggage, which was not more than a mile or two, I had the canopy of heaven for my hospital, and the ground for my hammock. I found a spot where the dry leaves had collected between the knolls; I made up a bed of these, and nestled in it, having no other friend present but the sun to smile upon me. I had nothing to eat or drink, not even water, and was unable to go after any myself, for I was sick indeed. In the evening, one of my messmates found me out, and soon after brought me some boiled hog's flesh (it was not pork) and turnips, without either bread or salt. I could not eat it, but I felt obliged to him notwithstanding; he did all he could do - he gave me the best he had to give, and had to steal that, poor fellow; - necessity drove him to do it to satisfy the cravings of his own hunger, as well as to assist a fellow sufferer.

The British, soon after this, left the White Plains, and passed the Hudson, into New Jersey. We, likewise, fell back to New Castle and Wright's mills. Here a number of our sick were sent off to Norwalk, in Connecticut, to recruit. I was sent with them as a nurse. We were billetted among the inhabitants. I had, in my ward, seven or eight *sick soldiers,* who were (at least, soon after their arrival there,) as well in health as I was: all they wanted was a cook and something for a cook to exercise his functions upon. The inhabitants here were almost entirely what were in those days termed tories. An old lady, of whom I often procured milk, used always, when I went to her house, to give me a lecture on my opposition to our good king George. She had always said, (she told me,) that the regulars would make us fly like pigeons. My patients would not use any of the milk I had of her, for fear, as they said, of poison; I told them I was not afraid of her poisoning the milk, she had not wit enough to think of such a thing, nor resolution enough to do it if she did think of it.[78]

Joseph Plumb Martin

Joseph Plumb Martin's term of service expired on 25 December 1776 so he was discharged and did not participate in the Battle of Trenton that followed White Plains.

Battle of Trenton, 26 December 1776

Washington's army was demoralized by the continued retreats and lack of any victory. They had been ousted from New York after the Battle of White Plains by the British and Hessians and had retreated into Pennsylvania. The vast majority of troops that had started at the Battle of Long Island were gone, lost as killed, wounded, captured, deserted or expired enlistments such as Private Martin. New blood arrived in the form of militia units and recruits but these were dwindling. Washington wrote home that he thought that the "game was about up." He needed a victory and as the year ended Washington planned an attack to reverse his fortunes. He would have 2,400 troops to accomplish this. The American plan provided an attack from three directions. General John Cadwalader would execute a diversionary attack against the British garrison at Bordentown, New Jersey. General James Ewing would seize the bridge over Assumpink Creek to prevent reinforcements from reaching Trenton while the main attack force of 2,400 would cross the Delaware River to attack Trenton. General Greene would attack from the north and General Sullivan from the South. It would be a predawn attack.

Colonel Johann Rall commanded three regiments of Hessian soldiers, about 1,400 troops, and had stopped at the small town, Trenton, New Jersey. It was cold, Christmas, and the troops were exhausted.

At this time John Honeyman entered the scene. Honeyman claimed to be a Tory. He was a butcher and weaver who traded with the British and Hessians. He had easy access through the lines and could gather intelligence for the Patriots. Honeyman's role in the battle has been disputed ever since. Even Central Intelligence Agency analysts have recently evaluated the Honeyman story and concluded it was doubtful. Historians such as David Hackett Fisher who wrote a book about the battle also did not believe the Honeyman story but thoroughly evaluated the evidence.

> John Honeyman, a supposed double agent who was said to have visited German commander Johann Rall on the eve of the battle and lulled him into a state of security. This story comes to us from a family legend, and the absence of direct evidence is explained by its adherents as a consequence of the deep secrecy that surrounded Honeyman's work, which they believe was known only to the man himself, his wife, and General Washington. Stryker included this story in his history and published the record of a grand jury which on June 5, 1777, indicted Honeyman for giving "aid and comfort" to the enemy. Stryker thought it significant that no record of punishment could be found, and that its absence proved the authenticity of the legend. But negative evidence is always a weak foundation. Surviving legal records from the Revolution are notoriously incomplete. This document in itself proves nothing about Honeyman's alleged espionage.[79]

The Honeyman family is convinced that he was a Patriot hero, Washington mentioned nothing of Honeyman, and Rall took any secret he had to the grave since he was mortally wounded during the battle and died the next day. Still, the thought that a good spy would leave no trace behind is a very good argument for the lack of evidence supporting the Honeyman family claim. On the eve of the battle, other authentic British spies confirmed to the British that Washington's army was on the verge of collapse. Brazilla Haines, a Burlington County Tory stayed overnight in the American camp and reported to his masters that "they had only two field pieces" and "there were not above eight hundred, near one half boys and all of them militia."[80] It is likely that Haines unknowingly misled the British because he saw only one of the American camps and based his report on that one alone.

Washington Crossing the Delaware (Creative Commons)

Washington's attack was delayed due to bad weather. Eventually, crossing of the Delaware River progressed with no loss of life and the troops and artillery arrived on the other shore. By then the weather had cleared, but the landing was three hours late. Washington had written a note before the crossing that said "Victory or Death" and this became the password for the surprise attack.[81] Washington led the attack on Trenton riding back and forth along the line. At 0800 hours, the Americans hit a Hessian outpost about one mile from Trenton. The Hessians realized that they were under attack as Washington led his troops in the advance. They fired three volleys while the Hessians fired one in return and pulled back. Firing increased as the Americans entered Trenton and artillery fire from the other side of the Delaware River added to Hessian discomfort as Washington rode to the high ground to direct the attack as Generals Sullivan and Greene executed the plan. The bad weather had ruined the gun powder of many of the troops and Washington ordered the use of the bayonet. He was resolved to take Trenton.

Washington at Trenton (Library of Congress)

At around seven-thirty A.M., the operation was nearly derailed by a preposterous blunder committed by an old Washington colleague. General Adam Stephen had fought with Washington in Braddock's campaign and vied with him for a seat in the House of Burgesses. The day before the Delaware crossing, he had dispatched a company of Virginians to scout enemy positions in Trenton. Now, as he neared the town, Washington was shocked to meet these fifty Virginians and learn that they had exchanged fire with Hessian sentries, raising the appalling specter that the Hessians had been alerted to the Continental Army's advent. Under questioning, Captain George Wallis told Washington they had acted under instructions from Stephen.

Washington summarily hauled the latter into his presence. "You, sir!" Washington scolded him. "You, sir, may have ruined all my plans by having put them on their guard." Those present were amazed by the vivid show of temper, but Washington soon regained his self-mastery and told the Virginians to fall in with his column.

The mythology of the Battle of Trenton portrays the Hessian mercenaries as slumbering in a drunken stupor after imbibing late-night Christmas cheer. In fact, Colonel Johann Gottlieb Rall had kept his men on high alert, and they felt frazzled and exhausted from constant drills and patrols. Quite shrewdly, Washington had worn them down by irregular raids and small skirmishes in the surrounding countryside. If the Hessians were caught off guard that morning, it was only because they thought the forbidding weather would preclude an attack. These tough, brawny hirelings, with a reputation for ferocity, inspired healthy fear among the Americans. But handicapped by their patronizing view of the Americans, they couldn't conceive of something of quite the scale and daring that Washington attempted. "I must concede that on the whole we had a poor opinion of the rebels, who previously had never successfully opposed us," said Lieutenant Jakob Piel. Having received multiple warnings of the surprise attack, Rall was so certain of the superiority of his men that he dismissed these reports with blithe bravado: "Let them come."[82]

When Sullivan entered Trenton from the south the Hessians withdrew to their barracks, while Greene entered from the north. Rall attempted to form the three Hessian regiments but they were quickly overrun by the Americans and fled the town. Rall's attempt to rally and retake the town failed and he was mortally wounded. The Hessians suffered the same problem endured by the Americans. Wet gun powder caused many muskets to fail. The Hessians scattered and some escaped but many were trapped and surrendered to the Americans. Total Hessian casualties were twenty-two killed, eighty-three wounded, and 896 captured including the wounded. All four Hessian colonels were killed during the battle and Rall died the following night. American casualties were two dead and five wounded including James Monroe, a future president of the United States who was badly wounded by a musket ball in the shoulder.[83]

The importance of this battle was disproportionate to its size. The fact that it was a decisive victory dispelled the gloom hanging over the army from a series of defeats. Washington was quoted as saying "This is a glorious day for our country." Congress was elated and confidence in the army was restored. The victory proved to the American troops that the brutal Hessians could be beaten. Enlistments in the Patriot cause quickly increased. The victory included the capture of a large amount of supplies that were desperately needed by the Americans such as food, ammunition, and shoes. Lord Howe was stunned by the loss and a British column under Lord Cornwallis was sent marching from New York to avenge the defeat. About one hundred of the Queen's American Rangers were with Cornwallis.[84] The British far outnumbered the American army and clashed with the Americans at Trenton late in the day on 2 January. Washington slipped away in the dark leaving some troops to stoke the fires while he escaped.[85] Washington remained in New Jersey and achieved a second victory at Princeton on 3 January 1777.[86]

> The Pennsylvania militia have just broken in the face of heavy musket fire and grape shot. Suddenly, Washington appears among them, urging them to rally and form a line behind him. A detachment of New England Continentals joins the line, which first holds and then begins to move forward with Washington front-and-center astride his white English charger. The British troops are placed behind a fence at the crest of a hill. Within fifty yards bullets begin to whistle and men in the front of the American line begin to drop. At thirty yards Washington orders a halt and both sides exchange volleys simultaneously. An aide, Colonel Edward Fitzgerald, covers his face with his hat, certain that his commander, so conspicuous a target, was cut

down. But while men on both sides of him have fallen, Washington remains atop his horse, untouched. He turns toward Fitzgerald, takes his hand, and says: "Away my dear Colonel, and bring up the troops. The day is ours." And it was.[87]

Farewell to the Queen's American Rangers – 30 January 1777

While the Queen's American Rangers had performed well in the battles of 1776, the new Inspector-General of Britain's American Provincials, Alexander Innes found the Queen's American Rangers to be less than satisfactory when he examined the unit in January, 1777. He found a "number of persons very improper to hold any Commission" in the rangers and recommended a "thorough reformation" of the unit. Howe reviewed the report and decided that Robert Rogers should retire with pay. Major Christopher French of the 22nd Regiment was selected to replace Rogers on 30 January 1777.[88] The unhappiness with Rogers focused on Rogers recruiting practices and found that he recruited "low-born....undesirable elements." All but two of Rogers' officers were also discharged.[89] The report and its result reflected the general contempt of British regular army officers for the provincials. Incredibly, Howe later relented and allowed Rogers and others to remain on duty, and they were dispatched to accomplish recruiting duty. When word reached Washington he noted that Rogers was one of several "Villains, whose crimes are of great enormity . . . Rogers is an Active instrument in the Enemy hands, and his Conduct has particular claim to our notice."[90] The irony of sending Rogers on recruiting duty after he was fired for recruiting practices was lost on Howe. As one might expect, reports of atrocities committed by the rangers piled up after Rogers and others recruited more persons who were "low-born....undesirable elements." By the time Major John Graves Simcoe, fourth commander of the Queen's American Rangers took command, recruiting standards had been upgraded and it was becoming a first rate unit.

John Graves Simcoe (1694-1771) (Wikipedia)

By this time Robert Rogers was sinking into obscurity. He seldom appeared in the news. His brother James was dispossessed because he would not join the Patriots. James fled to Montreal and was given command of Loyalist ranger company. Betsy petitioned for divorce in January, 1778. She noted "infidelity, uncleanliness & drunken barbarity." The New Hampshire House of Representatives passed a resolution to dissolve the marriage on 28 February 1778.[91] Betsy married an Irish sea captain, John Roche in late spring of 1778. They remained married until his death in 1811.

Rogers sought permission to raise a Loyalist regiment in October 1778, but his request was denied. He requested permission to return to London to obtain financial relief (again) and to seek help for his effort to raise a regiment. While he was at sea on 19 November 1778, the New Hampshire legislature addressed the problem of dealing with Loyalists.

> An Act to Prevent the Return to this State of Certain Persons Therein Named [who] have Joined or Shall Join the Enemies Thereof." Seventy-six men were named; near the top of the list was "Maj. Robert Rogers." Some of his Old French War rangers were also listed, among them Stephen Holland, Enos Stevens, John Stinson, Samuel Stinson, and William Stark. Anyone who returned would be jailed and deported. Anyone who dared to come back after their first attempt would, "on Conviction . . . suffer the pain of Death.[92]

Rogers stayed in London collecting endorsements for his plan to raise a Loyalist unit and returned to America in April, 1779. On 16 June he wrote to Amherst who was now in London busy organizing British home defense forces against a possible invasion by France/Spain that never materialized.

> I have been honoured by the Commander in Chief here with a warrant to raise two more Battalions, one of which is called the King's Rangers – so that I shall have the highest Happiness, as a Subject, of giving two Battalions to their majesties, the third will be

called Rogers's Rangers... I flatter myself that my good Lord Amherst, will not forget an old Soldier, who has had the Honour to share in some of his glorious fateagues in America last War – but procure him some little Addition to his present rank in the British Army.[93]

Robert Rogers

He wrote again to Amherst on 11 September reporting recent success.

I have the honor to acquaint you I am after being present at the destruction of the Rebel Fleet at Penobscot setting out for Annapolis Royal the rendezvous of my first Battalion, which is at present in a most eligible train - from whence I push thro' to Canada, from which place in a short time I flatter myself your Lordship will hear of a spirited attack by my Indians & Rangers, on the middle Frontier, to the great detriment of the Rebels – and such credit to myself as may entitle me to expect that assistance, Generosity & patronage I have ever receiv'd from your Lordship.[94]

Robert Rogers

The letter was more myth than fact. By now, Robert Rogers' drinking was unmanageable and his brother James wrote "The conduct of my brother of late has almost unman'd me – when I was last at Quebec I wrote to him in regard to his conduct and as often he promised to reform – I am sorry his good talents should so unguarded fall a prey to Intemperance."[95] Rogers continued his recruiting efforts and ran up bills for alcohol and other expenses sending requests for payment to his superiors that were paid just to get rid of him. Rogers continued reckless spending and thus landed in jail for his debts in April 1780. He managed to get himself out of jail and December found him on board the schooner *Success* bound for New York. He still held the rank of Lieutenant Colonel although he was accomplishing very little for the Crown. The *Success* had barely cleared port when the Pennsylvania privateer, *Patty* came along side. The boarding party discovered the famous passenger and

Rogers was arrested and taken to Philadelphia as a prisoner-of-war where he was jailed on 7 January 1781. An exchange was proposed that involved a junior American officer who would be returned by the British for Rogers. Washington objected on the basis that it would establish a bad precedent: a junior exchanged for a senior. The British were told that if they reduced Rogers to an equivalent rank the trade could occur. Rogers was loaded on-board a transport for New York City where a transfer could be pursued. The ship landed on 1 September 1781 and Rogers was eventually freed. Rogers remained in British held New York City for two years doing very little except pub hopping. The last of the British troops and refugees left for Great Britain in mid-November 1783 and Rogers was apparently among them. Many of the arrivals were offered land in Nova Scotia where as one Patriot remarked " . . . specially created, and designed, by an over ruling Providence, for the dismal habitation of those pests of society, the Tories, Refugees, and Ingrates of America, where, on ground as rocky as their hearts, may they long continue."[96] Rogers declined the offer and remained in London.

Little is known of Robert Rogers last years. He spent much of his time in pubs and Debtors' prison. He had his small retirement pay but that did not cover much. A curious report appeared in The *Boston Gazette* on 12 September 1785.

> New London [Connecticut], Sept. 2. Tuesday last sailed, Ship *Peter Holden,* Wm. Dodds, Commander, for New-York, in whom went passenger, Col. Rogers, his Lady and suit consisting of a female bear, two dogs, a bitch, a brace of quails, and a young robin. – This redoubtable commander boasts of having, with seven others, taken three hundred rebels Cows, *Coupe de main,* and conducted them safely to New-York.[97]

Rogers' stay in America did not last long. This was the last time Rogers saw America. By early November Rogers and his consort were back in London. On 12 November 1785

Rogers was back in Debtors' prison. He was finally discharged on 11 May 1789. Robert Rogers died in his apartment on Blackman Street in London on 18 May 1795.

Epilogue

The Rangers

The Ranger Handbook, Today
Recognizing that I volunteered as a Ranger, fully knowing the hazards of my chosen profession, I will always endeavor to uphold the prestige, honor, and high esprit de corps of the Rangers.
Acknowledging the fact that a Ranger is a more elite soldier who arrives at the cutting edge of battle by land, sea, or air, I accept the fact that as a Ranger my country expects me to move further, faster and fight harder than any other soldier.
Never shall I fail my comrades. I will always keep myself mentally alert, physically strong and morally straight and I will shoulder more than my share of the task whatever it may be, one-hundred-percent and then some.
Gallantly will I show the world that I am a specially selected and well-trained soldier. My courtesy to superior officers, neatness of dress and care of equipment shall set the example for others to follow.
Energetically will I meet the enemies of my country. I shall defeat them on the field of battle for I am better trained and will fight with all my might. Surrender is not a Ranger word. I will never leave a fallen comrade to fall into the hands of the enemy and under no circumstances will I ever embarrass my country.
Readily will I display the intestinal fortitude required to fight on to the Ranger objective and complete the mission though I be the lone survivor.
Rangers Lead The Way!!!

— ***Ranger Handbook SH 21-76***

The earliest mention of American rangers occurred long before Rogers' Rangers.

> In 1622, after the Berkeley Plantation Massacre ... grim-faced men went forth to search out the Indian enemy. They were militia—citizen soldiers—but they were learning to blend the methods of Indian and European warfare...As they went in search of the enemy, the words *range, ranging and Ranger* were frequently used ... The American Ranger had been born.[1]

Some consider Benjamin Church (c. 1639-1718) as the father of American rangers. He designed a force to emulate the Indian methods of warfare and Church's Rangers operated under the tutelage of the Indian allies of the Colonial Governments. Church's Rangers fought King Philip's War (1675-1676) and Queen Anne's War (1702-1713). Successors of Church's Rangers principally John Gorham's Rangers would fight in King George's War (1744-1748) leading up to Robert Rogers in the French and Indian War. Following the War of Independence, twelve companies of rangers were raised during the War of 1812. These were employed to protect the western frontier. The most famous ranger in the U. S. Civil War was John Mosby. Mosby's Rangers raided Union supplies and diverted significant Union forces to protect supplies, trains, and installations.

During World War II, General Lucien Truscott proposed that a U. S. Army ranger group be established along the lines of the British commandos. This was done and two ranger battalions under Colonel William O. Darby fought in North Africa and Italy. At the Battle of Cisterna (30 January – 2 February 1944) in Italy, the rangers were badly defeated. Trapped in open ground and behind enemy lines, the rangers were forced to surrender. Of the total of 767 men only seven escaped and returned to Allied lines. The rest were killed or captured. New ranger units were formed and participated in the D-Day invasion. In the Pacific theater, the 6th Ranger Battalion participated in the invasion of the Philippines and executed the raid to free prisoners at the Cabanatuan POW Camp. In the Burma campaign, Merrill's Marauders under the command of Colonel Frank Merrill cut off Japanese forces and their supply lines in the Hukawng Valley. Ranger units were disbanded at the end of the war.

At the outbreak of the Korean War, the 8th Army Ranger Company was created and was led by LT Ralph Puckett in August 1950. This became the model for other ranger companies and a total of sixteen ranger companies were formed. During the war, ranger companies were attached to other units rather than creating separate ranger battalions and regiments. The same approach was followed in Vietnam. These units accomplished patrolling, ambushes and night raids.

During the Korean War, the Ranger School was established at Fort Benning, Georgia to train soldiers in the crafts developed by Robert Rogers two hundred years earlier. Upon graduation from the school these ranger qualified individuals were not necessarily assigned to ranger units, but to army units world-wide providing a base of people to train others. When the Korean War ended in 1953, ranger units were again deactivated as they had been after World War II.

In Vietnam, Long Range Reconnaissance Patrols (LRRPs) were the army's rangers. These were small heavily armed reconnaissance teams that would help in the effort to locate infiltrating North Vietnamese units from North Vietnam. These platoons were attached to every U. S. brigade and division. Irvin (Bugs) Moran tells the story of the LRRP at the Dak To battle in the Central Highlands of Vietnam.

Irvin (Bugs) Moran in 1967 (Bugs Moran)

The 173rd LRRP first arrived in the tri-border area of Dak To in June of 1967. The Brigade's three parachute infantry battalions were engaging North Vietnamese Army (NVA) units in the mountains surrounding the Dak To basecamp at this time, and LRRP teams were needed for reconnaissance patrols. Our platoon at this time consisted of 35 to 38 enlisted members and one officer. The teams consisted of five or six men who conducted long range missions that could last for five to seven days.

Infiltrations were done at either first or last light via choppers. These LRRP missions in the Dak To area that summer of 1967 were extremely dangerous and exhausting. The jungle terrain in this mountainous tri-border area has been described as some of the wildest and rugged jungle environments in the entire Southeast Asia region. Attempting to move silently through these unforgiving mountain ridges and ravines was extremely difficult. The trees were double and sometimes triple canopy which gave the entire area a very dark and dreary appearance. In addition to the North Vietnamese, LRRP teams ran into just about every species of animals that called this godforsaken place home. Open areas that allowed for ingress and egress by choppers were very hard to find, and if a team was compromised and pursued by NVA units, extraction by ropes (McGuire rigs) was the only way out.[2]

Our 173rd LRRP teams located and observed numerous NVA units moving both in and out of the Dak To area that June, July and August of 1967, and some teams were compromised resulting in very up close and personal engagements. Teams located both old and fresh bunker complexes in all four compass directions surrounding the Dak To basecamp. Some missions intended for five to seven days ended abruptly such as my first mission just west of the Dak To basecamp in July. As our five-man team exited the chopper, we immediately received intensive fire from an undetermined sized NVA unit that was located right next to the LZ. The choppers were able to successfully extract us, resulting in a mission of roughly 15 minutes. Our goal of locating the NVA had been accomplished!

To the relief of most LRRP members, we were taken out of the Dak To area during the first part of September 1967. These Dak To missions had been exceedingly difficult, and everyone was looking forward to easier missions in the mountains west of the coastal area of Tuy Hoa. The 173rd LRRP had no desire to return to that death shrouded place called Dak To.

Fate intervened. During the first week of November 1967, our platoon was alerted for a move from the beaches of our basecamp in Tuy Hoa back to Dak To. The 173rd parachute battalions had already returned to Dak To and were being hit hard. We arrived back at the Dak To basecamp around November 7th, and virtually all six to seven teams were immediately inserted by choppers into the mountains surrounding the Dak To airstrip. Most teams observed heavy NVA activities in this entire tri-border area. While on these missions, our teams were kept apprised of all the enemy contacts being made by the three 173rd battalions. All teams were extracted and returned to the Dak To basecamp as the battle for Hill 875 developed. When LRRP teams were out on missions, major air assets were held in standby for immediate extraction of a team in trouble. At this time, these assets were needed for aid and relief of the embattled 173rd line companies on Hill 875. The LRRP members were extremely frustrated. We knew we could get onto that hill faster than any other unit, but brigade headquarters would not allow it. Our commanding officer at the time, Lt. Jim Parkes, took three team leaders down to the chopper pads at the Dak To airstrip and volunteered to repel onto the hill with LZ clearing kits, ammo and medical supplies. Saner minds prevailed and this plan was also denied. Lt. Parkes was allowed to board a chopper headed to Hill 875 on November 20th with the plan of kicking out LZ clearing kits over the makeshift command post. This chopper received horrendous small arms fire while over the hill and Lt. Parkes received career ending wounds. His extreme valor that day is not known to many.

When Hill 875 was taken on November 23th, our teams were again inserted on missions surrounding Dak To with the intent of locating the NVA units retreating back into Laos and Cambodia via the infamous Ho Chi Minh trails. On December 1st, a large NVA unit was located just east of the area where the borders of Laos and Cambodia join Vietnam. I was point man on this mission. We ran headlong into the NVA point element and were able to eliminate it. We had no doubt that this NVA unit was retreating back into either Laos or Cambodia after the heavy fighting of the past few weeks. It quickly became apparent that this NVA unit knew it had run into a small reconnaissance team, and they immediately started pursuing us through the steep mountainous terrain. We succeeded in finding a very small opening in the triple canopy jungle, and three choppers snatched six of us out via McGuire rig ropes. Two team members dangled 120 feet below each of the three choppers as we flew 20 minutes at 5,000 feet back to a 4th Division fire support base. This panoramic view of the Dak To mountains was priceless, but not one that anyone wanted to see again. Our 173rd LRRP left the Dak To area in the middle of December. These 1967 missions in Dak To tested the abilities and perseverance of every platoon member. The memories of these missions of almost 50 years ago are still with us today.[3]

Irvin (Bugs) Moran, 173rd LRRP

Following the Vietnam War, the army reorganized rangers to create separate battalions and ultimately in 1986 the 75th Ranger Regiment of three battalions was formed. This was the first time that ranger battalions had been formed since World War II and it was based on the need to have larger units available to be deployed in special operations. The 75th Ranger Regiment has continued to serve in the War on Terror since it was established. No discussion of modern warfare would be complete without credit to our brave and loyal canine companions who served with us.

> 1st Ranger Battalion started its Multi-Purpose Canine (MPC) Program in the spring/summer of 2007 with just four original handlers. The program expanded to twelve handlers and twelve dogs in 2009 so that every line platoon would have a dog team designated to them. I myself made my way to the canine section in February 2009 after passing a three-day selection process conducted by the senior handlers, trainer, and the kennel master. I had re-enlisted back in 2007 during a deployment in the hopes of making my way to the K9 Program. I spent much of my childhood in the Midwest on a farm, and had always taken a liking to being around working dogs so it just seemed natural that I ended up in the K9 Program. I served three deployments to Afghanistan as a MPC handler. Out of my ten total combat rotations while in the Regiment, those are

by far some of my most memorable. There are no words to describe the bond between handler and dog, and seeing firsthand the morale boost that a dog brings to the team was amazing to witness.

Once the Ranger platoon learns to trust you and sees firsthand what you and your dog are capable of "bringing to the fight" it becomes that much easier to work together. These dogs are worth their weight in gold on the battlefield when utilized correctly and to their full potential. It is without a doubt, a very gratifying position because you truly get out of it what you put into it as a dog handler. On any given night on deployment, I was utilized by the platoon during many different aspects from route clearance, interior/ exterior detection of explosives on target, and the most exciting of all, chasing squirters who were running from the target. Obviously that's the most exciting, but it's only a small portion of what the K9 team brings to the table every night. You learn to be ready on the fly because nothing ever really goes as planned, but you always resort back to the basics and provide the team with the best K9 asset that you can while learning from your experiences. The more missions you go on with your dog, the better your team becomes.

My longest deployment was the spring/summer/fall of 2010 in Kandahar, Afghanistan. My assigned platoon was one of the ones that surged a month or so before the rest of the battalion, and we were to become what was known as "Team Merrill" that spring. Our mission set included conducting stay over day missions and clearing NAIs throughout Afghanistan. Now, as a dog handler, this brought up some concerns that were later laid to rest in my own mind. Taking a dog out all night on target, and then throughout the day in 100-degree heat was not something we had done before. Anyone who has been around our Belgian Malinois and Dutch Shepherds will tell you that these dogs will go until they drop dead, they love to work that much! So it was that much more of a responsibility on me, as a handler, to monitor my K9. Dogs can't talk to you like another Ranger can, to tell you he's hurt or tired. You just had to know and monitor your dog while trusting your instincts. I am truly grateful that I never had any issues and I'll go ahead and say it- 'My' Belgian Malinois was a freaking stud!

That summer would also turn out to be one of the worst for 1st Ranger Battalion, as we lost six Rangers that deployment, and one EOD augmentee lost his legs. I can remember clear as day after one ROD in early June 2010; we were standing on the airfield just off the tail of the CH-47. We had just returned back from a more than 36-hour mission as the guys walked by me. Almost all of them patted my dog on the head or pet him with watering eyes because we all knew we had just lost a brother that day, Doc Peney, and another was severely wounded. I do not know what in my mind told me to do it, but I just did it and I saw firsthand the morale and comfort that a dog could bring to a team at a time like that. For lack of a better term, it was *amazing to* witness and it felt good at that moment to be able to do that for my brothers.

Being deployed in Kandahar and living right next to the airfield also allowed me the opportunity to go out with other Ranger platoons throughout Afghanistan so I stayed busy that summer as a dog handler. As an attachment, you never turn down a mission, even if it's with another platoon. It was a fulfilling deployment as a dog handler because I was able to utilize and experience every aspect of being a dog handler. As I said before though, it was a deployment full of hardship and loss, but we all pulled through and stuck together like any Ranger Battalion does. I will always look back on my time in Battalion with a smile because of the bonds made, the brotherhood shared, and the life experiences I gained. As another Ranger buddy once said, "I am proud to look back and say I was blessed to WALK AMONG GIANTS!" I still to this day resort back to some of the basic K9 handler skills I learned at the very beginning and use them in my private sector job as a K9 Handler today – it just stays with you.

I think 1/75 has done an outstanding job with its K9 Program, we have one of the best trainers out there and he has molded a lot of guys into great handlers and produced some outstanding MPC Teams for 1/75. The assistant trainer, being one of the original four handlers at 1/75, is also worth his weight in gold for his vast knowledge of the MPC's and the ins and outs of being on target. I don't know what the future holds with the wars dwindling down, but I truly hope that Battalion does not view the working dog program as something they can do without, these dogs have proven their worth over the last decade of war. Sooner or later, even if the wars completely trickle off, they're going to be needed again somewhere, and it would be a damn shame to start all over again after all that has been gained.[4]

Lyne, 1/75th

A Death at Mount Vernon, 14 December 1799

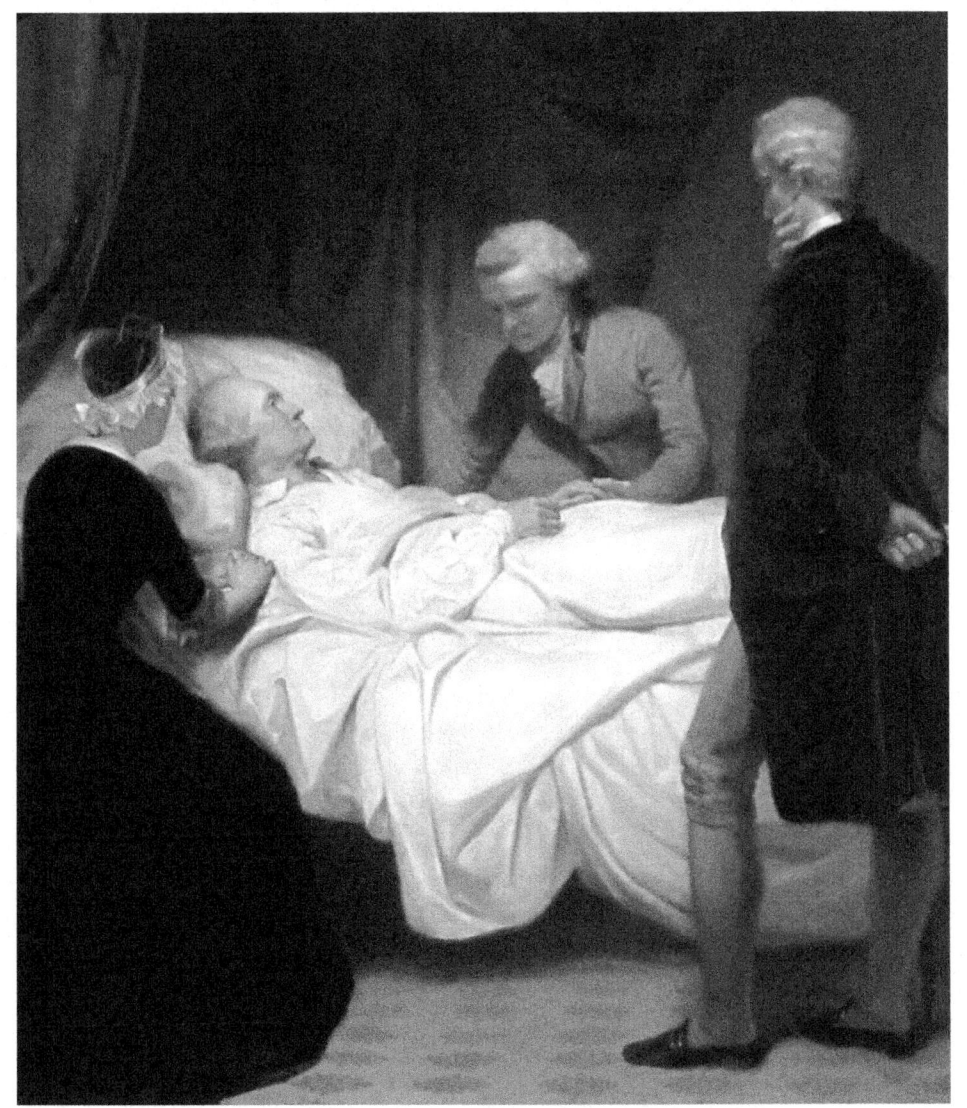

George Washington (1727-1799) (Wikipedia)

The night dragged slowly on. The two younger doctors, not being intimates of the family, waited downstairs. From the windows of the second - floor room, lamplight threw glistening squares on meager snow. Within, Dr. Craik sat, as he had for hours, staring into the fire. Washington's body servant,

Christopher, stood by the bed, a post he had not deserted since morning, although Washington had several times motioned him to sit down. A group of house servants – "Caroline, Molly and Charlotte," and some others – stood near the door. Lear was hovering around the head of the bed, intently trying to interpret every gesture and do what he could to ease the sufferer. Martha was sitting near the foot of the bed.

No one thought to look at a clock, so we only know for sure that it was approaching midnight when Washington withdrew his hand from Lear's and felt his own pulse. Lear called Craik, who came to the bedside. Washington lifted his arm and then his "hand fell from his wrist." As Lear reached out for the limp hand, Craik put his own hand over Washington's eyes. There was no struggle, not even a sigh.

In a calm, controlled voice, Martha asked, "Is he gone?" Unable to speak, Lear held up his hand in a signal of assent.[5]

James Thomas Flexner

And so the great man died perhaps the most respected and loved Patriot in American history.

Saint Mary-Newington Churchyard, London

Saint Mary-Newington Churchyard in 1827 (Wikipedia)

Robert Rogers was buried on 20 May 1795 in Saint Mary-Newington Churchyard, London.[6] Robert Rogers was quickly forgotten after his death in 1795. Betsy had remarried and they had not been in contact for years. The new country was not interested in the exploits of their Loyalist cousins and neighbors who had betrayed the revolution. This would remain so until nearly a century after his death when Joseph Burbeen Walker published his paper, *Life and Exploits of Robert Rogers,*

The Ranger in 1885. Walker captured Robert Rogers and his times.

> No man has been universally great. Individuals who have made themselves prominent among their fellows have done so by achievements in special directions only, and confined to limited portions of their lives. Particularly true is this remark when applied to Major Robert Rogers, the Ranger, who, in our last French war, greatly distinguished himself as a partisan commander, and gained as wide fame as did any other soldier of equal rank and opportunity. I do not introduce him here as a saint, for, as is well known, no quality of sanctity ever entered his composition; but rather, as the resolute commander of resolute men, in desperate encounters with a desperate foe; as a man eminently fitted for the rough work given him to do.[7]
>
> **Joseph Burbeen Walker**

The following article appeared in London's *Morning Post and Fashionable World* on 25 May 1795. It is probably as good an epitaph as any.

> Lieutenant Col. Rogers, who died on Thursday last in the Borough, served in America during the late war, in which he had the command of a body of Rangers, with which he performed prodigious feats of valour. He was a man of uncommon strength, but adversity, and a long confinement in the Rules of the King's Bench [a London prison] had reduced him to the most miserable state of wretchedness.[8]

This tribute in the London newspaper was far more respectful than any mention of Robert Rogers in America at that time. One man's traitor is another's patriot.

Michael A. Eggleston, Nokesville, Virginia, 2017

Biographical Sketches

This section provides a biographical summary of those mentioned in this history. When known, years of birth and death are provided in parentheses for each person.

Joseph-Louis Ainsse (1744-1802) – Canadian interpreter and fur trader who testified at the court-martial of Robert Rogers.

James Abercromby (1706-1781) – With the outbreak of the Seven Years' War in 1756, he was promoted to major general and ordered to the British Colonies. He commanded a brigade at Louisbourg in 1757 and became Commander-in-Chief of the British forces in North America in December 1757. He was removed from command after the disastrous defeat at Carillon and was replaced by Jeffery Amherst.

William Alexander (1726-1783) – Also known as Lord Stirling. An American general during the War of Independence. Although he was born in America, he claimed the Scottish title of Lord Stirling after the death of his father. Alexander was captured by the British at the Battle of Long Island, but his successful delay allowed Washington and most of the army to escape. Alexander was exchanged by the British and promoted to major general in the American army. He was known as a brave and successful tactician. He died shortly after the end of the war and is buried in NYC opposite the New York Stock Exchange in Churchyard of Trinity Church,

Jeffery Amherst (1717-1797) – born in Kent, Great Britain. Amherst served in the War of the Austrian Succession before being appointed as British commander in the New World succeeding James Abercromby. He ordered Rogers' raid on Saint Francis and his mission to receive the surrender of the French in the west.

Jerome Atecouando – an Abenaki sachem and diplomat from Saint Francis. He attempted to negotiate neutrality with the British before the French and Indian War.

Attakullakulla (1705-1780) "Little Carpenter" – a Cherokee chief who was an ally to the British.

Elias Avery (1736-1759) – an ensign under Robert Rogers who participated in the Saint Francis Raid. He was with Rogers when the village was reconnoitered, and later led one of the parties returning from Saint Francis.

Lieutenant Governor William Bull (1683-1755) – was lieutenant governor of South Carolina from 1738 to 1755 and acting governor from 1738-44.

Daniel Barnes, Jr. (1736-1813) Colonial soldier who served in the French and Indian War. He is thought to have been the "Barnes" who buried treasure along the trail back from the Saint Francis Raid. Barnes served during the War of Independence as a captain in Colonial Jonathan Ward's Massachusetts continental regiment that fought at the Battle of Bunker Hill and other battles. Barnes retired as a major to Chelsea, Vermont where he died in 1813.

Jonathan Barns (d. 1761) – Colonial soldier taken prisoner by the Abenaki who become a renegade and helped the Indians track the Saint Francis raiders.

William Barrington (1717-1793) – a British politician who served two periods as Secretary at War during Britain's involvement in the Seven Years' War and the War of Independence.

Francois-Marie Picote de. Belestre (1716-1793) – was the commandant of Fort Detroit who surrendered to Robert Rogers in 1760. After the French and Indian War he joined the British army and defended Fort Saint Jean against American forces in 1775. He became a colonel in the British Army before his death in 1793.

Joseph Blanchard (1704-1758) – a colonel and commander of the New Hampshire provincials, he gave Rogers his first command.

Henry Bouquet (1719-1765) – a British officer who commanded the expedition to Fort Pitt during the Pontiac War.

Francois Charles de. Bourlamaque (1716-1763) – French general who accompanied Montcalm to America. He was commander of Carillon (later Fort Ticonderoga).

Edward Braddock (1695-1755) – organized the first large British force in North America. He commanded the British army that moved west to attack the French stronghold at the Forks of the Ohio in 1755. He was defeated and killed at the Battle of the Monongahela.

John Bradstreet (1714-1774) – captured Fort Frontenac in 1758. He was commander of bateau men during the French and Indian War.

Moses Brewer – ranger captain who served on the Saint Francis Raid and resigned after the raid on 24 November 1759.

Thomas Brown (b. 1740) – as a 16-year-old private he fought at the Battle on Snowshoes. His journal provides a detailed record of his experience as a prisoner of the Indians after he was wounded and captured.

Arthur Browne – a rector in Portsmouth, New Hampshire. His daughter, Elizabeth married a fellow member of the Masonic Lodge, Robert Rogers.

Charles Bulkeley (d.1758) – *stopped* the mutiny on Rogers' Island. Fought valiantly and was killed in the Battle on Snowshoes.

Jonathan Burbank – a ranger captain who was ambushed by an Abenaki war party. He was mistaken for Robert Rogers and was killed and horribly mutilated.

John "Gentleman Johnny" Burgoyne (1722-1792) – a British general best known for his surrender to the Americans after the battle of Saratoga, a decisive battle in the War of Independence.

Captain Butterfield – a provincial officer who left with Rogers on the Saint Francis Raid but was ordered to turn back and return with those who were sick or wounded.

William Byrd (1728-1777) – a colonel of the Second Virginia Regiment in 1756 who was sent to relieve Fort Loudoun during the Cherokee War but arrived too late.

John Campbell, Earl of Loudoun (1705-1782) – was sent to North America to serve as Commander-in-Chief and Governor General of Virginia in 1756. He asked Robert Rogers to write down the principles of successful bush warfare, which produced Rogers' Rules of Ranging.

Guy Carleton (1724-1808) – twice served as Governor of the Province of Quebec, from 1768 to 1778. During the War of Independence he was the commander-in-chief of all British forces in North America in 1782 and 1783.

Jonathan Carver (1710-1780) – an early explorer of North America who was also a mapmaker and surveyor. He was commissioned by Robert Rogers to search for the Northwest Passage after the war. He later published his discoveries.

Pierre-Joseph Celoron (1693-1759) – leader of the "Lead Plate Expedition" to reinforce the claims of France in the Ohio Valley. He buried lead plates on the route of his expedition claiming the land for France and evicted British traders along the way.

Jane Chandler – was a prisoner of the Abenaki freed by Robert Rogers during the Saint Francis Raid. At that time she was more Abenaki than white and caused nothing but problems on the return trip from Saint Francis which she survived.

Jacob Cheeksunkun (Captain Jacob) – *son* of Naunauphtaunk, he accompanied Captain Quinton Kennedy on his 1759 mission to Wolfe. Cheeksunkun was captured with Kennedy and was later released.

Benjamin Church (1639-1718) – a surgeon and captain of the first ranger force in America commissioned by the Governor of the Plymouth Colony. He is considered by some to be the father of the United States Army Rangers.

Henry Clinton (1730-1795) – a British army officer, best known for his service during the War of Independence. He was the British Commander-in-Chief in North America from 1778 to 1782.

Claude-Pierre de. Contrecour (1705-1775) – a member of the Troupes de la Marine who occupied the forks of the Ohio in 1755.

Martha Dandridge Custis Washington (1731-1802) – at age 18, she married Daniel Parke Custis, a rich planter two decades her senior. Two years after his death she married George Washington of Virginia.

Captain James Dalyell (d.1763) – commanded the British force sent to relieve the besieged Fort Detroit during Pontiac's Rebellion. He died in the Battle of Bloody Run in Detroit.

William O. Darby (1911-1945) – leader of Darby's Rangers during World War II. He was killed in action at the end of the war while trying to cut off a German retreat at Trento, Italy.

Marechal-de-Camp Jean-Armand, Baron de. Dieskau (1701-1767) – was defeated and captured by the British under William Johnson's forces at Lake George in 1755.

Robert Dinwiddie (1692-1770) – was lieutenant governor of Virginia. He sent George Washington west to engage the French. The venture ended when Washington defeated the French at the Battle of Jumonville Glen.

Arthur Dobbs (1689-1765) – served as Governor of colonial

North Carolina (1754-65). His support for expeditions to find the Northwest Passage aroused Rogers' interest in the venture.

General Jean Daniel Dumas (1721-1794) – fought against Braddock at the Battle of Monongahela and led the French Canadian and Abenaki force in the pursuit of Rogers' Rangers following the Saint Francis Raid.

John Evans – entered the rangers in 1756. Participated in the Saint Francis Raid and was discharged on 25 October 1760.

John Forbes (1707-1759) – adjutant general to Lord Loudoun, he captured Fort Duquesne in 1758.

Benjamin Franklin (1706-1790) – was one of the Founding Fathers of the United States. He was a Freemason whose accomplishments in many fields include author, printer, political theorist, politician, postmaster, scientist, inventor, civic activist, statesman, and diplomat.

Thomas Gage (1721-1787) – arrived with Braddock and fought at the Battle of the Monongahela. He participated in two British defeats: Braddock's defeat and the British assault on Carillon. He was an unrelenting enemy of Robert Rogers. Gage commanded British forces in America (1768-1775) and was replaced by William Howe after Boston.

George III, King of Great Britain (1738-1820) – his long reign (1760-1820) saw the end of the Seven Years' War and the loss of the colonies in North America.

Joseph-Louis Gill, or "Magouaouidombaouit" (1719-1798)

– son of New England captives he became principal chief of the Saint Francis Indians. He was away when Rogers' Rangers attacked Saint Francis village and took his wife and two sons prisoner.

Marie-Jeanne Gill – the wife of Chief Gill was captured during the Saint Francis Raid and was among the captives taken by the rangers for their return. She tried to trick the rangers leading them on a route to the French. A Stockbridge Indian slit her throat when the deceit was discovered.

Carty Gilman – a counterfeiting co-conspirator with the Rogers brothers and others. He was arrested in the roundup of counterfeiters.

Henry Gladwin (1729-1791) – British commander of Fort Detroit who successfully defended the fort during a long siege by Chief Pontiac during Pontiac's Rebellion.

John Gorham (1709-1751) – New England ranger who commanded Gorham's Rangers during King George's War.

Nathan Hale (1755-1776) – *a* young schoolteacher selected by George Washington to spy on the British in New York. He was caught by Robert Rogers and hanged by the British.

Moses Hazen (1733-1803) – ranger captain who was on the Kennedy mission when he was a private. He was later promoted. During the War of Independence he fought for the American cause and raised a regiment called "Congress's Own." At the end of the war he was promoted to general and retired to Vermont.

William Haviland (1718-1784) – a British colonel in the 27th Foot who cut Rogers' unit and this led to the ranger defeat at the Battle on Snowshoes.

Chief Hendrick Theyanoguin (1691-1755) – a Mohawk chief who accompanied Sir William Johnson to the Battle of Lake George where he was killed.

Alexander Henry (1739-1824) – born in New Jersey, he was one of the leading pioneers of the British-Canadian fur trade following the British conquest of New France.

Stephen Hoit (d. 1759) – a ranger who participated in the Saint Francis Raid. He led one of the parties that returned from the raid but died along the way back.

John Honeyman (1729-1822) – an alleged spy for Washington who, it is said, provided misleading information to the Hessians before the Battle of Trenton.

Joseph Hopkins (Born b. 1731) – a turncoat British colonial officer who entered the service of France. He wrote a letter to Robert Rogers that incriminated Rogers in a French plot. It appears to have been an effort to discredit Rogers and it resulted in Rogers' court-martial.

George Augustus, Viscount Howe (1725-1758) – *a* friend of Robert Rogers that supported ranger tactics. He was a highly regarded British officer who was killed during the attack on Carillon in 1758 during the French and Indian War.

William Howe (1729-1814) – a British officer during the French and Indian War who was with Wolfe at Louisbourg and Quebec. He replaced Gage as commander of British forces in America during the War of Independence.

William Johnson (1715-1774) – as superintendent of Indian Affairs he was a rival of Robert Rogers. He defeated the French at the Battle of Lake George and is alleged to have conspired with Thomas Gage to discredit Robert Rogers.

Joseph Coulon DeVillers de Jumonville (1718-1754) – was born in Quebec and killed in an engagement with the Americans commanded by George Washington during the French and Indian War.

Quinton Kennedy (d. 1762) – was captured by Indians in 1759 while trying to carry dispatches from Amherst to Wolfe. His capture triggered the Saint Francis Raid. Kennedy was later released and fought in the Cherokee War.

Jean-Baptiste Levrault de Langis, or Langy (1723-1760) – a French partisan fighter who often engaged Robert Rogers in fierce skirmishes in the woods.

Charles-Michel Mouet de. Langlade (1729-1801) – an officer in Troupes de la Marine. He opposed Rogers at the Battle on Snowshoes.

Francois-Gaston Duc de Levis (1719-1787) – served as second in command to Montcalm at Quebec. When Montcalm was killed, Levis took command and later defeated the British outside Quebec in April 1760.

Francois-Marie le Marchand de Lignery (1703-1759) – a colonial military leader in the province of New France during the French and Indian War. He died of wounds sustained in the 1759 Battle of La Belle-Famille.

Charles Le Moyne de. Longueuil (1687-1755) – governor of Montreal (1749-55 and governor of New France for a short time after the death of Governor Jonuiere.

4th Earl of Loudoun – See John Campbell (1705-1782) – served as Britain's Commander-in-Chief in America from mid-1756 to early 1758 and presided over an era of British defeats.

Paul-Louis Dazemard de. Lusignan (1691-1764) – *a* Canadian born officer, Lusignan, was Commandant of Crown Point (1751-58) and afterward of Carillon, ile aux Noix, Saint-Jean, and Chambly.

Governor Lyttelton (1724-1808) – governor of South Carolina in 1755.

Joseph Marin de la Malgue (1719-1774) – a dangerous enemy of Robert Rogers. He was at the Battle of Monongahela and turned the battle against the British.

Francis "Swamp Fox" Marion (c.1732-1795) – a guerrilla leader who fought against the British in South Carolina. His earlier career was spent fighting the Cherokees during the French and Indian War.

Joseph Plumb Martin (1760-1850) – veteran of the War of Independence who published his recollections in 1830. Martin's book provides a soldier's view of the war and is a valuable reference for historians since he describes details of the battles that he witnessed.

Frank Merrill (1903-1955) – World War II U. S. Army guerilla leader who fought against the Japanese in the Burma Campaign. He led the 5307th Composite Unit called "Merrill's Marauders." The unit specialized in operating deep behind enemy lines.

John Millan – published Rogers' *Journals and Concise Account of North America in London*, October 1765.

Robert Monckton (1726-1782) – British general who was second in command to Wolfe at Quebec. Later he served as Royal Governor of New York and departed the colonies in 1763 and never returned.

George Monro (1700-1757) – British commander at Fort William Henry. He defended the fort against the French and their Indian allies in 1757. After a resolute defense, he surrendered and this was followed by an Indian massacre of the inhabitants, an event recounted in James Fenimore Cooper's book, *The Last of the Mohicans*. Monro survived the massacre but died suddenly three months later.

Archibald Montgomery (1726-1796) – Scottish officer and commander during the Cherokee war in South Carolina. He also fought with Washington and Bouquet at Fort Duquesne in 1758. He defeated the Cherokees, in 1760 at the Battle of Etchocy and again in 1761, at the Battle of War-Woman's Creek.

Louis-Joseph de, Marquis de. Montcalm (1712-1759) – commanded French forces in North America from 1756 to his death in 1759 at Quebec. He led France to victory at Oswego (1756), Fort William Henry (1757), and Carillon (1758).

John S. Mosby (1833-1916) – a Confederate guerilla leader during the Civil War. Known as the "Gray Ghost," he commanded the 43rd Battalion of Virginia that was called Mosby's Rangers. They conducted raids often behind Union lines.

James Murray (1722-1794) – a British officer who served with Wolfe at Quebec and later defended the city.

Oconostota (1712-1783) – a Cherokee leader who allied his tribe with the British. He also became an ally of Attakullakulla.

Amos Ogden – commanded the provincials during the Saint Francis Raid and although wounded he survived the long return from the raid.

Billy Phillips – ranger sharpshooter at the Battle on Snowshoes where he was captured. He escaped and joined Robert Rogers on the Saint Francis Raid.

William Pitt, 1st Earl of Chatham (1708-1778) – a British political leader during the French and Indian War, he served as Prime Minister of Great Britain (1766-1768).

Pontiac, or "Ponteach!" (1712?-1769) – Ottawa chief who led an uprising given his name against the British in western America near Detroit in 1763. He met Robert Rogers who made him the hero of the second oldest American play: "Ponteach, or, The Savages of America: a Tragedy."

Nathaniel Potter – personal secretary to Robert Rogers. When they quarreled, he accused Rogers of treason.

Ralph Puckett (1926-) – Born in Tilton, Georgia on 8 December 1926. He graduated from the U. S. Military Academy in 1949 and served in the Korean War. The Eighth Ranger Company was formed in August 1950 commanded by LT Ralph Puckett. This unit held Hill 205 overlooking Chongchon River in Korea against overwhelming odds. During the battle Puckett was badly wounded and after the war commanded the Mountain Ranger Division of the U. S. Army Infantry School Ranger Department. Colonel Puckett retired from the U. S. Army in 1971 and resides in Columbus, Georgia.

Israel Putnam (1718-1790) a captain in Rogers' Rangers who was captured at the Battle of Fort Anne, but escaped. He also fought in Pontiac's Rebellion During the War of Independence he was an American general who distinguished himself at the Battle of Bunker Hill.

Johann Rall (1726-1776) – Hessian commander defeated by George Washington at the Battle of Trenton during the War of Independence. Rall was mortally wounded in the battle and died that night.

Benjamin Roberts – former Indian department commissary at Michilimackinac. He leveled charges of treason against Robert Rogers that led to Rogers' court-martial.

Arthur Rogers – a child of Robert and Elizabeth Rogers born on 12 February 1769 in Portsmouth, NH. He inherited the Rogers' home and died in 1841 in Portsmouth.

Elizabeth Browne Rogers (1741-1813) – wife of Robert Rogers and daughter of a Portsmouth, New Hampshire minister, Arthur Browne. She married Rogers on June 30, 1761. They had one son, Arthur born in 1769. She successfully filed for divorce in 1775, claiming long separations, drunkenness, and infidelity and subsequently married a sea captain John Roche.

James and Mary McFatridge Rogers – parents of Robert Rogers and his brothers.

James Rogers (1726-1792) – brother of Robert Rogers. He served with Rogers' Rangers as a Captain during the French and Indian War. He fought with the British commanding the King's Rangers during the War of Independence.

Richard Rogers (d. 1757) ranger captain and younger brother of Robert Rogers. He died from smallpox in 1757.

Father Pierre-Joseph-Antoine Roubaud (1724-c.1789) – a Jesuit priest who served as a missionary to the Abenaki at Saint Francis during the French and Indian War. He later assisted the British during the War of Independence.

Sabbatis – son of Chief Gill who was carried away by Robert Rogers on his return from the Saint Francis Raid. Rogers befriended Sabbatis who later returned to Saint Francis.

Samadagwis (d. 1759) – Mohegan ranger who was on the Saint Francis Raid. He tried to warn the Abenaki of the raid, was wounded in the attack and died the next day.

John Shepherd – ranger captain who served until 25 June 1759 when he resigned due to bad health. During the War for Independence he sided with the British and enlisted in the Queen's American Rangers.

William Shirley (1694-1771) – British governor of Massachusetts (1741-59). He gave Robert Rogers his first command. Shirley briefly commanded all British forces in the New World following the death of Braddock.

Silverheels a friendly Indian chief who helped Washington at the Battle of Jumonville Glen. He supplied warriors and warned Washington of the French advance.

John Graves Simcoe (1752-1806) – a British army general and the first Lieutenant Governor of Upper Canada from 1791 until 1796. During the War of Independence he commanded the Queen's Rangers and fought against the Americans. At the Battle of Brandywine legend has it that he ordered his men not to fire upon three fleeing rebels, one of these was George Washington.

Thomas Speakman or Spikeman (d.1757) – ranger captain who was captured, tortured, and killed by Indians after the Battle on Snowshoes.

Archibald Stark (1730-1819) – brother of John Stark. He was commissioned in the rangers in 1758 and was discharged in 1760.

Caleb Stark – son of John Stark who recalled meeting with Robert Rogers years later.

John Stark (1728-1822) – a boyhood friend of Robert Rogers, he served in the rangers as a Captain and later during the War of Independence he defeated the British at the Battle of Bennington, in 1777.

William Stark (1724-1776) – brother of John Stark. He fought for the British during the War of Independence and died when he was thrown by a horse during the Battle of Long Island. His brother John, the Patriot, said "was the best thing William ever did in his life."[1]

Samuel Stevens – located at Fort #4, he was ordered to rendezvous with the Rogers' Rangers who were returning from Saint Francis. Lieutenant Stevens arrived at rendezvous with the supplies for Rogers, but left before the starvation-ridden group straggled in. He was court-martialed and dismissed.

Lord Stirling see William Alexander.

Owen Sullivan (d.1756) - the most famous counterfeiter in colonial America. He enlisted Robert Rogers in his counterfeiting schemes. Sullivan was finally caught and hanged in 1756.

John Sullivan (1740-1795) – an American general in the War of Independence, a delegate in the Continental Congress, Governor of New Hampshire and a United States federal judge.

Theyanoguin, or "Hendrick" (1680-1755) – a Christian Mohawk who was a close friend of Sir William Johnson. As a sachem he provided help and advice to Johnson and was killed at the Battle of Lake George in 1755.

Charles Townshend (1725-1767) – Lord of the Admiralty and friend of Robert Rogers. Townshend supported Rogers' efforts to find the Northwest Passage.

William Trent (1715-1787) – a former fur trader, he was sent by Virginia Lieutenant Governor Dinwiddie to occupy the forks of the Ohio River and establish a fort.

William Tryon (1729-1788) – royal governor of North Carolina (1765-1771) and New York (1771-1788). As governor of New York, he hatched the conspiracy that sought to hand over NYC to the British in 1776. The plot that included the assassination of George Washington failed.

George (James) Turner – lieutenant in Moses Brewer's company during the Saint Francis Raid.

Tute, James (1738-1782) – ranger captain who served with distinction on the Saint Francis Raid. He also helped Jonathan Carver with the expedition to find the Northwest Passage that had been commissioned by Robert Rogers.

Francois-Pierre de Rigaud, de. Vaudreuil (1703-1779) – governor of Montreal from 1757 to 1760.

Pierre de Rigaud, de. Vaudreuil de Cavagnia, Marquis de Vaudreuil (1698-1778) – Canadian born Governor-general of Louisiana and New France.

Joseph Waite (d.1776) – ranger captain who fought in the Battle on Snowshoes and commanded a party on the return from Saint Francis. During the War of Independence he fought against the British and died after the Battle of Valcour Island.

Reverend Timothy Walker (1705-1782) – first minister of Rumford (earlier Penacook, later Concord) from 1730 to 1782.

Daniel Webb (1700-1773) – **was** the British commander who refused to send help to Fort William Henry when it was under attack by the French.

Eleazar Wheelock (1771-1779) – founded Dartmouth College. He died during the War of Independence on April 24, 1779 and is buried in Hanover.

Benning Wentworth (1696-1770) – royal governor of the colony of New Hampshire and a fellow mason of Rogers in Portsmouth.

Richard Whitworth (1734-1811) – member of Parliament and supporter of the search for the Northwest Passage. He was a confidant of Robert Rogers and sought to help him obtain financing for an expedition.

Ephrain Williams (1714-1755) – a British colonel who led a regiment including Rogers' Rangers against the French at Crown Point. He was killed in an ambush at the Battle of Lake George.

Samuel Willyamos (also spelled Williams) – British captain with Rogers' Rangers who was injured in route to Saint Francis village. Due his injuries he was forced to return to Crown Point with other injured and ill soldiers.

James Wolfe (1727-1759) – British commander killed while winning the Battle of Quebec in 1759.

Appendix A, Names, Acronyms and Terms

abbatis – a rampart made of felled trees placed with sharpened branches facing out toward the enemy.

Abenaki – an Indian tribe, one of the Algonquian-speaking peoples of northeastern North America.

atalapose – an Indian word meaning a sliding place.

Bateau – a shallow-draft, flat-bottomed boat.

Bolthole – a place where a person can escape and hide.

Broadsheet – largest of newspaper formats. It is printed on one side and is usually displayed rather than folded and read.

Brother Jonathan – the national personification and emblem of New England similar to the later characterization, Uncle Sam that represented the entire U. S.

Cabatnatuan POW Camp – World War II Japanese prisoner-of-war camp that was subject of a successful effort to liberate prisoners at the end of the war called "The Great Raid."

cadet – a trainee promoted to officer rank after successful completion of training.

Canister – a cylindrical container loaded with small lead balls and fired from a cannon.

Carillon – built by the French at a narrows near the south end of Lake Champlain in northern New York, it was used during the French and Indian War. It was renamed Fort Ticonderoga after it was taken by the British.

Cartouch – a paper cartridge with bullet and powder that was loaded into the muzzle of a musket.

CH-47 – a heavy lift helicopter called the Chinook. It was extensively used in the Vietnam War.

Cockade – a rosette or knot worn in a hat as a badge of rank.

Chameleon – a lizard that has the ability to change color in order to blend into its surroundings.
Crown Point – a fort in New York on the shore of Lake Champlain used in the 18th century during the French and Indian War.
Debtors' Prison – a prison for people who were unable to pay debt used through the mid-19th century.
Disabligeing Langweg – uncooperative language.
Draw drafts – writing a check to be paid later.
EOD – explosive ordnance disposal.
Express – a communication.
FOB – forward operating base.
Fort Anne – built to protect the harbor of Annapolis Royal, Nova Scotia. It was used during the French and Indian War and was a British outpost during the War of Independence.
Fort Benning – located in Georgia. It is used today as the U. S. Army Infantry School.
Fort Brewerton – located at Brewerton in Oswego County, New York. It was erected by the British in 1759 to defend the passage from Albany to the port of Oswego.
Fort Cumberland – an 18th-century frontier fort at the current location of Cumberland, Maryland. It was an important military and economic center during the French and Indian War.
Fort Detroit – located in the current city of Detroit, Michigan. It was built by the French to keep the British from moving into the west and to monopolize the fur trade in central North America.
Fort Duquesne – established by the French in 1754 after the Battle of Jumonville Glen in 1754. It is located at the confluence of the Monongahela and Allegheny rivers in today's downtown Pittsburgh, Pennsylvania. It was destroyed by the British in 1758 and replaced by Fort Pitt named after the British Prime Minister, William Pitt.

Fort Edward –located in Washington County, New York at the falls on the Hudson River. It was constructed by General Phineas Lyman in 1755 because it commands the Hudson River and Champlain River valleys.

Fort George – located in Ontario, Canada it was the site of several battles fought during the War of 1812. It was built by the British Army after Jay's Treaty (1796) required Britain to withdraw from Fort Niagara.

Fort Loudoun – located in northern Virginia at Winchester. It was constructed by George Washington during the French and Indian War. Washington and his militia regiment were headquartered at the fort for two years.

Fort Michilimackinac – 18th-century French, and later British, fort and trading post at the Straits of Mackinac. It was built around 1715 and abandoned in 1783. It was located along the Straits, which connect Lake Huron and Lake Michigan. Mackinaw City, Michigan is at the site of the fort.

Fort Necessity – following the Battle of Jumonville Glen, Washington needed to defend against an imminent attack by French soldiers and built a 'fort of necessity' in late May and early June, 1754. A battle occurred there in July and the British were defeated and forced to return to Virginia.

Fort Niagara – this French fort was located near Youngstown, New York on the eastern bank of the Niagara River at its mouth on Lake Ontario. It fell to the British during the French and Indian War in July 1759

Fort Number Four – during French and Indian War it was the northernmost British settlement along the Connecticut River in New Hampshire. It is now known as Charlestown, New Hampshire.

Fort Ontario – located on the east side of the Oswego River on high ground overlooking Lake Ontario, it was one of several forts erected by the British to protect the area around the east end of Lake Ontario. It was built in 1755, during the French and

Indian War in order to bolster defenses already in place at Fort Oswego on the opposite side of the river.

Fort Oswego – 18th-century trading post in the Great Lakes region that is now within the city of Oswego, New York. It was the site of a battle between French and British forces in 1756 during the French and Indian War in which the British lost.

Fort Pitt – the site of the Indian siege in Pontiac's War that failed. S*ee also* Fort Duquesne.

Fort Prince George – was the first of five forts that were built to control the strategic "Forks of the Ohio" (the confluence of the Monongahela and Allegheny rivers) in Pittsburgh, Pennsylvania. The site was originally a trading post established by Ohio Company trader William Trent. It was used during the French and Indian War.

Fort St. Frederic – a French fort built on Lake Champlain to secure the region against British colonization and control the lake. It was located in the town of Crown Point, New York across the lake from Vermont. It was destroyed by the French when British army under General Jeffery Amherst advanced against the French. Crown Point was built by the British next to the ruins of Fort St. Frederic.

Fort Ticonderoga – see Carillon.

Fort Toulouse – a historic fort near the city of Wetumpka, Alabama established to counter the growing influence of the British colonies of Georgia and Carolina. It was abandoned in 1763 when France ceded its territory to Great Britain.

Fort Wentworth – built in 1755 at the junction of the Upper Ammonoosuc River and Connecticut River, in Northumberland, New Hampshire. It was used during the French and Indian War but fell into disrepair and could not be used by Rogers Rangers during their return from the Saint Francis Raid.

Fort William Henry – a British fort ordered by Sir William Johnson in September 1755. It was located at the southern end of Lake George in New York. When the British surrendered to the French and their Indian allies in 1757, notorious atrocities were committed by the Huron tribes.

Freemasonry – a fraternal organization that traces its origins to the local fraternities of stonemasons, which from the end of the fourteenth century regulated the qualifications of stonemasons and their interaction with authorities and clients. The basic unit of Freemasonry is the Lodge. The earliest known American Lodges were in Pennsylvania in 1715. After the American Revolution, independent U.S. Grand Lodges formed themselves within each state.

Gorget – a piece of armor protecting the throat.

Grape or grape shot – large lead balls in cylindrical container loaded and fired from a cannon.

Hessians – German mercenaries hired by Britain to fight in some of their 18th- century wars. They took their name from their home, the German state of Hesse-Kassel.

Intolerable Acts – a series of punitive laws passed by the British Parliament in 1774 after the Boston Tea party that triggered the War of Independence.

K9 – *a* domestic dog trained to perform specific tasks such as patrolling, assistance, guarding.

Livres – a unit of French currency.

LOC – Library of Congress.

Loyalist – American colonists who remained loyal to Great Britain during the War of Independence. They were also called Tories

LRRP – long range reconnaissance patrol.

LZ – landing zone.

Mahican or Mohican – Eastern Algonquian Indian tribe that settled in the upper Hudson River Valley and western New England.

Moneymaker – a counterfeiter.

MPC – Multi-Purpose Canine Program.

NAI – Named Area of Interest.
Northwest Passage – a water route connecting the northern Atlantic and Pacific Oceans.
NVA – North Vietnamese Army.
NYC – New York City
oral traditions – is the technique of passing oral traditions from the eldest people to the very young had long helped to ensure that accuracy was maintained over time. For generations, Abenaki children grew up continuing to learn the details of the historical, medicinal, spiritual, occupational, and other knowledge their families carried until they, themselves, were old enough to pass them on.[1]
Patriot – a person who supports their country and is prepared to defend it against enemies.
Philibeg – a kilt.
ROD – remain over day.
Rogers' Island – an island in the Hudson River, in Washington County, New York. It was used as a training location by Robert Rogers during the French and Indian War.
RPG – rocket propelled grenade
Rules of the King's Bench – a prison in south London from medieval times until it closed in 1880. It was used as a debtors' prison and for other offenses.
Sachem – the paramount chief in an Indian tribe.
SAW – squad automatic weapon.
Spoils of war – goods taken by force as part of a military or political victory.
Stamp Act – an act by the British Parliament that imposed a direct tax on the colonies of British America for printed materials in the colonies. It required that materials be produced on stamped paper from London that carried an embossed revenue stamp.
Squirter – someone running for cover.

tourbillon – in a watch, a tourbillon counters the effects of gravity by mounting the escapement and balance wheel in a rotating cage, to negate the effect of gravity when the timepiece is stuck in a certain position.

Tory – see Loyalists.

Tricorne – a style of three cornered hat popular during the 18th century that fell out of style by 1800.

Troupes de la Marine – formations of soldiers assigned to French ships but also used in land battles.

Wampum – shell beads used by early Native Americans for gift exchange.

War on Terror – the international military campaign that started after the 11 September attacks on the United States. It is also known as the Global War on Terrorism (GWOT).

Withies – a strong flexible willow stem.

Appendix B, Chronology

1744
March: Start of King George's War between Great Britain and France.

1753
French troops from Canada march south; seize and fortify the Ohio Valley. Britain protests the invasion and claims Ohio for itself.

1754
22 May: Battle of Jumonville Glen (in present day Pennsylvania) starts the French and Indian War.

1755
January: Rogers arrested for counterfeiting.
9 July: Defeat of General Braddock's forces by the French along the Monongahela River near present day Pittsburgh.
8 September: Battle of Lake George.

1756
17 May: The Seven Years' War begins as Great Britain declares war on France. The North American conflict expands to Europe, Africa, Asia and South America.
August: Battle of Oswego.

1757
21 January: Ambush.
9 August: Great Britain defeated at Fort William Henry.
6 December: Ranger mutiny on Rogers' Island.

1758
13 March: Battle on Snowshoes.
8 July: British assault on Carillon repulsed.
8 August: Battle of Fort Anne.
December: Washington leaves the army.

1759
27 July: French fortress at Carillon falls to the British and is renamed Fort Ticonderoga.
September – November: Robert Rogers' Saint Francis Raid.
13 September: Defeat of the French at Quebec.
25 December: The 100 Toes Expedition.

1760
25 May: The ranger raid to destroy villages.
8 September: Montreal falls to the British ending the conflict in North America.
29 November: Fort Detroit surrenders to Robert Rogers.

1761
30 June: Rogers marries Elizabeth Browne.
December: The Cherokee War ends.

1763
10 February: Treaty of Paris ends the Seven Years' War including the French and Indian War in the Colonies.[1]
27 April: Ottawa Chief Pontiac unites many American Indian nations in an effort to drive British off their land.
7 May: Start of Pontiacs War.
31 July: Battle of Bloody Run.

1764
January: Rogers arrives in New York City and is imprisoned for his debts.

1765
Summer: Rogers in London for the first time. Publishes The Journals and The Savages in America.

1766
9 January: Rogers arrives in New York City aboard a ship from London.
25 July: Pontiac's War ends.
10 August: Rogers moves to Michilimackinac.
3 September: Carver departs in the attempt to find the Northwest Passage.

1767
6 December: Rogers arrested for treason.

1768
4 September: Charles Townshend dies in London.
20 October: Rogers' court-martial.
31 October: Rogers acquitted of all charges.
19 December: General Gage orders release of Robert Rogers from prison and he is allowed the freedom of Montreal.

1769
1 March: Deputy Judge-Advocate in London approves verdict of Court-Martial.
20 April: Pontiac murdered.
3 June: Gage allows Rogers to go to London.

18 July: Rogers departs for London.

1770-1771
Rogers in London petitioning for funds.

1772-1773
Rogers committed to London debtors' prison.

1774
4 August: Rogers released from debtors' prison.

1775
19 April: War for Independence begins: Battles of Lexington and Concord.
4 June: Rogers sails for North America.
14 June: Continental Army created. Washington appointed commanding general.
17 June: Battle of Bunker (Breed's) Hill.
2 July: Washington takes command of the army.
August: Rogers arrives in America and goes to Williamsburg, Virginia.
December: Rogers arrives in Boston.

1776
17 March: British evacuate Boston.
June: The plot to kill George Washington.
26 June: Rogers arrested for treason.
4 July: Congress declares independence.
8 July: Rogers escapes and joins General Howe's army on Staten Island.
6 August: The Queen's American Rangers is organized.
27 August: British victory at the Battle of Long Island.
15 September: British seize New York City.
22 September: The execution of Nathan Hale.

28 October: Battle of White Plains.
26 December: Battle of Trenton.

1777
3 January: Battle of Princeton.
30 January: Rogers leaves the rangers.
16 August: Americans commanded by John Stark win at Battle of Bennington.
19 December: Washington withdraws to Valley Forge.

1778
28 February: Elizabeth Rogers divorces Robert.

1779
April: Rogers in London; returns to America.

1780
April: Rogers jailed for his debts.
December: Rogers released from jail.

1781
7 January: Rogers captured and jailed as a prisoner-of-war.
1 September: Rogers transported to New York City.

1782
Rogers in New York City seeking an exchange.

1783
November: British troops and refugees leave America for Great Britain.

1784
Rogers in London.

1785
September: Rogers' last visit to America.

1786-1794
Rogers in London

1795
18 May: Robert Rogers dies in London.

Appendix C,
Rogers' Ranging Rules

Below are listed Rogers' Rules of Ranging. These were developed by Robert Rogers and sent by letter to Lord Loudoun at his request on 27 October 1757. They were intended to govern the conduct of the rangers and are still quoted today.

> 1. All Rangers are to be subject to the rules and articles of war; to appear at roll-call every evening on their own parade, equipped each with a firelock, sixty rounds of powder and ball, and a hatchet, at which time an officer from each company is to inspect the same, to see they are in order, so as to be ready on any emergency to march at a minute's warning; and before they are dismissed the necessary guards are to be drafted, and scouts for the next day appointed.

> 2. Whenever you are ordered out to the enemy's forts or frontiers for discoveries, if your number be small, march in a single file, keeping at such a distance from each other as to prevent one shot from killing two men, sending one man, or more, forward, and the like on each side, at the distance of twenty yards from the main body, if the ground you march over will admit of it, to give the signal to the officer of the approach of an enemy, and of their number, & c.

> 3. If you march over marshes or soft ground, change your position, and march abreast of each other, to prevent the enemy from tracking you (as they would do if you marched in a single file) till you get over such ground, and then resume your former order, and march till it is quite dark before you encamp, which do, if possible, on a piece of ground that may afford your sentries the advantage of seeing or hearing the enemy at some considerable distance, keeping one half of your whole party awake alternately through the night.

4. Some time before you come to the place you would reconnoitre, make a stand, and send one or two men in whom you can confide, to look out the best ground for making your observations.

5. If you have the good fortune to take any prisoners, keep them separate till they are examined, and in your return take a different route from that in which you went out, that you may the better discover any party in your rear, and have an opportunity, if their strength be superior to yours, to alter your course, or disperse, as circumstances may require.

6. If you march in a large body of three or four hundred, with a design to attack the enemy, divide your party into three columns, each headed by a proper officer, and let these columns march in single file, the columns to the right and left keeping at twenty yards distance or more from that of the center, if the ground will admit, and let proper guards be kept in the front and rear, and suitable flanking parties as a due distance as before directed, with orders to halt on all eminences, to take a view of the surrounding ground, to prevent your being ambushed, and to notify the approach or retreat of the enemy, that proper dispositions may be made for attacking, defending, & c, and if the enemy approach in your front on level ground, form a front of your three columns or main body with the advanced, guard, keeping out your flanking parties, as if you were marching under the command of trusty officers, to prevent the enemy from pressing hard on either of your wings, or surrounding you, which is the usual method of the savages, if their number will admit of it, and be careful likewise to support and strengthen your rear guard.

7. If you are obliged to receive the enemy's fire, fall or squat down, till it is over, then rise and discharge at them. If their main body is equal to yours, extend yourselves occasionally; but if superior, be careful to support and strengthen your flanking parties, to make them equal with theirs, that if possible you may repulse them to their main body, in which case push upon them with the greatest resolution, with equal force in each flank and in the center, observing to keep at a due distance from each other, and advance from tree to tree, with one half of the party before the other ten or twelve yards. If the enemy push upon you, let your front fire and

fall down, and then let your rear advance thro' them and do the like, by which time those who before were in front will be ready to discharge again, and repeat the same alternately, as occasion shall require; by this means you will keep up such a constant fire, that the enemy will not be able easily to break your order, or gain your ground.

8. If you oblige the enemy to retreat, be careful, in your pursuit of them, to keep out your flanking parties, and prevent them from gaining eminences, or rising grounds, in which case they would perhaps be able to rally and repulse in their turn.

9. If you are obliged to retreat, let the front of your whole party fire and fall back, till the rear has done the same, making for the best ground you can; by this means you will oblige the enemy to pursue you, if they do it at all, in the face of a constant fire.

10. If the enemy is so superior that you are in danger of being surrounded by them, let the whole body disperse, and every one take a different road to the place of rendezvous appointed for that evening, which must every morning be altered and fixed for evening ensuing, in order to bring the whole party, or as many of them as possible, together, after any separation that may happen in the day; but if you should happen to be actually surrounded, form yourselves into a square, or if in the woods, a circle is best, and, if possible, make a stand till the darkness of the night favours your escape.

11. If your rear is attacked, the main body and flankers must face about to the right or left, as occasion shall require, and form themselves to oppose the enemy, as before directed; and the same method must be observed, if attacked in either of your flanks, by which means you will always make a rear of one of your flank-guards.

12. If you determine to rally after a retreat, in order to make a fresh stand against the enemy, by all means endeavour to do it on the most rising ground you can come at, which will give you greatly the advantage in point of situation, and enable you to repulse superior numbers.

13. If general, when pushed upon by the enemy, reserve your fire till they approach very near, which will them put them into the greater surprise and consternation, and give you an opportunity of rushing upon them with your hatchets and cutlasses to the better advantage.

14. When you encamp at night, fix your sentries in such a manner as not to be relieved from the main body till morning, profound secrecy and silence being often of the last importance in these cases. Each sentry, therefore, should consist of six men, two of whom must be constantly alert, and when relieved by their fellows, it should be done without noise; and in case those on duty see or hear anything, which alarms them, they are not to speak, but one of them is silently to retreat, and acquaint the commanding officer thereof, that proper dispositions may be made; and all occasional sentries should be fixed in like manner.

15. At the first dawn of day, awake your whole detachment; that being the time when the savages choose to fall upon their enemies, you should by all means be in readiness to receive them.

16. If the enemy should be discovered by your detachments in the morning, and their numbers are superior to yours, and a victory doubtful, you should not attack them till the evening, as then they will not know your numbers, and if you are repulsed, your retreat will be followed by the darkness of the night.

17. Before you leave your encampment, send out small parties to scout round it, to see if there be any appearance or track of an enemy that might have been near you during the night.

18. When you stop for refreshment, choose some spring or rivulet if you can, and dispose your party so as not to be surprised, posting proper guards and sentries at a due distance, and let a small party waylay the path you came in, lest the enemy should be pursuing.

19. If, in your return, you have to cross rivers, avoid the usual fords as much as possible, lest the enemy should have discovered, and be there expecting you.

20. If you have to pass by lakes, keep at some distance from the edge of the water, lest, in case of an ambuscade, or an attack from the enemy, when in that situation, your retreat should be cut off.

21. If the enemy pursue your rear, take a circle till you come to your own tracks, and there form ambush to receive them, and give them the first fire.

22. When you return from a scout, and come near our forts, avoid the usual roads, and avenues thereto, lest the enemy should have headed you, and lay in ambush to receive you, when almost exhausted with fatigues.

23. When you pursue any party that has been near our forts or encampments, follow not directly in their tracks, lest you should be discovered by their rear guards, who, at such a time, would be most alert; but endeavour, by a different route, to head and meet them in some narrow pass, or lay in ambush to receive them when and where they least expect it.

24. If you are to embark in canoes, bateaux, or otherwise, by water, choose the evening for the time of your embarkation, as you will then have the whole night before you, to pass undiscovered by any parties of the enemy, on hills, or other places, which command a prospect of the lake or river you are upon.

25. In paddling or rowing, give orders that the boat or canoe next the sternmost, wait for her, and the third for the second, and the fourth for the third, and so on, to prevent separation, and that you may be ready to assist each other on any emergency.

26. Appoint one man in each boat to look out for fires, on the adjacent shores, from the numbers and size of which you may form some judgement of the numbers that kindled them, and whether you are able to attack them or not.

27. If you find the enemy encamped near the banks of a river, or lake, which you imagine they will attempt to cross for their security upon being attacked, leave a detachment of your party on

the opposite shore to receive them, while, with the remainder, you surprise them, having them between you and the lake or river.

28. If you cannot satisfy yourself as to the enemy's number and strength, from their fire, & c. conceal your boats at some distance, and ascertain their number by a reconnoitering party, when they embark, or march, in the morning, marking the course they steer, & c. when you may pursue, ambush, and attack them, or let them pass, as prudence shall direct you. In general, however, that you may not be discovered by the enemy on the lakes and rivers at a great distance, it is safest to lay by, with your boats and party concealed all day, without noise or show, and to pursue your intended route by night; and whether you go by land or water, give out parole and countersigns, in order to know one another in the dark, and likewise appoint a station for every man to repair to, in case of any accident that may separate you.

Such in general are the rules to be observed in the Ranging service; there are, however, a thousand occurrences and circumstances which may happen that will make it necessary in some measure to depart from them and to put other arts and stratagems in practice; in which case every man's reason and judgment must be his guide, according to the particular situation and nature of things; and that he may do this to advantage, he should keep in mind a maxim never to be departed from by a commander, viz. to preserve a firmness and presence of mind on every occasion.[1]

Robert Rogers

Appendix D, The Ranger Roster[1]

Most of the rangers are listed as from New Hampshire, since at that time; Vermont was a part of New Hampshire. Massachusetts is second most common origin. Stockbridge Mohegan Indians joined the rangers in large numbers but few are identified. Rank of each ranger is shown. If unknown, the listing is "Ranger." Some provincials accompanied the rangers on campaigns and these are identified as "provincial" in the roster. There were also a few regulars and these are identified as such. There were other rangers not listed. They entered and left the rangers, but no record of them survives. Rangers recruited during the War of Independence are not listed.

Abbott, Nathaniel of Andover, Massachusetts. First Lieutenant. Served at Forts Edward and William Henry.
Addleton, Daniel. Ranger. Recruited by James Rogers, October 1757.
Adison, James. Ranger. Served at Forts Edward and William Henry.
Aker, William. Ranger. Served at Forts Edward and William Henry.
Albany, William. Ranger. On the Saint Francis Raid.
Anderson, Hugh. Ranger. Recruited by James Rogers, October 1757.
Andrew, Isaac. Clerk.
Annis, William. Ranger. Captain Bulkeley's Company.
Anthony, David. Private. Captain Bulkeley's Company.
Archibald, James. Sergeant. From Manchester, New Hampshire. Served at Forts Edward and William Henry.
Atherton (Etherington), Phineas of Lancaster, Massachusetts. Second Lieutenant.
Avery, Elias. Lieutenant. On the Saint Francis Raid.
Baker, Robert. Ranger. Captured with Thomas Brown in January 1757.
Baldwin (Balmding), Isaac. Sergeant.
Ballard, Samuel. Ranger. Killed on the Saint Francis Raid.
Balset, Thomas. Ranger. On the Saint Francis Raid.
Banck (Bank), Josiah. First Lieutenant.

Barnes, Daniel Jr. of Marlborough, Massachusetts. Ranger.
Barnes, George. of Durham, New Hampshire. Provincial. A captive of the Abenaki freed during the Saint Francis Raid.
Barnes, Jonathan. Sergeant. Served in Rogers' Own. He died of smallpox between 24 February and 24 August 1757.
Barns (Burns), Jonathan. Provincial. The renegade who helped the Abenaki track the rangers after the Saint Francis Raid. He was later hanged for his crimes.
Bates, Oliver. Sergeant. Captain Bulkeley's Company.
Beeman, Samuel. Sergeant.
Bennett, Elisha. Ranger. Served at Forts Edward and William Henry.
Bernard, Francis. Cadet. Not commissioned.
Beverly, Thomas. Sergeant.
Beverly, William. Sergeant.
Bewer, Eliab. Ensign. Captain Bulkeley's Company.
Bill, Judah. Private. Captain Bulkeley's Company.
Bolton (Botton), John. Sergeant.
Bolton, Joseph. Cadet.
Bolton, Joseph. Sergeant.
Boujour, John. A Swiss volunteer. Cadet. Not commissioned.
Bowen, Peter. Ranger. On the Saint Francis Raid.
Boyce, Richard "One-eyed Pete." A British volunteer, Cadet.
Bradbury, Sanders. Sergeant.
Bradley, Benjamin. Sergeant. On the Saint Francis Raid.
Brewer, David of Sudbury, Massachusetts. Captain.
Brewer, Elias of Sudbury, Massachusetts. Ensign.
Brewer, Jason. Sergeant.
Brewer, Jonathan from Massachusetts. Captain.
Brewer, Moses from Massachusetts. Captain.
Bridge, Benjamin. Cadet. Captain Bulkeley's Company.
Brigham, Nathan. Lieutenant. Provincial. On the Saint Francis Raid.
Britton, Samuel. Private. Captain Bulkeley's Company.
Brown, Benjamin. Ranger. Recruited by James Rogers, October 1757.
Brown, Boaz. Private. Captain Bulkeley's Company.
Brown, John. Ranger. From Manchester, New Hampshire. Served at Forts Edward and William Henry.
Brown, Thomas. Ranger. Born in Charlestown near Boston.

Captured by Indians, but returned to his home.
Bryant, Nath. Sergeant.
Buck, Thomas. Sergeant.
Bucknam, Edward. Ranger. On the Saint Francis Raid.
Buford, George. Sergeant.
Bulkeley, Charles of Littleton, Massachusetts. Captain. Killed in Battle on Snowshoes.
Bunbary, Henry William. Ranger. On the Saint Francis Raid.
Burbank, Jonathan of New Hopkinton, Massachusetts. Captain. Served at Forts Edward and William Henry.
Burbank, Nathaniel (or Caleb). Sergeant.
Burbeen, Paul. Paymaster.
Burns, Boston. Private. Captain Bulkeley's Company.
Burnside, Ambrose. Ranger. On the Saint Francis Raid.
Burnside, Thomas. Ranger. On the Saint Francis Raid.
Butler, John of Boston, Massachusetts. First Lieutenant.
Butterfield, Jonas. Sergeant.
Cahail, John. Ranger. Recruited by James Rogers, October 1757.
Cahoon (Calhoun), Samuel. Sergeant.
Cahoon, Robert. Sergeant.
Caldwell, John. Ensign.
Campbell, Archibald, Jr., a Scottish volunteer. Ensign.
Campbell, Archibald, Sr., Scottish Volunteer, Second Lieutenant.
Campbell, George. Second Lieutenant. On the Saint Francis Raid.
Campbell, James. Ranger. On the Saint Francis Raid.
Campbell, Robert. Private. Captain Bulkeley's Company.
Campbell, Samuel. Ranger. On the Saint Francis Raid.
Cargill (Also spelled Gargill or Cargyll), Abernathan (Abernethy) of Newcastle, Maine. Second Lieutenant. On the Saint Francis Raid.
Carruthers, Francis, a British volunteer. Ensign.
Castleman, John. Sergeant.
Chalmers, Ronald, a British volunteer. Cadet. Not commissioned.
Cheeksaunkun, Jacob of Stockbridge, Massachusetts. Captain. Stockbridge Mohegan Warrior. On Saint Francis Raid.[2]
Christopher, John, a British volunteer. Lieutenant.
Clark, Abram. Private. Captain Bulkeley's Company.
Clark (Clarke), James of Merrimack Valley, New Hampshire. Second Lieutenant. Served at Forts Edward and William Henry.
Clark (Clarke), John. Ensign.

325

Clark, Samuel. Private. Captain Bulkeley's Company.
Clark, William. Sergeant.
Cleaveland, Ephraim. Sergeant.
Clim, Philip. Private. Captain Bulkeley's Company.
Clish, Thomas. Private. Captain Bulkeley's Company.
Coleman, James. Private. Captain Bulkeley's Company.
Collingwood, (First name not listed), a British volunteer. Cadet.
Collins, John. Ranger. On the Saint Francis Raid.
Colton, Isaac. From Manchester, New Hampshire. Served at Forts Edward and William Henry.
Conally, Christopher. Private. Captain Bulkeley's Company.
Conally, Daniel. Private. Captain Bulkeley's Company.
Costalow, Edward. Ranger. Recruited by James Rogers, October 1757.
Craige, John. Sergeant.
Creed, Francis from England. Second Lieutenant.
Crofton, Edward of England. First Lieutenant.
Crofton, Walter, a British volunteer. Lieutenant.
Crosby, Samuel. Private. Captain Bulkeley's Company.
Crosby, William. Private. Captain Bulkeley's Company. Died 2 August 1757.
Crotty, Andrew, a British volunteer. Lieutenant.
Cumings, John. Ranger. Recruited by James Rogers, October 1757.
Cunningham, Samuel. Private. Captain Bulkeley's Company.
Cunningham, Thomas (William). Second Lieutenant. Captain Bulkeley's Company. From Manchester, New Hampshire. Served at Forts Edward and William Henry.
Curtis, Frederick. Ranger. On the Saint Francis Raid.
Cutter, Ameriah Ruhamah of North Yarmouth, Massachusetts. Surgeon.
Cymbal, Ebn. Ranger. Recruited by James Rogers, October 1757.
D'Arcy, Robert of New York City. First Lieutenant.
Danforth, Jonathan. Private. Captain Bulkeley's Company.
Darling, Benjamin. Ranger. Recruited by James Rogers, October 1757.
Davis, John. Sergeant.
Dawson, Hendrick. Private. Captain Bulkeley's Company.
Day, Isaac (Harvard). Ranger. Recruited by James Rogers, October 1757.
De Bien (Beaubien), Beau. (This was a dog, carried on the rolls as

sergeant).[3]
Degart, Peter. Second Lieutenant.
Dekefar, Luthainsans, a Swiss volunteer. Cadet. Not commissioned.
Denbow, Elijah. Sergeant.
Devine, William. Ranger. Recruited by James Rogers, October 1757.
Dewey, James. Clerk.
Dickey, Matthew. Ranger. Recruited by James Rogers, October 1757.
Dickinson, Daniel. Ranger. Recruited by James Rogers, October 1757.
Dinsmore, John. Sergeant. Captain Bulkeley's Company.
Dodd, Benjamin. Ranger. On the Saint Francis Raid.
Douglas, Phineas. Private. Captain Bulkeley's Company.
Douglas, Samuel. Private. Captain Bulkeley's Company.
Drew, Zebulon (Lemuel). Sergeant.
Drought, Thomas, a British volunteer. Lieutenant.
Dudley, Charles. Ranger. From Manchester, New Hampshire. Served at Forts Edward and William Henry.
Dunbar, James. Lieutenant. British regular. Commanded the British regulars during the Saint Francis Raid.
Duquipe, Joseph. Second Lieutenant. Stockbridge Mohegan Warrior.
Dutton, Joshua. Private. Captain Bulkeley's Company.
Dwyer, Daniel. Ranger. Captain Bulkeley's Company.
Eastman, Amos. Ranger.
Eastman, Joseph. Deacon.
Edmunds, John. Corporal.
Edmunds. Jonathan. Private. Captain Bulkeley's Company.
Ekins, Lawrence. Clerk. Deserter.
Elrington, Richard, a British volunteer. Lieutenant.
Emerson, Jacob. Private. Captain Bulkeley's Company.
Etowaukaum, Jonas. Ensign. Stockbridge Mohegan Warrior.
Evans
, David. Ranger. On the Saint Francis Raid.
Evans, John. Sergeant. On the Saint Francis Raid.
Farmer, Thomas. Ranger. Captain Bulkeley's Company.
Farnham, Timothy. Sergeant.
Farnsworth, Matthias. Private. Captain Bulkeley's Company.
Farrer (Ferror), Abel. Sergeant.

Farrington, Jacob of Andover, Massachusetts. Second Lieutenant. On the Saint Francis Raid.
Farron, Benoni. Sergeant.
Faulkner, James of Charlestown, New Hampshire. First Lieutenant.
Ferrin, Benjamin. Sergeant.
Fisk, Samuel. Corporal.
Fitch, William. Private. Captain Bulkeley's Company.
Fitch, Zachariah. Private. Captain Bulkeley's Company.
Fitche. Lieutenant. On the Saint Francis Raid.
Flagg, John. Private. Captain Bulkeley's Company.
Flagg, Joseph. Private. Captain Bulkeley's Company.
Flanders, Philip. Sergeant.
Fletcher, John of Chesterfield, New Hampshire. First Lieutenant.
Forseys, Benjamin. Captain Bulkeley's Company.
Forseys, Thomas. Captain Bulkeley's Company.
Fossit, Benjamin. Second Lieutenant.
Foster, Rowling. Ranger. From Manchester, New Hampshire. Served at Forts Edward and William Henry.
Fowler, Ebner. Sergeant.
Fraser, William, a Scottish volunteer. Lieutenant.
Fraser, William, Jr., a Scottish volunteer. Ensign.
Frazier, Simon. Ranger. On the Saint Francis Raid.
French, Abner. Sergeant.
Frisbough, (First name not listed), a British volunteer. Cadet. Not commissioned.
Frost, John. Ranger. From Manchester, New Hampshire. Served at Forts Edward and William Henry.
Fugard, Samuel. Provincial. Killed during the Saint Francis Raid.
Gates, Jonathan. Private. Captain Bulkeley's Company.
Geer, (First name not listed). Sergeant.
Gibs, Robert. Cadet.
Gilman, David of Exeter, New Hampshire. Ensign.
Gilman, Samuel of Exeter, New Hampshire. Second Lieutenant.
Gilson, Amasa. Ranger. Captain Bulkeley's Company.
Glenny, James. Private. Captain Bulkeley's Company. Died 10 August 1757.
Glenny, William. Private. Captain Bulkeley's Company. Died 13 August 1757.
Gold, Samuel. Private. Captain Bulkeley's Company.
Goodwin, Luxford. Sergeant.

Graham, John, a Scottish volunteer. Captain.
Graham & Comp. Captain Bulkeley's Company.
Grant, Allen, a British volunteer. Lieutenant. On the Saint Francis Raid.
Grant, Noah. Lieutenant. Provincial. On the Saint Francis Raid.
Greenough, Daniel. Sergeant.
Grise, James. Ranger. From Manchester, New Hampshire. Served at Forts Edward and William Henry.
Grover (Glover), Thomas. Sergeant.
Hackett, James. Sergeant.
Hair, William. First Lieutenant.
Hale (Hald), Josiah. Sergeant.
Hall, Benjamin. Sergeant.
Haltain, Thioridare. Ranger. On the Saint Francis Raid.
Hamilton, John. Lieutenant.
Hamilton, Samuel. Sergeant.
Hans, Charles. Private. Captain Bulkeley's Company.
Hartman, John. Ranger. From Manchester, New Hampshire. Served at Forts Edward and William Henry.
Hartwell, Daniel. Private. Captain Bulkeley's Company.
Hartwell, Francis. Ranger. On the Saint Francis Raid.
Hartwell, Solomon. Private. Captain Bulkeley's Company.
Hay, David. Ranger. On the Saint Francis Raid.
Hazen, (First name not listed). Ensign.
Hazen, Moses of Haverhill, Massachusetts. Captain. Also served in the War of Independence with the Patriots.
Heddy, Lpher. Sergeant.
Henry, James. Sergeant. From Manchester, New Hampshire. Served at Forts Edward and William Henry.
Hewit, John. Ranger. On the Saint Francis Raid.
Hewit, Thomas. Private. Captain Bulkeley's Company.
Hildreth, Amaziah. Private. Captain Bulkeley's Company.
Hill, James. Lieutenant.
Hill, Henry. Sergeant.
Hobbs, Humphrey of Southegan (now Amherst, New Hampshire). Captain. Served at Forts Edward and William Henry.
Holden, William from New Hampshire. Second Lieutenant.
Holden, William. Sergeant.
Hodgkins, Jonathan. Private. Captain Bulkeley's Company.
Hodscase, Timothy. Ranger. From Manchester, New Hampshire.

Served at Forts Edward and William Henry.
Holland, Stephen of Rumsford, New Hampshire. Second Lieutenant. He fought for the British during the War of Independence
Holmes, (First name not listed). Sergeant.
Holmes, Robert from New Hampshire. First Lieutenant.
Hopkins, Joseph. Sergeant.
Horst, Engelbertus. Cadet. Not commissioned.
Howard, Jonathan. Sergeant.
Hoyt (Hoit), Stephen. Sergeant. On the Saint Francis Raid.
Huik, Richard. Ranger. On the Saint Francis Raid.
Humble, Charles. Lieutenant.
Humphries, Ashboll. Sergeant.
Hutchings (Hutchins), Benjamin of Boston, Massachusetts. Ensign.
Hutchins, William. Sergeant.
Irwin, William. Lieutenant.
Jacob, Captain.
Jacob, "Duke." Ranger. On the Saint Francis Raid.
Jacquis, Robert. Sergeant.
Jenkins. Lieutenant. Died on the Saint Francis Raid of starvation.
Johnson, Joseph. Second Lieutenant. Stockbridge Mohegan Warrior.
Johnson, Nathaniel. Corporal. From Manchester, New Hampshire. Served at Forts Edward and William Henry.
Johnson, Noah of Dunstable, New Hampshire. Captain. Served at Forts Edward and William Henry.
Jones, Moses. Sergeant. Provincial. On the Saint Francis Raid.
Keeser (Keiser), George. Ensign.
Kellock, Ephraim. Private. Captain Bulkeley's Company. Died 24 July 1757.
Kelsey, Moses. Sergeant.
Kennedy, Samuel. First Lieutenant. From Goffstown, New Hampshire. Served at Forts Edward and William Henry. Killed in battle, 21 January 1757.
Kent, Michael. Cadet. Killed at Rogers' Rock, 13 March 1758.
Kidder, Joseph. Private. Captain Bulkeley's Company.
Kilson, Andrew. Sergeant.
Kimball, Ebenezer. Captain Bulkeley's Company.
Kirkwood, Robert. Ranger.
Kiser, John. Ranger. From Manchester, New Hampshire. Served at

Forts Edward and William Henry.

Knowlton, Thomas. Ranger. Fought at Fort Anne in 1758. Later served in the War for Independence and was killed at Long Island.

Koonehaunt, Joseph. Sergeant. Stockbridge Mohegan Warrior.

Lain, Joseph. Sergeant.

Lawrence, Abel. Private. Captain Bulkeley's Company.

Lawrence, Thomas from New Hampshire. First Lieutenant.

Lee, Daniel (or Jacob). Ranger. On the Saint Francis Raid.

Leighton, Francis. Private. Captain Bulkeley's Company.

Leiton, John. Ranger. From Manchester, New Hampshire. Served at Forts Edward and William Henry.

Lervi, Peter. Ranger. On the Saint Francis Raid.

Lessly, John. Private. Captain Bulkeley's Company.

Letch, Samuel. Ranger. From Manchester, New Hampshire. Served at Forts Edward and William Henry.

Libby, Job. Sergeant.

Linn, Nicholas. Private. Captain Bulkeley's Company.

Lock, Joshua of Worcester, Massachusetts. Second Lieutenant.

Logan, Edward. Ranger. On the Saint Francis Raid.

Lord, Thomas. Sergeant.

Lottridges, Robert. Captain Bulkeley's Company.

Lownsbury, Josiah. Sergeant.

Lysaught, Cornelius. Lieutenant.

Mahanter, Piller. Ranger. From Manchester, New Hampshire. Served at Forts Edward and William Henry.

Mackres, Samuel. Ranger. On the Saint Francis Raid. In John Stark's company.

MacLeane, Allan. Ranger. On the Saint Francis Raid.

MacLeane, Francis. Ranger. On the Saint Francis Raid.

MacLeane, Kenny. Ranger. On the Saint Francis Raid.

MacLeane, Lauchlan. Ranger. On the Saint Francis Raid.

Martin, Joshua of Goffstown, New Hampshire. Ensign. Served at Forts Edward and William Henry.

Martin, Peter. Private. Captain Bulkeley's Company. Died 18 July 1757.

Mars, James. Ranger. From Manchester, New Hampshire. Served at Forts Edward and William Henry.

Mater, John. Ranger. Recruited by James Rogers, October 1757.

Maukhquampoo, Jeremiah. Ranger.

Maunaummaug, John. Ranger.

Maxell, Thompson. Sergeant. On the Saint Francis Raid. From Bedford, Massachusetts.

McBean, Donald. Cadet. Not commissioned.

McCally, Alexander. Private. Captain Bulkeley's Company.

McClellan, William. Private. Captain Bulkeley's Company. Died 30 July 1757.

McClenning, William. Sergeant.

McCormick, Caesar. Second Lieutenant.

McCoy, Charles. Ranger. Recruited by James Rogers, October 1757.

McCracken (McCrackon), Joseph. Sergeant.

McCullough, (First name not listed). Sergeant.

McCurdy, John of Dunbarton, New Hampshire. Captain. Served at Forts Edward and William Henry.

McCurdy, John of Haverhill, Massachusetts. Clerk.

McDaniel, Ranal. Sergeant.

McDonald, Gregory. Ensign. Killed in Battle on Snowshoes.

McDougal, John. Lieutenant.

McDuffe (Duffy), John of Londonderry, New Hampshire. First Lieutenant.

McGee, William. Private. Captain Bulkeley's Company.

McIntire (McIntyre), Peter. Sergeant.

McKalley, John. Private. Captain Bulkeley's Company.

McKane, (First name not listed). Sergeant.

McKeen, William. Ranger. From Manchester, New Hampshire. Served at Forts Edward and William Henry.

McMullen, Andrew of Worchester, Massachusetts. First Lieutenant. On the Saint Francis Raid.

McNeal, Andrew. Private. British regular. On the Saint Francis Raid.

McNeil (McNeal), James. Sergeant. From Manchester, New Hampshire. Served at Forts Edward and William Henry.

McNee, Robert. Private. Captain Bulkeley's Company.

Menzies, Charles. Lieutenant.

Merry, Ralph. Ranger. On the Saint Francis Raid.

Michel, John. Ranger. From Manchester, New Hampshire. Served at Forts Edward and William Henry.

Middleton, John. Private. Captain Bulkeley's Company.

Millet, Thomas. Ensign.

Miscoukukk, Jacob. Ranger.

Mitchell, John. Sergeant.
Monfel, (No first name given). Cadet. Not commissioned.
Moore, Increase. Second Lieutenant.
Moore, William. Sergeant.
Moore (Morris), William of Stratham, New Hampshire. Second Lieutenant.
Morgan, James. Ranger. From Manchester, New Hampshire. Served at Forts Edward and William Henry.
Morris, William. Ensign. Captain Bulkeley's Company.
Munroe, Abram. Private. Captain Bulkeley's Company.
Munroe, Edmund. Ensign.
Munroe, Nathan. Private. Captain Bulkeley's Company. Died 5 August 1757.
Murfey, Daniel. Ranger. Recruited by James Rogers, October 1757.
Murphy, Daniel. Ranger. On the Saint Francis Raid. In Campbell's party.
Murray, David. Sergeant.
Napkin, Wonk. Ranger. On the Saint Francis Raid. From Jacob's Stockbridge Ranger Company. In Cambell's party.
Naunauphtaunk, Jacob of Stockbridge, Massachusetts. Captain. Stockbridge Mohegan Warrior.
Neale, James of Amoskeag, New Hampshire. Captain.
Nepash, Daniel. Ranger. On the Saint Francis Raid. From Jacob's Stockbridge Ranger Company. In Cambell's party.
Nichols, James. Private. Captain Bulkeley's Company.
Nicholson, William. Lieutenant.
Noble, Mark of Dunbarton, New Hampshire. First Lieutenant.
Notgrass, Andrew. Private. Captain Bulkeley's Company.
Nutt, David. Ranger. From Manchester, New Hampshire. Served at Forts Edward and William Henry.
O'Brien, Morris. Ranger. On the Saint Francis Raid. In Campbell's party.
Ogden, Amos from New Jersey. Captain. Wounded during the Saint Francis Raid.
Ogden, Nathaniel. Second Lieutenant.
Oliver, Robert. Cadet. Not commissioned.
Osgood, James. Sergeant.
Page, Caleb, Jr. of Rumford and Dunbarton, New Hampshire. Ensign.
Paige, Caleb. Ensign. Served at Forts Edward and William Henry.

Killed before 21 January 1757.
Parker, Phineas. Corporal.
Parker, William. Sergeant.
Parnell, Robert, Sergeant. Killed in Battle on Snowshoes.
Patten, John. First Lieutenant.
Patterson, John. Ranger. On the Saint Francis Raid.
Patterson, Walter. Lieutenant.
Pen, William. Ensign.
Perry, Abraham. Ensign.
Perry, Charles. Cadet. Not commissioned.
Perry, Ebenezer. Corporal.
Phillip, (First name not listed). Sergeant. Stockbridge Mohegan Warrior. On Saint Francis Raid.
Phillips, Henry. Lieutenant. Captain Bulkeley's Company.
Phillips, John. Private. Captain Bulkeley's Company.
Phillips, William Hendrick of Albany, New York. Second Lieutenant. On Saint Francis Raid.
Pomeroy, Robert. Ranger. On the Saint Francis Raid.
Pool, William. Private. Captain Bulkeley's Company.
Porter, Noah from Connecticut. First Lieutenant.
Pottinger, James from England. First Lieutenant. Killed in Battle on Snowshoes.
Prentice, Jonah. Private. Captain Bulkeley's Company.
Prentice, William. Private. Captain Bulkeley's Company.
Price, Richard. Ranger. On the Saint Francis Raid.
Ransom, William. Sergeant.
Reed, Thomas. Second Lieutenant.
Reed, Timothy. Ensign.
Reinhault, Ericke. Cadet. Not commissioned.
Rice, Samuel. Private. Captain Bulkeley's Company.
Ridge, William. Ranger. On the Saint Francis Raid.
Robb, Alexander. Sergeant. Captain Bulkeley's Company.
Robbins, Nathan. Private. Captain Bulkeley's Company.
Roberts, Benjamin. Lieutenant. Accused Rogers of treason at Michilimackinac.
Robertson, John. Lieutenant.
Rogers, Charles of New Hampshire. Second Lieutenant.
Rogers, James. Lieutenant. From Goffstown, New Hampshire. Served at Forts Edward and William Henry.
Rogers, James, Jr., of Methuen, Massachusetts. Major.

Rogers, John. Ranger. Recruited by James Rogers, October 1757.
Rogers, Patrick. Private. Captain Bulkeley's Company.
Rogers, Richard of Methuen, Massachusetts. Captain.
Rogers, Robert of Methuen, Massachusetts. Lieutenant Colonel and Commander. Commanded the Saint Francis Raid.
Rolph, Francis of Boston, Massachusetts. Ensign.
Rolphs, Mr. Captain Bulkeley's Company.
Ross, Andrew, Scottish volunteer. Ensign. Killed in Battle on Snowshoes.
Rossier, John. Sergeant.
Russell, Richard. Private. Captain Bulkeley's Company. Died 28 July 1757.
Samadagwis. Ranger. A traitor, killed at Saint Francis.
Sanborn (Samborn), Tristrum. Sergeant.
Scott, Abram. Ranger. Recruited by James Rogers, October 1757.
Scott, Alexander. Private. Captain Bulkeley's Company.
Scott, Benjamin. Ranger. Recruited by James Rogers, October 1757.
Scott, William. Ranger. Recruited by James Rogers, October 1757.
Scott, William (Petersburough). Ranger. Recruited by James Rogers, October 1757.
Schlosser, John Charles. Ensign.
Seagraves, John. Sergeant.
Senter, Joseph of Londonderry, New Hampshire. First Lieutenant.
Sever, Jacob. Sergeant.
Severance, Martin. Sergeant. On Saint Francis Raid.
Severance, Matthew. Sergeant.
Shepherd, John of Canterbury, New Hampshire. Captain.
Shepherd, Samuel, Jr., Ensign.
Sherwin, Ebenazer. Ranger. Recruited by James Rogers, October 1757.
Sherwin, Elnathan. Ranger. Captain Bulkeley's Company.
Shur, George. Ranger. Captain Bulkeley's Company.
Silaway, Jonathan. Ranger. From Manchester, New Hampshire. Served at Forts Edward and William Henry.
Simond, James. Ranger. From Manchester, New Hampshire. Served at Forts Edward and William Henry.
Simonds, Nathan. Sergeant. Captain Bulkeley's Company.
Simpson, Pileh. Ranger. From Manchester, New Hampshire. Served at Forts Edward and William Henry.

Sixbury, Hendrick. Private. Captain Bulkeley's Company.
Skell, Jacob. Ensign.
Smith, Aaron. Private. Captain Bulkeley's Company.
Smith, Abel. Ranger. Captain Bulkeley's Company.
Smith (Smyth), Lawrence, a British volunteer, Ensign.
Smith, Nathaniel. Ranger. From Manchester, New Hampshire. Served at Forts Edward and William Henry.
Smith, William. Ranger. On the Saint Francis Raid.
Soper, George. Ranger. On the Saint Francis Raid.
Southward, Isaac. Private. Captain Bulkeley's Company.
Spraguer, John. Ranger. Recruited by James Rogers, October 1757.
Sparrow, John. Ranger. On the Saint Francis Raid.
Spaulding, Benjamin. Private. Captain Bulkeley's Company.
Spaulding, Oliver. Ranger. Recruited by James Rogers, October 1757.
Speakman, Thomas of Boston, Massachusetts. Captain. Also listed as Spikeman. Killed while a prisoner with Thomas Brown in January 1757.
Squanton, Benjamin. Ranger. From Manchester, New Hampshire. Served at Forts Edward and William Henry.
Stark, Archibald of Londonderry, New Hampshire. First Lieutenant.
Stark, John of Londonderry, New Hampshire. Captain.
Stark, Samuel of Londonderry, New Hampshire. Ensign.
Stark, William of Londonderry, New Hampshire. Captain.
Stearns, Elezar. Private. Captain Bulkeley's Company.
Sterling, Hugh. Lieutenant.
Stevens, Enos. He fought for the British during the War of Independence.
Stevens, Samuel of New Hampshire. Second Lieutenant. Led the relief party to Fort Number Four after the Saint Francis Raid.[4]
Stevens (Stephens), Simon of Deerfield, Massachusetts. Captain. On the Saint Francis Raid.
Stewart, Philip. Private. Captain Bulkeley's Company.
Stewart, William. Ranger. Captain Bulkeley's Company.
Stewart, William of Albany, New York. Adjutant.
Still, No first name given. Cadet. Not commissioned.
Stimson, John. He fought for the British during the War of Independence.
Stimson, Samuel. He fought for the British during the War of Independence.

Stinson, Samuel. Ranger. Recruited by James Rogers, October 1757.
Stockwell, Emmons. Ranger. On the Saint Francis Raid.
Stone, David of Petersham, Massachusetts. First Lieutenant.
Stone, Nathan. First Lieutenant.
Stuard, William. Ranger. Recruited by James Rogers, October 1757.
Stuart, James. Private. Captain Bulkeley's Company.
Stuart, John. Ranger. On the Saint Francis Raid.
Stuart, Robert. Ranger. On the Saint Francis Raid.
Stuart, William. Ranger. On the Saint Francis Raid. In Campbell's party.
Stubens. (Stevens) (First name not listed). First Lieutenant.
Swan, Jer. Ranger. Recruited by James Rogers, October 1757.
Swan, William. Corporal.
Sweeny, Bryan. Sergeant.
Taylor, Leonard. Ranger. Recruited by James Rogers, October 1757.
Taylor, Nathaniel. Ranger. Recruited by James Rogers, October 1757.
Taylor, Nathan. Private. Captain Bulkeley's Company.
Taylor, William. Private. Captain Bulkeley's Company.
Thompson, Jonathan (Enlisted Albany). Ranger. Recruited by James Rogers, October 1757.
Thribout, (First name not listed). Second Lieutenant.
Titwood, Joshua. Ranger. From Manchester, New Hampshire. Served at Forts Edward and William Henry.
Toby, Simon. Ranger. From Manchester, New Hampshire. Served at Forts Edward and William Henry.
Townsend, Jacob. Sergeant.
Truett, Robert. Sergeant.
Trull, John. Private. Captain Bulkeley's Company.
Turner, George (James). Second Lieutenant. On the Saint Francis Raid.
Tute, James of Hardwick, Massachusetts. Captain. Later participated in the search for the Northwest Passage.
Uhhaunwaumut, Solomon of Stockbridge, Massachusetts. Captain. Stockbridge Mohegan Warrior.
Vanderheyden, David. Private. Captain Bulkeley's Company.
Vanelieu, Gibson. Ensign.

Van Tyne, Richard. First Lieutenant.

Ven Bebber, Henry. Cadet. Not commissioned. From Manchester, New Hampshire. Served at Forts Edward and William Henry.

Vearland, Jacob of Albany, New York. Surgeon.

Wackerberg, Andrew. Cadet. Not commissioned.

Wadleigh, John. Ranger. From Manchester, New Hampshire. Served at Forts Edward and William Henry.

Waite, Benjamin. Ensign.

Waite, Jason. Sergeant.

Waite, Joseph from Massachusetts. Captain. Also spelled Wait. Second in command of the Saint Francis Raid.

Wallace, David. Private. Captain Bulkeley's Company.

Wallace, Hugh. British regular. On the Saint Francis Raid.

Wallace, Solomon. Private. Captain Bulkeley's Company.

Walter, Charles Joseph. Second Lieutenant.

Wansant, Andrew. Ranger. On the Saint Francis Raid. In Rogers' party.

Ward, Nicholas. Lieutenant.

Wardoman, George. Cadet. Not commissioned.

Ware, Daniel. Ranger. Recruited by James Rogers, October 1757.

Warren, James. Sergeant.

Warren, Jonas. Sergeant. Captain Bulkeley's Company.

Warren, William. Ranger. From Amesbury. On the Saint Francis Raid. Captured in retreat and escaped in 1760.

Waupunjscot, Hendrick. Sergeant.

Wauwaumpequvnaunt, John. Clerk. Stockbridge Mohegan Warrior.

Webster, Ebenezer. Cadet.

Welch, James. Ranger. From Manchester, New Hampshire. Served at Forts Edward and William Henry.

Wellesley (First name not listed). Sergeant.

Wells, Aggrippe "Captain Grip." Ranger. From Deerfield, Massachusetts. On the Saint Francis Raid.

Wells, Phillip. Sergeant.

Wendecker, George. Ranger. Deserter.

Wendell, Henry Isaac from Mohawk Valley, New York. Captain.

Wheeler, Ebenezer. Provincial. Killed during the Saint Francis Raid.

Wheeler, Ephraim. Corporal.

Wheeler, William. Ranger. From Manchester, New Hampshire. Served at Forts Edward and William Henry.

White, James, a British volunteer. Ensign. Killed in Battle on Snowshoes.
Wilcox, John. Lieutenant.
Williams, Benjamin. Sergeant.
Williams, John. Ranger. On the Saint Francis Raid.
Willis, David. Private. Captain Bulkeley's Company.
Willison, William. Private. Captain Bulkeley's Company.
Wills, Philip. Ranger. From Manchester, New Hampshire. Served at Forts Edward and William Henry.
Willson, Elijah. Private. Captain Bulkeley's Company.
Wilson, Andrew. Sergeant.
Wilson, John of Petersham, Massachusetts. Ensign.
Wnaumpos, Abraham. Sergeant. On Saint Francis Raid.
Wriesberg, Daniel. Lieutenant. From Hanover, New Hampshire.
Wrightson, John. Captain.
Young, Stephen. Ranger. From Manchester, New Hampshire. Served at Forts Edward and William Henry.
Young, Walter. Lieutenant.

Bibliography

Books

Alden, John R. *George Washington, a Biography*. Norwalk: Easton Press, 1993.

Allison, William Thomas, Jeffrey Grey, and Janet G. Valetine. *American Military History, A Survey from Colonial Times to the Present*. Upper Saddle River: Pearson Education, Inc., 2013.

Anderson, Fred. *Massachusetts Soldiers & Society in the Seven Years' War*. Chapel Hill: The University of North Carolina Press, 1984.

_____ *George Washington Remembers, Reflections on the French and Indian War*. Lanham: Rowman & Littlefield Publishers, In., 2004.

_____ *Crucible of War. The Seven Years' War and the Fate of Empire in British North America, 1754-1766*. New York: Vintage Books, 2000.

Andrist, Ralph K. *The Founding Fathers, George Washington in his Own Words, Volume 1*. New York: Newsweek Book Division, 1972.

Association of Graduates, United States Military Academy. *The Register of Graduates and Former Cadets of the United States Military, 2015*. West Point: Association of Graduates, 2015.

Bahmanyar, Mir. *Shadow Warriors, A History of the U. S. Army Rangers*. New York: Osprey Publishing, 2003.

Baker, Mark Allen. *Spies of Revolutionary Connecticut, From Benedict Arnold to Nathan Hale*. Charleston: The History Press, 2014.

Bartley, Scott A. *Vermont Families in 1791, Volume 1, Special Publication Number 1*. Camden: Picton Press, 1992.
_____. *Vermont Families in 1791, Volume 2, Special Publication Number 5*. Camden: Picton Press, 1997.

Berleth, Richard. *Bloody Mohawk, The French and Indian War & American Revolution on New York's Frontier*. New York: Black Dome Press Corp., 2009.

Berton, Pierre. *Flames Across the Border, The Canadian-American Tragedy, 1813-1814*. Boston: Little, Brown and Company, 1981.

Billias, George Athan. *George Washington's Opponents, British Generals and Admirals in the American Revolution*. New York: William Morrow and Company, Inc., 1969.

Black, Robert W. *Ranger Dawn: the American Ranger from the Colonial Period to the Mexican War*. Pennsylvania: Stackpole Books, 2009.

Bliven, Bruce, Jr. *Under Guns, New York: 1775-1776*. New York: Harper & Row, Publishers, 1972.

Borneman, Walter R. *The French and Indian War: Deciding The Fate of North America*. New York: Harpers Perennial, 2006.

Bowen, Catherine Drinker. *Miracle at Philadelphia, The Story of the Constitutional Convention, May to September 1787*. Boston: Little, Brown and Company, 1966.

Bigelow, Ella A. *Historical Reminiscences of Early Times in Marlborough, Massachusetts and Prominent Events from 1860-1910*. Marlborough: Times Publishing Company, Printers, 1910.

Browne, G. Waldo. *With Rogers' Rangers, Wood Ranger Tales*. New York: A. Wessels Company, 1907.

Bruchac, Joseph. *The Winter People*. New York: Puffin Books, 2002.

Bruchac, Marge. *Malian's Song*. Hanover: University Press of New England, 2005.

Brumwell, Stephen. *White Devil, A True Story of War, Savagery, and Vengeance in Colonial America*. Boston: DaCapo Press, 2005.

Burpee, Lawrence J. *Searching for the Western Sea, The Story of the Exploration of North Western America*. New York: Musson Book Company, 1908.

Butterfield, L. H., ed., *Diary of John Adams, vol. 2, 1771-1781, entry of September 21*. Cambridge: 1962.

Callahan, North. *Henry Knox, General Washington's General*. New York: A. S. Barnes and Company, 1958.

Calloway, Colin G. *Western Abenakis of Vermont, 1600-1800, War, Migration, and the Survival of an Indian People*. Norman: University of Oklahoma Press, 1987.

Carmer, Carl. *The Hudson*. New York: Holt, Rinehart and Winston, 1939.

Campbell, William W. *The Border Warfare of New York, During the Revolution, or The Annals of Tryon County*. New York: Baker & Scribner, 1849.

Carnes, Mark C. and John A. Garraty. *American Destiny, Narrative of a Nation, Volume I, To 1877*. New York: Pearson Education, Inc., 2012.

Carver, Jonathan. *Travels Through the Interior Parts of North America in the Years 1766, 1767, and 1768*. Dublin: 1779.

Chernow, Ron. *Washington, A Life*. New York: Penguin Books, 2010.

Chet, Guy. *Conquering the American Wilderness, The Triumph of European Warfare in the Colonial Northeast*. Boston: University of Massachusetts Press, 2003.

Clark, Ronald W. *A Biography, Benjamin Franklin*. New York: Random House, 1983.

Commager, Henry Steele and Richard B. Morris. *The Spirit of 'Seventy-Six, The Story of the American Revolution as Told by the Participants*. New York: Bonanza Books, 1983.

Cuneo, John R. *Robert Rogers of the Rangers*. New York: Oxford University Press, 1987.

Corning, A. Elwood. *Washington at Temple Hill*. Newburgh: The Lanmere Publishing Company, 1932.

Cox, Caroline. *A Proper Sense of Honor, Service and Sacrifice in George Washington's Army*. Chapel Hill: The University of North Carolina Press, 2004.

Clinton, Henry. *The American Revolution, The British Commander-In-Chief's Narrative of his Campaigns, 1775-1782*. New Haven: Yale University Press, 1954.

Dann, John C. *The Revolution Remembered, Eyewitness Accounts of the War for Independence*. Chicago: University of Chicago Press, 1980.

Day, Gordon M. In *Search of New England's Native Past: Selected Essays by Gordon M. Day (Native Americans of the Northeast)*. Amherst: University of Massachusetts Press, 1998.

Delgado, James P. *Across the Top of the World, The Quest for the Northwest Passage*. Vancouver: Douglas & McIntyre, 1999.

Joint Publication 1-02. Washington, D. C.: Department of Defense, 2010.

Joint Publication 3-05. Washington, D. C.: Department of Defense, 2014.

Drimmer, Frederick. *Captured by Indians, 15 Firsthand Accounts, 1750-1870*. New York: Dover Publications, Inc., 1961.

Eggleston, Michael A. *Exiting Vietnam, The Era of Vietnamization and American Withdrawal Revealed in First-Person Accounts*. Jefferson: McFarland & Company, Inc., Publishers, 2014.

_____ *The 5ᵗʰ Marine Regiment Devil Dogs in World War I*. Jefferson: McFarland & Company, Inc., Publishers, 2016.

_____ *Dak To and the Border Battles of Vietnam, 1967-1968*. Jefferson: McFarland & Company, Inc., Publishers, 2017.

Ellis, Joseph J. *His Excellency, George Washington*. New York: Vintage Books, 2004.

Fenn, Elizabeth A. *Pox Americana, The Great Smallpox Epidemic of 1775-82*. Phoenix Mill: Hill and Wang, 2001.

Ferling, John E. *Setting the World Ablaze: Washington, Adams, Jefferson, and the American Revolution*. New York: Oxford University Press, 2000.

Ferris, Robert G. *Explorers and Settlers, Historic Places Commemorating the Early Exploration and Settlement of the United States*. Washington, D.C.: National Park Service, 1968.

Fischer, David Hackett. *Washington's Crossing*. New York: Oxford University Press, Inc., 2004.

Fleming, Thomas. *Washington's Secret War. The Hidden History of Valley Forge*. New York: Smithsonian Books, 2005.

Flexner, James Thomas. *Washington, The Indispensable Man*. Boston: Little, Brown and Company, 1969.

Force, Peter, ed., *American Archives, vol. 4, Series 3, 1775, Pennsylvania Committee of Safety Minutes, Friday, September 23, 1775*.

Fowler, William M., Jr. *Empires at War, The French and Indian War and the Struggle for North America, 1754-1763*. New York: Walker & Company, 2005.

Fritz, Jean. *Traitor, The Case of Benedict Arnold*. New York: The Putnam and Grosset Group, 1981.

Gara, Donald J. *Queen"s American Rangers*. Yardley: Westholme Publishing, 2015.

Gelb, Norman. *Jonathan Carver's Travels Through America, 1766-1768, An Eighteen-Century Explorer's Account of Uncharted America*. New York: John Wiley & Sons, Inc., 1993.

Goodrich, S. G. *A Pictorial History of the Western World*. Hartford: Wm. W. House, 1858.

Gross, Robert A. *The Minutemen and Their World*. New York: Hill and Wang, 1976.

Hawke, David Freeman. *Franklin*. New York: Harper & Row, Publishers, 1976.

Headley, J. T. *Washington and His Generals, Volume 1*. New York: Baker and Scribner, 1848.
_____. *Washington and His Generals, Volume 2*. New York: Baker and Scribner, 1848.

Hemenway, Abby Marta. *The Vermont Historical Gazetteer, A Magazine Embracing a History of Each Town, Civil, Ecclesiastical, Biographical, and Military in Three Volumes, Volume I*. Burlington: Miss A. M. Hemenway, 1867.
_____. *The Vermont Historical Gazetteer, A*

Magazine Embracing a History of Each Town, Civil, Ecclesiastical, Biographical, and Military, Volume II. Burlington: Miss A. M. Hemenway, 1871.

Hirschfeld, Fritz. *George Washington and Slavery: A Documentary Portrayal.* Columbia: University of Missouri Press, 1997.

Hudson, Charles and Joseph Allen. *History of the Town of Marlborough, Middlesex County.* Boston: T. R. Marvin & Son, 1862.

Hurd, Duane Hamilton. *History of Clinton & Franklin Counties, New York.* Plattsburg: Clinton County American Revolution Bicentennial Commission, 1978.

Hutson, James (July–August 2003). *"Nathan Hale Revisited— A Tory's Account of the Arrest of the First American Spy."* Information Bulletin. *The Library of Congress.*

Isaacson, Walter. *A Benjamin Franklin Reader.* New York: Simon & Schuster, 2003.

Katcher, Philip R. N. *Encyclopedia of British Provincial, and German Army Units 1775-1783.* Harrisburg: Stackpole Company, 1973.

Kayworth, Alfred E. and Raymond G. Potvin. *The Scalp Hunters, Abenaki Ambush at Lovewell Pond – 1725.* Boston: Braden Books, Inc., 2002.

Ketchum, Richard M. *Decisive Day, The Battle of Bunker Hill.* Garden City: Doubleday & Company, Inc., 1974.

King, Duane H. *The Memoirs of Lt. Henry Timberlake: The Story of a Soldier, Adventurer, and Emissary to the Cherokees, 1756-1765*. Cherokee: Museum of the Cherokee Indian Press, 2007.

Kirkwood, Robert. *Through So Many Dangers: The Memoirs and Adventures of Robert Kirk, Late of the Royal Highland Regiment*. Fleischmanns: Purple Mountain Press, 2004.

Koke, Richard J. *Accomplice in Treason, Joshua Hett Smith and the Arnold Conspiracy*. New York: The New-York Historical Society, 1973.

Langguth, A. J. *Patriots, The Men Who Started the American Revolution*. New York: Simon & Schuster, 1988.

Lengel, Edward G. *General George Washington: A Military Life*. New York: Random House, 2005.

Letters of Delegates to Congress, Vol. 4. "William Whipple to John Langdon, Philadelphia, July 1, 1776." Library of Congress.

Liss, David. *The Whiskey Rebels*. New York: Ballantine Books, 2008.

Loescher, Burt Garfield. *The History of Rogers Rangers, Volume I, The Beginnings, Jan 1755-April 6, 1758*. San Francisco: Heritage Books, Inc., 1946.
_____. *Genesis Rogers Rangers, The First Green Berets, Volume II*. San Francisco: Heritage Books, Inc., 1969.
_____. *The History of Rogers Rangers, Volume III, Officers and Non-Commissioned Officers*. San

Francisco: Heritage Books, Inc., 1957.

_____. *The History of Rogers Rangers, Volume IV, The St. Francis Raid*. San Francisco: Heritage Books, Inc., 2008.

Long, J. C. *Lord Jeffery Amherst, A Soldier of the King*. New York: The MacMillian Company, 1933.

Lord, Walter. *The Dawn's Early Light, The Climactic shaping of the "Land of the Free" during the Hazardous Events of 1814 in Washington, Baltimore, and London*. New York: W. W. Norton & Company, Inc., 1972.

Lucier, Armand Francis. *French and Indian War Notices Abstracted from Colonial Newspapers, Vol. 1: 1754-1755*. Bowie: Heritage Books, 1999.

_____. *French and Indian War Notices Abstracted from Colonial Newspapers, Vol. 2: 1756-1757*. Bowie: Heritage Books, 2007.

_____. *French and Indian War Notices Abstracted from Colonial Newspapers, Vol. 3: January 1 1758 to September 17, 1759*. Bowie: Heritage Books, 2007.

_____. *French and Indian War Notices Abstracted from Colonial Newspapers, Vol. 4: September 17, 1759 to December 30, 1760*. Bowie: Heritage Books, 2007.

_____. *French and Indian War Notices Abstracted from Colonial Newspapers, Vol. 5: January 1, 1761 to January 17, 1763*. Bowie: Heritage Books, 2007.

_____. *Newspaper Datelines of the American Revolution, Vol. 3: May 1, 1776 to November 1, 1776*. Westminster: Heritage Books, 2004.

Luzader, John. *Decision on the Hudson, The Saratoga Campaign of 1777*. Washington, D. C.: National Park Service,

1975.

Mackenzie, Frederick. *Diary of Frederick Mackenzie.* Cambridge: Harvard University Press, 1930.

Malone, Dumas. *Jefferson The Virginian, Volume 1.* Boston: Little, Brown and Company, 1948.
_____. *Jefferson and The Rights of Man, Volume 2.* Boston: Little, Brown and Company, 1951.
_____. *Jefferson and The Ordeal of Liberty, Volume 3.* Boston: Little, Brown and Company, 1962.
_____. *Jefferson The President, First Term, 1801-1805, Volume 4.* Boston: Little, Brown and Company, 1970.
_____. *Jefferson The President, Second Term, 1805-1809, Volume 5.* Boston: Little, Brown and Company, 1974.
_____. *Jefferson The Sage of Monticello, Volume 6.* Boston: Little, Brown and Company, 1981.

Mante, Thomas. *The History of the Late War in North-America, and the Islands of the West-Indies, including the Campaigns of MDCCLXIII and MDCCLXIV Against His Majesty's Indian Enemies.* London: W. Strahan, and T. Cadell in the Strand, 1772.

Marston, Daniel. *Essential Histories, The Seven Years' War.* New York, Osprey Publishing, 2001.

Martin, James Kirby and Mark Edward Lender. *A Respectable Army, The Military Origins of the Republic, 1763-1789.* Wheeling: Harlan Davidson, Inc., 1982.

Martin, Joseph Plumb. *Narrative of Some of the Adventures, Dangers and Sufferings of a Revolutionary Soldier; Interspersed with Anecdotes of Incidents that Occurred within his Own Observation Written by Himself.* Hallowell: Glazier, Masters & Company, 1830.

McLynn, Frank. *1759, The Year Britain Became Master of the World.* New York: Grove Press, 2004.

Meacham, Jon. *Thomas Jefferson, The Art of Power.* New York: Random House, 2012.

Metcalf, Harrison, ed., *Laws of New Hampshire, Vol. 4: Revolutionary War Period, 1776-1784.* Bristol, 1916.

Mevers, Frank C., ed., *The Papers of Josiah Bartlett.* "Langdon to Bartlett, Portsmouth, June 3, 1776." Hanover: University Press of New England, 1979.

Middlekauff. Robert. *The Glorious Cause, The American Revolution, 1763-1789.* New York: Oxford University Press, 1982.

Millett, Alan R., Peter Maslowski, and William B. Feis. *For the Common Defense, A Military History of the United States from 1607 to 2012.* New York: Free Press, 2012.

Nagel, Paul C. *Descent from Glory, Four Generations of the John Adams Family.* New York: Oxford University Press, 1983.

Navarre, Robert. "The Journal of Pontiac's Conspiracy," in Milo Milton Quaife, *The Siege of Detroit in 1763: The Journal of Pontiac's Conspiracy and John Rutherford's Narrative of a Captivity.* Chicago: Lakeside Press, 1958.

Nebenzahl, Kenneth. *Atlas of the American Revolution.* Chicago: Rand McNally & Company, 1974.

Nelson, Paul David. *General Sir Guy Carleton, Lord Dorchester, Soldier-Statesman of Early British Canada.* Cranbury: Associated University Presses, 2000.

Nevins, Allan. *Ranger, The Adventurous Life of Robert Rogers of the Rangers.* Driffield: Leonaur, 2011.

New York Historical Society. *Narratives of the Revolution in New York.* Kingsport: Kingsport Press, 1975.

Novick, Peter. *That Noble Dream, The "Objectivity Question" and the American Historical Profession.* Cambridge: Cambridge University Press, 1998.

Oates, Stephen B. and Charles J. Errico. *Portrait of America, Volume 1 to 1877.* Boston: Houghton Mifflin Company, 2007.

O'Brien, Cormac. *Outnumbered, Incredible Stories of History's Most Surprising Battlefield Upsets.* Beverly: New York: Crestline, 2010.

O'Connor, Liam Patrick. "The American Spy: Winning the War from the Shadows." *The SAR Magazine, Sons of the American Revolution.* Louisville: Sons of the American Revolution, 2016.

Paine, Thomas. *Common Sense and Rights of Man.* Birmingham: Palladium Press, 2000.

Parkman, Francis. *Montcalm and Wolfe.* New York: The American Past, 1983.

Parkman, Francis and John Fiske. *The Works of Francis*

Parkman, Volume 9. Boston: Little, Brown and Company, 1897.

Parry, William Edward. *Three Voyages for the Discovery of a Northwest Passage from the Atlantic to the Pacific, Volume I*. Memphis: General Books, 2012.

Pell, H. G. *The Champlain Valley in the American Revolution*. New York: New York State American Revolution Bicentennial Commission, 1976.

Phelps, M. William. *The Life and Death of America's First Spy, Nathan Hale*. New York: Thomas Dunne Books, 2008.

Philbrick, Nathaniel. *Bunker Hill, A City, A Siege, A Revolution*. New York: Penguin Books, 2013.
_____ *Valiant Ambition, George Washington, Benedict Arnold, and the Fate of the American Revolution*. New York: Viking, 2016.

Porter, C. E. *The Military History of the State of New Hampshire from Its Settlement, in 1623, to the Rebellion, in1861*. Concord: McFarland and Jenks, 1866.

Randall, Willard Sterne. *Benedict Arnold, Patriot and Traitor*. New York: William Morrow and Company, Inc., 1990.
_____ *George Washington: A Life*. New York: Henry Holt & Company, 1997.

Ranger Handbook SH 21-76

Rasmussen, William M. S.; Tilton, Robert S. *George Washington-the Man Behind the Myths*. Charlottesville: University Press of Virginia, 1999.

Reid, W. Max. *The Mohawk Valley, Its Legends and Its History*. New York: The Knickerbocker Press, 1979.

Reynolds, Paul R. *Guy Carleton, A Biography*. Toronto: Gage Publishing Limited, 1980.

Roberts, Kenneth. *Northwest Passage, Book I*. Garden City: Doubleday & Company, Inc., 1937.
_____. *Northwest Passage, Book II*. Garden City: Doubleday & Company, Inc., 1937.

Rogers, Mary Cochrane. *A Battle Fought on Snow Shoes, Rogers' Rock, Lake George, March 13, 1758*. Derry: Self-Published, 1917.

Rogers, Robert. *Journals of Robert Rogers of the Rangers, The Exploits of Rogers & the Rangers in his Own Words During 1755-1761 in the French & Indian War*. Leonaur, Ltd., 2005.
_____ *Ponteach, or the Savages of North America: A Tragedy*. London: J. Millan, 1766.

Root, Jean Christie. *Nathan Hale*. Lexington: Self-Published.

Rose, Alexander. *Washington's Spies, The Story of America's First Spy Ring*. New York: Random House, 2006

Ross, John F. *War on the Run, The Epic Story of Robert Rogers and the Conquest of America's First Frontier*. New York: Bantam Books, 2011.

Royster, Charles. *A Revolutionary People at War, The Continental Army and American Colonies, 1775-1783*. New York: W. W. Norton & Company, 1979.

Sabine, William H. W., ed., *Historical Memoirs, From March 16, 1763 to July 25, 1778, of William Smith, Vol. II, entry of early 1776*. New York: Arno Press, 1969.

Sarles, Frank B. and Charles E. Shedd. *Colonials and Patriots, Historic Places Commemorating Our Forebears 1700-1785*. Washington: National Park Service, 1964.

Shields, Joseph W. *From Flintlock to M1*. New York: Coward-McCann, 1954.

Skovlund, Marty, Jr., *Violence of Action. The Untold Stories of the 75th Ranger Regiment in the War on Terror*. Colorado Springs: Blackside Concepts, 2014.

Smith, David. *William Howe and the American War of Independence*. New York: Bloomsbury Academic, 2015.

Smith, Paul H. *Letters of Delegates To Congress, 1774-1789, Volume 1*. Washington: Library of Congress, 1976.
_____ *Letters of Delegates To Congress, 1774-1789, Volume 4*. Washington: Library of Congress, 1979.

Sparks, Jared. *Life and Treason of Benedict Arnold*. Middletown: First Rate Publishers, 2016.

Spaulding, E. Wilder. *His Excellency, George Clinton, Critic of the Constitution*. New York: The MacMillan Company, 1938.

Spielvogel, Jackson J. *Western Civilization, Volume II, Since 1500*. London: Thomson Wadsworth, 2006.

Stark, Caleb. *Memoir and Official Correspondence of John Stark*. Concord: G. Parker Lyon, 1860.

Stark, John, Maj. Gen. *Reminiscences of the French War Containing Rogers' Expeditions with the New England Rangers under his Command as Published in London in 1765; with Notes and Illustrations. To which is Added an Account of the Life and Military Services of Maj. Gen. John Stark; with Notices and Anecdotes of Other Officers Distinguished in the French and Revolutionary Wars.* Concord: Luther Roby, 1831.

Steele, Ian K. *Betrayals, Fort William Henry & the Massacre.* New York: Oxford University Press, 1990.

Stein, Stephen J. *The Shaker Experience in America.* New Haven: Yale University Press, 1992.

Todish, Timothy J. *The Annotated and Illustrated Journals of Major Robert Rogers.* Fleischmanns: Purple Mountain Press, 2002.

Toll, Ian W. *Six Frigates, The Epic History of the Founding of the U. S. Navy.* New York: W. W. Norton & Company, 2006.

Treason? "Proceedings of a General Court Martial held in the City of Montreal."

Tryon, William. *The Correspondence of William Tryon and Other Selected Papers, Volume II, 1768-1818.* Raleigh: Division of Archives and History, Department of Cultural Resources, 1981.

Turabian, Kate L. *A Manual for Writers of Research Papers, Theses, and Dissertations, Chicago Style for Students and Researchers, Eighth Edition.* Chicago: The University of Chicago Press, 2010.

Utley, Robert M. & Wilcomb E. Washburn. *The American Heritage History of The Indian Wars*. New York: The American Heritage Publish Co., Inc., 1977.

Van Zandt, Roland. *Chronicles of the Hudson, Three Centuries of Travelers Accounts*. New Brunswick: Rutgers University Press, 1971.

Vaughan, Alden T. *New England Frontier, Puritans and Indians, 1620-1675*. New York: W. W. Norton & Company, 1979.

Walker, Joseph Burbeen. *Life and Exploits of Robert Rogers, the Ranger*. Boston: John N. McClintock, and Company, 1885.

Webster, J. Clarence. *The Journal of Jeffrey Amherst, Recording the Military Career of General Amherst in America from 1758 to 1763*. Chicago: University of Chicago Press, 1931.

Weidensaul, Scott. *The First Frontier, The Forgotten History of Struggle, Savagery, and Endurance in Early America*. Boston: Houghton Mifflin Harcourt, 2013.

Whitney, David C. *The People of the Revolution, The Colonial Spirit of '76, The Lives of Members of Congress and Other Prominent Men and Women of the Period*. Chicago: J. G. Ferguson Publishing Company, 1974.

Wiencek, Henry. *An Imperfect God: George Washington, His Slaves, and the Creation of America*. New York: Farrar, Straus and Giroux, 2013.

Willcox, William B. *Portrait of a General, Sir Henry Clinton in the War of Independence*. New York: Alfred A. Knopf, 1964.

Williams, Glyn. *Voyage of Delusions, The Quest for the Northwest Passage*. New Haven: Yale University Press, 2002.

Willson, Beckles. *The Life and Letters of James Wolfe*. London: Heinemann, 1909.

Wood, Gordon S. *The Creation of the American Republic, 1776-1787*. Chapel Hill: The University of North Carolina, 1969.

Wright, Esmond. *The Fire of Liberty, The American War of Independence Seen Through the Eyes of the Men and Women, the Statesmen and Soldiers Who Fought it*. New York: St. Martin's Press, 1983.

Wulff, Matt. *Robert Rogers' Rules for the Ranging Service, An Analysis*. Westminster: Heritage Books, 2007.

Young, Alfred F. *Masquerade, The Life and Times of Deborah Sampson, Continental Soldier*. New York: Alfred A. Knopf, 2004.

Zaboly, Gary Stephen, *A True Ranger: The Life and Many Wars of Major Robert Rogers*. Garden City Park: Royal Blockhouse llc, 2004.

Zinn, Howard. *A People's History of the United States*. New York: Harper Perennial Modern Classics, 1999.

Articles

The Boston Gazette, September 12, 1785.

Ewing, William S. "An Eyewitness Account by James Furnis of the Surrender of Fort William Henry, August 1757." *New York History, The Quarterly Journal of the New York State Historical Association* (July, 1961).

Day, Gordon M. "Rogers' Raid in Indian Tradition." *New Hampshire Historical Society Annual Meeting* (18 April 1962).

"Report from London dated May 3." *New Hampshire Gazette August 15, 1775.*

"A Heavy Firing." *Pennsylvania Gazette, December 7, 1758.*

"A Vast Country." *Pennsylvania Gazette, December 14, 1758.*

The Scots Magazine, October 1775.

Letters

The American Magazine, vol. 2, no 1, Spring-Summer 1986. "Rogers to Whitworth, New York, September 29, 1775."
Amherst Papers, WO 34, vol. 115, folio 71. "Rogers to Amherst, New York, June 16, 1779."

Gage Papers, American Series, Clements Library. "Gage to Johnson, June 12, 1766."

Gage Papers, American Studies, Clements Library. "Carleton to Gage, October 13, 1767."

George Washington Papers. "Reverend Eleazar Wheelock to George Washington, December 2, 1775."

George Washington Papers. "Washington to the Continental Congress, New York, June 27, 1776."

Johnson Papers. "Benjamin Roberts to Fred Christopher Spiesmacher, Michilimackinac, August 20, 1767".

Murphy, Cullen to Members of the Amherst College Community, 26 January 2016.

New York Gazette, 28 November 1768. "Extract of a Letter from Montreal, dated October 29, 1768."

"Rogers to Washington, Medford, December 14, 1775."

"Wheelock to Washington, December 2, 1775."

Web Sites

Acts of Parliament. https://en.wikisource.org/wiki/Portal:Acts_of_the_Parliament_of_the_United_Kingdom/George_II (accessed 20 December 2016).

Central Intelligence Agency. https://www.cia.gov/news-information/featured-story-archive/2010-featured-story-archive/intelligence-throughout-history-john-honeyman.html (accessed 21 February 2017).

Heritage Books. Heritagebooks.com (accessed 11 June 2016).

Known Volunteers in Rogers' Rangers. http://www.us-roots.org/colonialamerica/rogers/roster.html (accessed 27 March 2017).

Marge Bruchac. "Reading Abenaki Traditions and European Records of Rogers' Raid." http://vermontfolklifecenter.org/childrens-books/malians-song/additional_resources/rogers_raid_facts.pdf (accessed 23 May 2016).

Military Heritage. "The Seven Years' War." http://www.militaryheritage.com/7yrswar.htm (accessed 2 April 2016).

Newsbank. Readex.com (accessed 11 June 2016).

Newspapers. Newspapers.com (accessed 11 June 2016).
Northwest Passage. http://www.cbc.ca/news/canada/british-columbia/vancouver-maritime-museum-northwest-passage-1.3709993 (accessed 20 December 2016).

Ranger Hall of Fame. http://www.rangerhalloffame.com. (accessed 26 February 2017).

Studies in Intelligence. https://www.cia.gov/library/center-for-the-study-of-intelligence/csi-publications/csi-studies/studies/vol52no2/pdf/U-%20Studies%2052-2%20-Jun08-HoneymanCase-Web.pdf (accessed 21 February 2017).

Treasure Net. http:/www.treasurenet.com (accessed 25 July 2016).

U. S. Army Ranger Association. http://www.ranger.org (accessed 19 June 2016).

Wabanaki History. http://www.nedoba.org (accessed 1 July 2016).

Washington Proclamations. http://www.slate.com/blogs/the_vault/2016/10/21/george_washington_s_1776_evacuation_proclamation_to_the_city_of_new_york.html (accessed 25 May 2017).

History. http://www.history.com/topics/seven-years-war (accessed 12 August 2016).

http://www.cbc.ca/news/canada/british-columbia/vancouver-maritime-museum-northwest-passage-1.3709993 (accessed 6 June 2017).

https://en.wikisource.org/wiki/Portal: Acts_of_the_Parliament_of_the_United_Kingdom/George_II (accessed 6 June 2017).

Films

Roberts, Kenneth. *Northwest Passage,* DVD. Directed by King Vidor. Hollywood: Metro-Goldwyn-Mayer, 1940.

Unpublished Materials

Campbell, Lieutenant George. "Diary, 8 May-20 December, 1759."

Chapter Notes

[1] Newspapers were common as they are, today, but additionally, broadsheets were used to deliver news. These were large sheets printed on one side and displayed by printers in windows and in streets.

[2] William M. Fowler, Jr. *Empires at War, The French and Indian War and the Struggle for North America, 1754-1763* (New York: Walker & Company, 2005), 42.

[3] Allan Nevins. *Ranger, The Adventurous Life of Robert Rogers of the Rangers* (Driffield: Leonaur, 2011), 20-21.

[4] Gary Stephen Zaboly. *A True Ranger: The Life and Many Wars of Major Robert Rogers* (Garden City Park: Royal Blockhouse llc, 2004), 56.

[5] Burt Garfield Loescher. *The History of Rogers' Rangers, Volume IV, The Saint Francis Raid* (San Francisco: Heritage Books, Inc., 2008), 3.

[6] John R. Cuneo. *Robert Rogers of the Rangers* (New York: Oxford University Press, 1987), 183.

[7] Zaboly, *A True Ranger: The Life and Many Wars of Major Robert Rogers*, 431.

[8] As an example, a volume of over a thousand pages of William Tryon's eighteenth century papers was downloaded in less than a minute.

[9] While Daniel Barnes' career in the War of Independence is well documented, his role as a ranger is less clear and no documents clearly establish him as a ranger with Robert Rogers.

[10] Mark C. Carnes, and John A. Garraty. *American Destiny, Narrative of a Nation, Volume I, To 1877* (New York: Pearson Education, Inc.), 2012, 49.

[11] Carnes, *American Destiny, Narrative of a Nation, Volume I, To 1877*, 53.

[12] Fowler, *Empires at War, The French and Indian War and the Struggle for North America*, 12.

[13] Ibid., 2-3.

[14] Carnes, *American Destiny, Narrative of a Nation, Volume I, To 1877*, 93.

[15] Fowler, *Empires at War, The French and Indian War and the Struggle for North America*, 2.

[16] Fowler, *Empires at War, The French and Indian War and the Struggle for North America*, 12.

Chapter 1 War in the New World

[1] There is no record from Jenkins about his thoughts about the loss of his ear or the war that followed. He did describe the loss of his ear to the British Prime Minister, Robert Walpole.

[2] Frank McLynn. *1759, The Year Britain Became Master of the World* (New York: Grove Press, 2004), 335.

[3] McLynn, *1759 The Year Britain Became Master of the World,* 334-335.

[4] Abby Marta Hemenway. *The Vermont Historical Gazetteer, A Magazine Embracing a History of Each Town, Civil, Ecclesiastical, Biographical, and Military in Three Volumes, Volume II* (Burlington: Miss A. M. Hemenway, 1867), 273-274.

[5] John F. Ross. *War on the Run, The Epic Story of Robert Rogers and the Conquest of America's First Frontier* (New York: Bantam Books, 2011), 43-44.

[6] Cuneo, *Robert Rogers of the Rangers*, 4.

[7] Cuneo, *Robert Rogers of the Rangers*, 7.

[8] Ross, *War on the Run, The Epic Story of Robert Rogers and the Conquest of America's First Frontier,* 20-21.

[9] C. E. Porter, 278. *The Military History of the State of New Hampshire from Its Settlement, in 1623, to the Rebellion, in1861* (Concord: McFarland and Jenks, 1866), 278.

[10] There are several images of Robert Rogers. None are from life, but represent what the artist thought that Rogers might have looked like. This image is from 1776.

[11] Walter R. Borneman. *The French and Indian War: Deciding The Fate of North America* (New York: Harpers Perennial, 2006), 17.

[12] Fowler, *Empires at War, The French and Indian War and the Struggle for North America*, 14.

[13] Borneman, *The French and Indian War: Deciding The Fate of North America,* 18.

[14] Borneman, *The French and Indian War: Deciding The Fate of North America,* 19.

[15] Borneman, *The French and Indian War: Deciding The Fate of North America,* 22.

[16] Fowler, *Empires at War, The French and Indian War and the Struggle for North America*, 37.

[17] Ibid.

[18] Fowler, *Empires at War, The French and Indian War and the Struggle for North America*, 42.

[19] Armand Francis Lucier. *French and Indian War Notices Abstracted from*

Colonial Newspapers, Vol. 1: 1754-1755 (Bowie: Heritage Books, 1999), 75-78.

[20] Fowler, *Empires at War, The French and Indian War and the Struggle for North America*, 42.

[21] Fowler, *Empires at War, The French and Indian War and the Struggle for North America*, 43.

[22] Ron Chernow. *Washington, A Life* (New York: Penguin Books, 2010), 42.

[23] Inscription found on many colonial paper bills. Ross, *War on the Run, The Epic Story of Robert Rogers and the Conquest of America's First Frontier*, 60.

[24] Ross, *War on the Run, The Epic Story of Robert Rogers and the Conquest of America's First Frontier*, 64.

[25] Cuneo, *Robert Rogers of the Rangers*, 12.

[26] Ross, *War on the Run, The Epic Story of Robert Rogers and the Conquest of America's First Frontier*, 66.

[27] Ibid.

[28] Ross, *War on the Run, The Epic Story of Robert Rogers and the Conquest of America's First Frontier*, 68.

[29] Borneman, *The French and Indian War: Deciding The Fate of North America*, 42.

[30] Borneman, *The French and Indian War: Deciding The Fate of North America*, 55.

[31] Ibid.

[32] Braddock was a typical British flag office who had gained rank by longevity and loyal service. He was sixty, when he landed at Hampton Roads, Virginia to start his campaign. This was an old age for one who would be campaigning in the wilderness. He needed the work, so he accepted this command.

[33] Lucier, *French and Indian War Notices Abstracted from Colonial Newspapers, Vol. 1: 1754-1755*, 247-251.

[34] Fowler, *Empires at War, The French and Indian War and the Struggle for North America* 84-85.

[35] Ross, *War on the Run, The Epic Story of Robert Rogers and the Conquest of America's First Frontier*, 79.

[36] Ross, *War on the Run, The Epic Story of Robert Rogers and the Conquest of America's First Frontier*, 121-134.

[37] Armand Francis Lucier, *French and Indian War Notices Abstracted from Colonial Newspapers, Vol. 2: 1756-1757* (Bowie: Heritage Books, 2007),

193.

[38] Brown blamed Rogers for the capture of the rangers. Actually Rogers evacuated most of his wounded but missed some (including Brown) because it was dark.

[39] Frederick Drimmer, *Captured by Indians, 15 Firsthand Accounts, 1750-1870* (New York: Dover Publications, Inc., 1961), 62-69.

[40] Lucier, *French and Indian War Notices Abstracted from Colonial Newspapers, Vol. 2: 1756-1757*, 285-286.

[41] Ian K. Steele. *Betrayals, Fort William Henry & the Massacre* (New York: Oxford University Press, 1990), 143.

[42] Lucier, *French and Indian War Notices Abstracted from Colonial Newspapers, Vol. 4: September 17, 1759 to December 30, 1760*, 98.

[43] Beckles Willson. *The Life and Letters of James Wolfe* (London: Heinemann, 1909), 365.

[44] Ross, *War on the Run, The Epic Story of Robert Rogers and the Conquest of America's First Frontier*, 149.

[45] Ross, *War on the Run, The Epic Story of Robert Rogers and the Conquest of America's First Frontier*, 163.

[46] Mary Cochane Rogers. *A Battle Fought on Snow Shoes, Rogers' Rock, Lake George, March 13, 1758* (Derry: Self-Published, 1917), 1-7.

[47] Lucier, *French and Indian War Notices Abstracted from Colonial Newspapers, Vol. 3: January 1 1758 to September 17, 1759*, 41.

[48] Cuneo, *Robert Rogers of the Rangers*, 71.

[49] Borneman, *The French and Indian War: Deciding The Fate of North America*, 130.

[50] Borneman, *The French and Indian War: Deciding The Fate of North America*, 131-139.

[51] Lucier, *French and Indian War Notices Abstracted from Colonial Newspapers, Vol. 3: January 1 1758 to September 17, 1759*, 102.

[52] Lucier, *French and Indian War Notices Abstracted from Colonial Newspapers, Vol. 3: January 1 1758 to September 17, 1759*, 129-130.

[53] Lucier, *French and Indian War Notices Abstracted from Colonial Newspapers, Vol. 3: January 1 1758 to September 17, 1759*, 131.

[54] Ross, *War on the Run, The Epic Story of Robert Rogers and the Conquest of America's First Frontier*, 208-212.

[55] Steele, *Betrayals, Fort William Henry & the Massacre*, 111-112.

[56] Steele, *Betrayals, Fort William Henry & the Massacre*, 126.

[57] Steele, *Betrayals, Fort William Henry & the Massacre*, 127.

[58] Armand Francis Lucier, *French and Indian War Notices Abstracted from*

Colonial Newspapers, Vol. 4: September 17, 1759 to December 30, 1760 (Bowie: Heritage Books, 2007), 67.

Chapter 2 – The Saint Francis Raid
[1] Francis Parkman. *Montcalm and Wolfe* (New York: The American Past, 1983), 264.
[2] Lucier, *French and Indian War Notices Abstracted from Colonial Newspapers, Vol. 3: January 1 1758 to September 17, 1759*, 333.
[3] Sephen Brumwell. *White Devil, A True Story of War, Savagery, and Vengeance in Colonial America* (Boston: DaCapo Press, 2005) 146-147.
[4] Fowler, *Empires at War, The French and Indian War and the Struggle for North America*, 217.
[5] Robert Rogers. *Journals of Robert Rogers of the Rangers, The Exploits of Rogers & the Rangers in his Own Words During 1755-1761 in the French & Indian War.* (Leonaur, Ltd., 2005), 116.
[6] Lucier, *French and Indian War Notices Abstracted from Colonial Newspapers, Vol. 4: September 17, 1759 to December 30, 1760*, 115-116.
[7] McLynn, *1759 The Year Britain Became Master of the World*, 328-330.
[8] McLynn, *1759 The Year Britain Became Master of the World*, 330.
[9] Lucier, *French and Indian War Notices Abstracted from Colonial Newspapers, Vol. 4: September 17, 1759 to December 30, 1760*, 165.
[10] Loescher, *The History of Rogers' Rangers, Volume IV, The Saint Francis Raid*, 3.
[11] Loescher, *The History of Rogers' Rangers, Volume IV, The Saint Francis Raid*, 4.
[1] McLynn, *1759 The Year Britain Became Master of the World*, 341.
[2] Marge Bruchac. *Malian's Song* (Hanover: University Press of New England, 2005), 2.
[3] McLynn, *1759 The Year Britain Became Master of the World*, 335; Loescher, *The History of Rogers' Rangers, Volume IV, The Saint Francis Raid*, 33.
[4] Some historians dispute the presence of Mohawks on the expedition (see Loescher, *The History of Rogers' Rangers, Volume IV, The Saint Francis Raid*, 3.), but there is ample evidence that they went along on the expedition, at least at its start.
[5] McLynn, *1759 The Year Britain Became Master of the World*, 337.
[6] Ibid.
[7] Loescher, *The History of Rogers' Rangers, Volume IV, The Saint Francis Raid*, 14.

[8] Loescher, *The History of Rogers' Rangers, Volume IV, The Saint Francis Raid*, 15.
[9] This was portrayed in the film *Northwest Passage*.
[10] Loescher, *The History of Rogers' Rangers, Volume IV, The Saint Francis Raid*, 126.
[11] Lucier, *French and Indian War Notices Abstracted from Colonial Newspapers, Vol. 4: September 17, 1759 to December 30, 1760*, 13.
[12] McLynn, *1759 The Year Britain Became Master of the World*, 337.
[13] Ibid.
[14] Loescher, *The History of Rogers' Rangers, Volume IV, The Saint Francis Raid*, 17.
[15] Loescher, *The History of Rogers' Rangers, Volume IV, The Saint Francis Raid*, 20-21.
[16] Bruchac, *Malian's Song*, 4.
[17] McLynn, *1759 The Year Britain Became Master of the World*, 338.
[18] Ibid.
[19] Loescher, *The History of Rogers' Rangers, Volume IV, The Saint Francis Raid*, 21.
[20] McLynn, *1759 The Year Britain Became Master of the World*, 339.
[21] McLynn, *1759 The Year Britain Became Master of the World*, 339-341.
[22] Bruchac, *Malian's Song*, 4.
[23] Loescher, *The History of Rogers' Rangers, Volume IV, The Saint Francis Raid*, 30.
[24] McLynn, *1759 The Year Britain Became Master of the World*, 342.
[25] Gordon M. Day. "Rogers' Raid in Indian Tradition." *New Hampshire Historical Society Annual Meeting* (18 April 1962), 15-16 . McLynn was convinced that it was a wedding celebration.
[26] McLynn, *1759 The Year Britain Became Master of the World*, 341.
[27] Abenaki oral tradition identifies him as a Mohegan scout named Samadagwis who was later killed by Abenaki who were not aware of his effort to save their camp. Tradition indicates that he asked to be baptized before he was executed, but there is no record indicating that he was.
[28] Day, *New Hampshire Historical Society Annual Meeting*, 9.
[29] McLynn, *1759 The Year Britain Became Master of the World*, 341-342.
[30] Bruchac, *Malian's Song*, 9.
[31] Day, *New Hampshire Historical Society Annual Meeting*, 7.
[32] Loescher, *The History of Rogers' Rangers, Volume IV, The Saint Francis Raid*, 42.
[33] McLynn, *1759 The Year Britain Became Master of the World*, 343.

[34] The Abenaki survivors would not have had any difficulty in getting food given the proximity of French garrisons that could supply them and the fact that the French were converging on Saint Francis to deal with the Rangers.

[35] Loescher, *The History of Rogers' Rangers, Volume IV, The Saint Francis Raid*, 51.

[36] Day, *New Hampshire Historical Society Annual Meeting*, 5-7.

[37] Most records identify him only as "Barnes," but McLynn indicates he was George Barnes. Other records indicate that it was Daniel Barnes, Jr., from Marlborough, Massachusetts.

[38] The numbers of French and their Indian allies circulating near Saint Francis are somewhat confused in the various reports. It appears that a total of 400 were initially sent to Missisquoi Bay (reinforced by 300 more after the raid).

[39] Bruchac, *Malian's Song*, 5.

[40] Loescher, *The History of Rogers' Rangers, Volume IV, The Saint Francis Raid*, 39.

[41] McLynn, *1759 The Year Britain Became Master of the World*, 344.

[42] Brumwell, *White Devil, A True Story of War, Savagery, and Vengeance in Colonial America*, 203.

[43] McLynn, *1759 The Year Britain Became Master of the World*, 345.

[44] Loescher, *The History of Rogers' Rangers, Volume IV, The Saint Francis Raid*, 46.

[45] Loescher, *The History of Rogers' Rangers, Volume IV, The Saint Francis Raid*.

[46] Loescher, *The History of Rogers' Rangers, Volume IV, The Saint Francis Raid*, 56-57.

[47] Loescher, *The History of Rogers' Rangers, Volume IV, The Saint Francis Raid*, 75.

[48] Campbell, October 22-November 4, 1759 entries.

[49] Loescher, *The History of Rogers' Rangers, Volume IV, The Saint Francis Raid*, 76-78.

[50] Loescher, *The History of Rogers' Rangers, Volume IV, The Saint Francis Raid*, 58-59.

[51] Loescher, *The History of Rogers' Rangers, Volume IV, The Saint Francis Raid*, 61-63.

[52] Loescher, *The History of Rogers' Rangers, Volume IV, The Saint Francis Raid*, 80-83.

[53] Loescher, *The History of Rogers' Rangers, Volume IV, The Saint Francis Raid*, 101-104.
[54] Loescher, *The History of Rogers' Rangers, Volume IV, The Saint Francis Raid*, 97-99.
[55] Loescher, *The History of Rogers' Rangers, Volume IV, The Saint Francis Raid*, 78-80.
[56] McLynn, *1759 The Year Britain Became Master of the World*, 347-348.
[57] Brumwell, *White Devil, A True Story of War, Savagery, and Vengeance in Colonial America*, 223.
[58] McLynn, *1759 The Year Britain Became Master of the World*, 348.
[59] McLynn, *1759 The Year Britain Became Master of the World*, 348-350.
[60] Also, the French reported that women and children had been killed.
[61] Bishop de Pontbriand, Montreal, letter to a Bishop of France, November 5, 1759, *Documents Relative to the Colonial History of the State of New York, Volume X*, 1058.
[62] It was Father Roubaud who had detained Quinton Kennedy and turned him over to French authorities.
[63] Thomas Mante. *The History of the Late War in North-America, and the Islands of the West-Indies, including the Campaigns of MDCCLXIII and MDCCLXIV Against His Majesty's Indian Enemies* (London: W. Strahan, and T. Cadell in the Strand, 1772), 223-224.
[64] This event is portrayed in gory detail in the film *Northwest Passage*. The film is based upon the Kenneth Roberts' novel of the same name which is considered fiction. What most do not know is that Roberts was a thorough researcher and his "fiction" is in fact carefully written history with a fictional dialog added in. He published a Volume II to his *Northwest Passage* that includes many references including personal accounts of Rangers on the Saint Francis Raid.
[65] Loescher, *The History of Rogers' Rangers, Volume IV, The Saint Francis Raid*, 62-64.
[66] Brumwell, *White Devil, A True Story of War, Savagery, and Vengeance in Colonial America*, 229-230.
[67] Robert Kirkwood. *Through So Many Dangers: The Memoirs and Adventures of Robert Kirk, Late of the Royal Highland Regiment* (Fleischmanns: Purple Mountain Press, 2004), 5-41.
[68] Loescher, *The History of Rogers' Rangers, Volume IV, The Saint Francis Raid*, 43-44.
[69] Loescher, *The History of Rogers' Rangers, Volume IV, The Saint Francis Raid*, 69-76.

[70] Loescher, *The History of Rogers' Rangers, Volume IV, The Saint Francis Raid*, 62-64.
[71] Loescher, *The History of Rogers' Rangers, Volume IV, The Saint Francis Raid*, 80-83.
[72] Bruchac, *Malian's Song*, 6.
[73] Loescher, *The History of Rogers' Rangers, Volume IV, The Saint Francis Raid*, 83.
[74] Brumwell, *White Devil, A True Story of War, Savagery, and Vengeance in Colonial America*, 216.
[75] Loescher, *The History of Rogers' Rangers, Volume IV, The Saint Francis Raid*, 111-113.
[76] Lucier, *French and Indian War Notices Abstracted from Colonial Newspapers, Vol. 4: September 17, 1759 to December 30, 1760*. 64-67.

Chapter 3 – On to Montreal

[1] Borneman, *The French and Indian War: Deciding The Fate of North America*, 234.
[2] Game seemed to disappear and the winter was exceptionally cold. This fact was mentioned in the narrative of the Wait Party.
[3] Borneman, *The French and Indian War: Deciding The Fate of North America*, 234
[4] J. C. Long. *Lord Jeffery Amherst, A Soldier of the King* (New York: The MacMillian Company, 1933), 123-127.
[5] Loescher, *Genesis Rogers Rangers, The First Green Berets, Volume II*, 68-69.
[6] Loescher, *Genesis Rogers Rangers, The First Green Berets, Volume II*, 70.
[7] Lucier, *French and Indian War Notices Abstracted from Colonial Newspapers, Vol. 4: September 17, 1759 to December 30, 1760*, 98.
[8] Like most field soldiers, Rogers was not big on paperwork and as was the custom of the day, he had paid many of his Ranger costs with his own funds. It was now time to seek reimbursement and he was faced with an awesome British bureaucracy that wanted every penny justified. General Gage, his nemesis, was the ultimate bureaucrat and complained to Amherst ". . . .he was told that people take Receipts in Payment for Goods, & it is not usual to leave them behind in strange Places" (Brumwell, *White Devil, A True Story of War, Savagery, and Vengeance in Colonial America*, 250). Rogers continued to search for his receipts and would be partially successful in obtaining reimbursement from the Crown.

[9] Ross, *War on the Run, The Epic Story of Robert Rogers and the Conquest of America's First Frontier*, 271-272.
[10] Lucier, *French and Indian War Notices Abstracted from Colonial Newspapers, Vol. 4: September 17, 1759 to December 30, 1760*, 120.
[11] Brumwell, *White Devil, A True Story of War, Savagery, and Vengeance in Colonial America*, 250-251.
[12] Brumwell, *White Devil, A True Story of War, Savagery, and Vengeance in Colonial America*, 251.
[13] Borneman, *The French and Indian War: Deciding The Fate of North America*, 243.
[14] Long, *Lord Jeffery Amherst, A Soldier of the King*, 127.
[15] Loescher, *Genesis Rogers Rangers, The First Green Berets, Volume II*, 86-87.
[16] Loescher, *Genesis Rogers Rangers, The First Green Berets, Volume II*, 92.
[17] Loescher, *Genesis Rogers Rangers, The First Green Berets, Volume II*, 96-98.
[18] Loescher, *Genesis Rogers Rangers, The First Green Berets, Volume II*, 99-102.
[19] Lucier, *French and Indian War Notices Abstracted from Colonial Newspapers, Vol. 4: September 17, 1759 to December 30, 1760*, 173.
[20] Borneman, *The French and Indian War: Deciding The Fate of North America*, 248.
[21] Borneman, *The French and Indian War: Deciding The Fate of North America*, 250.
[22] Borneman, *The French and Indian War: Deciding The Fate of North America*, 273.
[23] John R. Alden. *George Washington, a Biography* (Norwalk: Easton Press, 1993), 147.
[24] David Hackett Fischer. *Washington's Crossing* (New York: Oxford University Press, Inc., 2004), 15-16; Joseph J. Ellis. *His Excellency, George Washington* (New York: Vintage Books, 2004), 38.
[25] John E. Ferling. *Setting the World Ablaze: Washington, Adams, Jefferson, and the American Revolution* (New York: Oxford University Press, 2000), 33-34.

Chapter 4 – Closing in
[1] Ross, *War on the Run, The Epic Story of Robert Rogers and the Conquest of America's First Frontier*, 291.

[2] Ross, *War on the Run, The Epic Story of Robert Rogers and the Conquest of America's First Frontier*, 287-288.
[3] Lucier, *French and Indian War Notices Abstracted from Colonial Newspapers, Vol. 4: September 17, 1759 to December 30, 1760*, 264.
[4] Ross, *War on the Run, The Epic Story of Robert Rogers and the Conquest of America's First Frontier*, 300.
[5] Ibid.
[6] Ross, *War on the Run, The Epic Story of Robert Rogers and the Conquest of America's First Frontier*, 307.
[7] Ross, *War on the Run, The Epic Story of Robert Rogers and the Conquest of America's First Frontier*, 309.
[8] Armand Francis Lucier. *French and Indian War Notices Abstracted from Colonial Newspapers, Vol. 5: January 1, 1761 to January 17, 1763* (Bowie: Heritage Books, 2007), 20.
[9] Ross, *War on the Run, The Epic Story of Robert Rogers and the Conquest of America's First Frontier*, 309-310.
[10] Ross, *War on the Run, The Epic Story of Robert Rogers and the Conquest of America's First Frontier*, 313.
[11] Zaboly, *A True Ranger: The Life and Many Wars of Major Robert Rogers*, 323.
[12] Ross, *War on the Run, The Epic Story of Robert Rogers and the Conquest of America's First Frontier*, 315.
[13] Ross, *War on the Run, The Epic Story of Robert Rogers and the Conquest of America's First Frontier*, 316.
[14] Ellis, *His Excellency, George Washington*, 31.
[15] This route follows the path of the modern Pennsylvania Turnpike.
[16] Ellis, *His Excellency, George Washington His Excellency, George Washington*, 25.
[17] Ellis, *His Excellency, George Washington*, 25-27.
[18] Ellis, *His Excellency, George Washington*, 32.
[19] Chernow, *Washington: A Life*, 90.
[20] Borneman, *The French and Indian War: Deciding The Fate of North America*, 158-159.
[21] "A Heavy Firing": *Pennsylvania Gazette*, December 7, 1758; "A Vast Country": *Pennsylvania Gazette*, December 14, 1758.
[22] Borneman, *The French and Indian War: Deciding The Fate of North America*, 163.

[23] The civilized tribes were composed of the five Native American nations—the Cherokee, Chickasaw, Choctaw, Creek (Muscogee), and Seminole.

[24] Duane H. King. *The Memoirs of Lt. Henry Timberlake: The Story of a Soldier, Adventurer, and Emissary to the Cherokees, 1756-1765* (Cherokee: Museum of the Cherokee Indian Press, 2007), xvii-xix.

[25] Brumwell, *White Devil, A True Story of War, Savagery, and Vengeance in Colonial America,* 265.

[26] Borneman, *The French and Indian War: Deciding The Fate of North America,* 256-260.

[27] Zaboly, *A True Ranger: The Life and Many Wars of Major Robert Rogers,* 325.

[28] Zaboly, *A True Ranger: The Life and Many Wars of Major Robert Rogers,* 334.

Chapter 5 – The Uneasy Peace

[1] Allan R. Millett, Peter Maslowski, and William B. Feis. *For the Common Defense, A Military History of the United States from 1607 to 2012* (New York: Free Press, 2012), 44.

[2] Robert Navarre. "The Journal of Pontiac's Conspiracy," in Milo Milton Quaife, *The Siege of Detroit in 1763: The Journal of Pontiac's Conspiracy and John Rutherford's Narrative of a Captivity* (Chicago: Lakeside Press, 1958), 22.

[3] This Indian nation was also called Ottawa or Odaawaa. It is said to mean traders.

[4] Zaboly, *A True Ranger: The Life and Many Wars of Major Robert Rogers,* 339.

[5] Zaboly, *A True Ranger: The Life and Many Wars of Major Robert Rogers,* 343.

[6] Rogers, *Ponteach,* 247.

[7] Long, *Lord Jeffery Amherst, A Soldier of the King* 187.

[8] Ibid.

[9] Cullen Murphy, Letter, 26 January 2016 to Members of the Amherst College Community.

[10] Zaboly, *A True Ranger: The Life and Many Wars of Major Robert Rogers,* 348.

[11] Zaboly, *A True Ranger: The Life and Many Wars of Major Robert Rogers,* 355.

[12] Zaboly, *A True Ranger: The Life and Many Wars of Major Robert Rogers,* 358.

[13] Zaboly, *A True Ranger: The Life and Many Wars of Major Robert Rogers*, 359.
[14] Zaboly, *A True Ranger: The Life and Many Wars of Major Robert Rogers*, 360.
[15] Book Title of Lawrence J. Burpee. *Searching for the Western Sea, The Story of the Exploration of North Western America* (New York: Musson Book Company, 1908).
[16] http://www.cbc.ca/news/canada/british-columbia/vancouver-maritime-museum-northwest-passage-1.3709993
[17] https://en.wikisource.org/wiki/Portal: Acts_of_the_Parliament_of_the_United_Kingdom/George_II
[18] Ross, *War on the Run, The Epic Story of Robert Rogers and the Conquest of America's First Frontier*, 353.
[19] Norman Gelb. *Jonathan Carver's Travels Through America, 1766-1768, An Eighteen-Century Explorer's Account of Uncharted America.* (New York: John Wiley & Sons, Inc., 1993), 13.
[20] Zaboly, *A True Ranger: The Life and Many Wars of Major Robert Rogers*, 369.
[21] Cuneo, *Robert Rogers of the Rangers*, 147-148.
[22] Cuneo, *Robert Rogers of the Rangers*, 180.
[23] Cuneo, *Robert Rogers of the Rangers*, 183.
[24] Zaboly, *A True Ranger: The Life and Many Wars of Major Robert Rogers*, 370.
[25] Zaboly, *A True Ranger: The Life and Many Wars of Major Robert Rogers*, 371
[26] Cuneo, *Robert Rogers of the Rangers*, 168.
[27] Zaboly, *A True Ranger: The Life and Many Wars of Major Robert Rogers*, 371-372.
[28] Gage to Johnson, June 12, 1766, Gage Papers, American Series, Clements Library.
[29] Zaboly, *A True Ranger: The Life and Many Wars of Major Robert Rogers*, 377.
[30] Ibid.
[31] Gelb, *Jonathan Carver's Travels Through America, 1766-1768, An Eighteen-Century Explorer's Account of Uncharted America*, 17.
[32] Gelb, *Jonathan Carver's Travels Through America, 1766-1768, An Eighteen-Century Explorer's Account of Uncharted America*, 20.
[33] Zaboly, *A True Ranger: The Life and Many Wars of Major Robert Rogers*, 377.

[34] Zaboly, *A True Ranger: The Life and Many Wars of Major Robert Rogers*, 140.

[35] Loescher, *The History of Rogers Rangers, Volume III, Officers and Non-Commissioned Officers*, 20-21.

[36] Burpee, *Searching for the Western Sea, The Story of the Exploration of North Western America*, 289-290.

[37] Zaboly, *A True Ranger: The Life and Many Wars of Major Robert Rogers*, 385.

[38] Cuneo, *Robert Rogers of the Rangers*, 218-219.

[39] Zaboly, *A True Ranger: The Life and Many Wars of Major Robert Rogers*, 417

[40] Zaboly, *A True Ranger: The Life and Many Wars of Major Robert Rogers*, 375.

[41] Daniel Claus to Johnson, Montreal, October 16, 1766 in Hough, Journals of Major Robert Rogers, note, 228.

[42] These included the Sioux, Chippewa, Fox, Sauk, Winnebagos and other western tribes. Some had traveled over 700 miles to attend the council

[43] Zaboly, *A True Ranger: The Life and Many Wars of Major Robert Rogers*, 386.

[44] Ibid.

[45] Zaboly, *A True Ranger: The Life and Many Wars of Major Robert Rogers*, 387.

[46] Zaboly, *A True Ranger: The Life and Many Wars of Major Robert Rogers*, 393.

[47] Ibid.

[48] Zaboly, *A True Ranger: The Life and Many Wars of Major Robert Rogers*, 392-393.

[49] Zaboly, *A True Ranger: The Life and Many Wars of Major Robert Rogers*, 382.

[50] Zaboly, *A True Ranger: The Life and Many Wars of Major Robert Rogers*, 389.

[51] Zaboly, *A True Ranger: The Life and Many Wars of Major Robert Rogers*, 390.

[52] Zaboly, *A True Ranger: The Life and Many Wars of Major Robert Rogers*, 391.

[53] "Benjamin Roberts to Fred Christopher Spiesmacher," Michilimackinac, August 20, 1767, Johnson Papers, V, 629-630.

[54] Zaboly, *A True Ranger: The Life and Many Wars of Major Robert Rogers*, 394

[55] Ibid.
[56] Carleton would later command British forces in America at the end of the War of Independence.
[57] Carleton to Gage, October 13, 1767, Gage Papers, American Studies, Clements Library.
[58] Cuneo, *Robert Rogers of the Rangers,* 227.
[59] Rogers to Elizabeth, 1768 (undated), Rogers/Roche Papers, Clemens Library.
[60] "Proceedings of a General Court Martial held in the City of Montreal," *Treason?,* 9-10.
[61] "Extract of a Letter from Montreal, dated October 29, 1768," New York Gazette, 28 November 1768.
[62] Zaboly, *A True Ranger: The Life and Many Wars of Major Robert Rogers,* 411.
[63] Cuneo, *Robert Rogers of the Rangers,* 245-246.
[64] Ibid.
[65] Zaboly, *A True Ranger: The Life and Many Wars of Major Robert Rogers,* 411.
[66] Nevins, *Ranger, The Adventurous Life of Robert Rogers of the Rangers,* 119.
[67] Cuneo, *Robert Rogers of the Rangers,* 246-247.
[68] Cuneo, *Robert Rogers of the Rangers,* 250.
[69] Cuneo, *Robert Rogers of the Rangers,* 251-252.
[70] Cuneo, *Robert Rogers of the Rangers,* 254-255.

Chapter 6 – War of Independence and After
[1] Alden, *George Washington, a Biography,* 101.
[2] Willard Sterne Randall. *George Washington: A Life* (New York: Henry Holt & Company, 1997), 262.
[3] John Stark, Maj. Gen. *Reminiscences of the French War Containing Rogers' Expeditions with the New England Rangers under his Command as Published in London in 1765; with Notes and Illustrations. To which is Added an Account of the Life and Military Services of Maj. Gen. John Stark; with Notices and Anecdotes of Other Officers Distinguished in the French and Revolutionary Wars* (Concord: Luther Roby), 1831.
[4] Zaboly, *A True Ranger: The Life and Many Wars of Major Robert Rogers,* 457.
[5] Zaboly, *A True Ranger: The Life and Many Wars of Major Robert Rogers,* 430.
[6] Ibid.

[7] *Diary of John Adams*, vol. 2, 1771-1781, edited by L. H. Butterfield, Cambridge, Massachusetts, 1962, entry of September 21, 1775, 177.
[8] Rogers to Whitworth (New York, September 29, 1775, *The American Magazine*, vol. 2, no 1, Spring-Summer 1986), 24.
[9] Pennsylvania Committee of Safety Minutes, Friday, September 23, 1775 in Peter Force, editor, *American Archives*, vol. 4, Series 3, 1775, 866.
[10] Report from London dated May 3, in *New-Hampshire Gazette* August 15, 1775.
[11] *The Scots Magazine*, October 1775, 553.
[12] *The Scots Magazine*, October 1775, 553.
[13] Zaboly, *A True Ranger: The Life and Many Wars of Major Robert Rogers*, 433.
[14] Ibid.
[15] Ibid.
[16] Ibid.
[17] Ibid.
[18] *Historical Memoirs, From March 16, 1763 to July 25, 1778, of William Smith*, ed. William H. W. Sabine, New York Times (Arno Press, 1969), Vol. II, entry of early 1776, 36.
[19] Zaboly, *A True Ranger: The Life and Many Wars of Major Robert Rogers*, 434.
[20] Reverend Eleazar Wheelock to George Washington, December 2, 1775, George Washington Papers.
[21] Zaboly, *A True Ranger: The Life and Many Wars of Major Robert Rogers*, 437.
[22] A quote by General John Burgoyne to Lord Rochfort . . . ." a rabble in arms flushed with success and insolence."
[23] Zaboly, *A True Ranger: The Life and Many Wars of Major Robert Rogers*, 435.
[24] Zaboly, *A True Ranger: The Life and Many Wars of Major Robert Rogers*, 435-436.
[25] Zaboly, *A True Ranger: The Life and Many Wars of Major Robert Rogers*, 436.
[26] The location was actually Breeds' Hill.
[27] John C. Dann. *The Revolution Remembered, Eyewitness Accounts of the War for Independence* (Chicago: University of Chicago Press, 1980), 4.
[28] Caleb Stark. *Memoir and Official Correspondence of John Stark* (Concord: G. Parker Lyon, 1860), 346.

[29] Zaboly, *A True Ranger: The Life and Many Wars of Major Robert Rogers*, 436.
[30] Rogers to Washington, Medford, December 14, 1775.
[31] Wheelock to Washington, December 2, 1775.
[32] Zaboly, *A True Ranger: The Life and Many Wars of Major Robert Rogers*, 437.
[33] Ibid.
[34] Ibid.
[35] Cuneo, *Robert Rogers of the Rangers,* 261
[36] Zaboly, *A True Ranger: The Life and Many Wars of Major Robert Rogers*, 439.
[37] Ibid.
[38] Zaboly, *A True Ranger: The Life and Many Wars of Major Robert Rogers*, 439.
[39] Langdon to Bartlett, Portsmouth, June 3, 1776, *The Papers of Josiah Bartlett*, edited by Frank C. Mevers, University Press of New England, Hanover, New Hampshire, 1979, 68.
[40] Chernow, *Washington, A Life,* 232.
[41] Chernow, *Washington, A Life,* 233.
[42] Armand Francis Lucier, *Newspaper Datelines of the American Revolution, Vol. 3* (Westminster: Heritage Books, 2004), 111.
[43] William Tryon. *The Correspondence of William Tryon and Other Selected Papers, Volume II, 1768-1818.* (Raleigh: Division of Archives and History, Department of Cultural Resources, 1981), 862.
[44] Bruce Blevin, Jr. *Under Guns, New York: 1775-1776* (New York: Harper & Row, Publishers, 1972), 143.
[45] Tryon, 862.
[46] Zaboly, *A True Ranger: The Life and Many Wars of Major Robert Rogers*, 443.
[47] Zaboly, *A True Ranger: The Life and Many Wars of Major Robert Rogers*, 440.
[48] Washington to the Continental Congress, New York, June 27, 1776, George Washington Papers.
[49] Zaboly, *A True Ranger: The Life and Many Wars of Major Robert Rogers*, 443.
[50] Ibid.
[51] William Whipple to John Langdon, Philadelphia, July 1, 1776, *Letters of Delegates to Congress, Vol. 4*, Library of Congress.

[52] Paul H. Smith. *Letters of Delegates To Congress, 1774-1789, Volume 4* (Washington: Library of Congress, 1979) 333.
[53] Smith, *Letters of Delegates To Congress, 1774-1789, Volume 4*, 419-420.
[54] Zaboly, *A True Ranger: The Life and Many Wars of Major Robert Rogers*, 444
[55] Ibid.
[56] Zaboly, *A True Ranger: The Life and Many Wars of Major Robert Rogers*, 445.
[57] Loescher. Genesis, 168-169.
[58] Zaboly, *A True Ranger: The Life and Many Wars of Major Robert Rogers*, 461.
[59] Chernow, *Washington, A Life*, 229.
[60] Smith, *Letters of Delegates To Congress, 1774-1789, Volume 4*, 63-64.
[61] Bliven, 331. Eisenhower's D-Day proclamation on 6 June 1944 bears a striking resemblance to Washington's.
[62] Zaboly, *A True Ranger: The Life and Many Wars of Major Robert Rogers*, 444.
[63] Lucier, *Newspaper Datelines of the American Revolution, Vol. 3*, 133.
[64] Chernow, *Washington, A Life*, 244-245.
[65] http://www.slate.com/blogs/the_vault/2016/10/21/george_washington_s_1776_evacuation_proclamation_to_the_city_of_new_york.html
[66] Smith, *Letters of Delegates To Congress, 1774-1789, Volume 4*, 465-66.
[67] Chernow, *Washington, A Life*, 253.
[68] Chernow, *Washington, A Life*, 249-250.
[69] Zaboly, *A True Ranger: The Life and Many Wars of Major Robert Rogers*, 446.
[70] Lucier, *Newspaper Datelines of the American Revolution, Vol. 3*, 261-263.
[71] A kind lady in Newburgh, New York sent the author an original copy of Joseph Plumb Martin's book that was published in 1830. This copy includes missing pages not found in one other original found in the 1950's.
[72] Joseph Plumb Martin. *Narrative of Some of the Adventures, Dangers and Sufferings of a Revolutionary Soldier; Interspersed with Anecdotes of Incidents that Occurred within his Own Observation Written by Himself* (Hallowell: Glazier, Masters & Company, 1830), 44.

[73] Martin, *Narrative of Some of the Adventures, Dangers and Sufferings of a Revolutionary Soldier; Interspersed with Anecdotes of Incidents that Occurred within his Own Observation Written by Himself,* 21-27.

[74] Hutson, James (July–August 2003). *"Nathan Hale Revisited— A Tory's Account of the Arrest of the First American Spy".* Information Bulletin. The Library of Congress.

[75] M. William Phelps. *The Life and Death of America's First Spy, Nathan Hale* (New York: Thomas Dunne Books, 2008), 170-193.

[76] Frederick Mackenzie. The famous quote attributed to Hale: "I only regret that I have but one life . . . ." is not mentioned by Mackenzie, but surely would have been if it had been actually stated by Hale. Based upon this and other sources, it appears that this famous quote is fiction. Mackenzie, Frederick. *Diary of Frederick Mackenzie.* (Cambridge: Harvard University Press, 1930), 61-62.

[77] Zaboly, *A True Ranger: The Life and Many Wars of Major Robert Rogers,* 450.

[78] Martin, *Narrative of Some of the Adventures, Dangers and Sufferings of a Revolutionary Soldier; Interspersed with Anecdotes of Incidents that Occurred within his Own Observation Written by Himself,* 44-49.

[79] Fischer, *Washington's Crossing,* 423

[80] Alexander Rose. *Washington's Spies, The Story of America's First Spy Ring* (New York: Random House, 2006), 42.

[81] Chernow, *Washington, A Life,* 272.

[82] Chernow, *Washington, A Life,* 275

[83] Fischer, *Washington's Crossing,* 247-255.

[84] Zaboly, *A True Ranger: The Life and Many Wars of Major Robert Rogers,* 453.

[85] James Thomas Flexner. *Washington, The Indispensable Man* (Boston: Little, Brown and Company, 1969) 96-97.

[86] Chernow, *Washington, A Life,* 276-284.

[87] Ellis, *His Excellency, George Washington,* 98-99.

[88] Zaboly, *A True Ranger: The Life and Many Wars of Major Robert Rogers,* 460.

[89] Ibid.

[90] Zaboly, *A True Ranger: The Life and Many Wars of Major Robert Rogers,* 461.

[91] Zaboly, *A True Ranger: The Life and Many Wars of Major Robert Rogers,* 462.

[92] *Laws of New Hampshire, Vol. 4: Revolutionary War Period, 1776-1784*, edited by Henry Harrison Metcalf, Bristol, New Hampshire, 1916, 177-180.
[93] Rogers to Amherst, New York, June 16, 1779, Amherst Papers, WO 34, vol. 115, folio 71.
[94] Rogers to Amherst, Halifax, September 11, 1779, Amherst Papers, vol. 155, folio 181.
[95] Zaboly, *A True Ranger: The Life and Many Wars of Major Robert Rogers*, 466
[96] Zaboly, *A True Ranger: The Life and Many Wars of Major Robert Rogers*, 468.
[97] *The Boston Gazette*, September 12, 1785.

Epilogue
[1] Robert Black. *Ranger Dawn: the American Ranger from the Colonial Period to the Mexican War*. (Pennsylvania: Stackpole Books, 2009), 7-8.
[2] The McGuire Rig was suspended from a helicopter and used to extract soldiers from areas without a suitable pick-up zone. It was simple, inexpensive, and effective. It was fashioned from a 2-inch wide, long nylon cargo tie-down strap with a quick-fit buckle on one end.
[3] Michael A. Eggleston. *Dak To and the Border Battles of Vietnam, 1967-1968* (Jefferson: McFarland & Company, Inc., Publishers, 2017), 60-62.
[4] Marty, Skovlund, Jr. *Violence of Action. The Untold Stories of the 75th Ranger Regiment in the War on Terror* (Colorado Springs: Blackside Concepts, 2014), 317-319.
[5] Flexner, *Washington, The Indispensable Man*, 402.
[6] Zaboly, *A True Ranger: The Life and Many Wars of Major Robert Rogers*, 473.
[7] Joseph Burbeen Walker *Life and Exploits of Robert Rogers, the Ranger* (Boston: John N. McClintock, and Company, 1885), 1.
[8] Zaboly, *A True Ranger: The Life and Many Wars of Major Robert Rogers*, 473.

Biographical Sketches
[1] Zaboly, *A True Ranger: The Life and Many Wars of Major Robert Rogers*, 445.

Appendix A, Names, Acronyms and Terms
[1] Bruchac, *Malian's Song*, 10.

Appendix B, Chronology
[1] Ross, *War on the Run, The Epic Story of Robert Rogers and the Conquest of America's First Frontier*, xxiii-xxiv.

Appendix C, Rogers' Rules of Ranging
[1] Ross, *War on the Run, The Epic Story of Robert Rogers and the Conquest of America's First Frontier,* 145.

Appendix D, The Ranger Roster
[1] Names below are from Loescher's listing of Rangers in his volume III, History of Rogers's Rangers. Loescher's list includes only officers and non-commissioned officers. Private soldiers and others listed below were extracted from Loescher's Volume IV as well as journals written during the French and Indian War. Many other sources provided names of Rangers not found in Loescher's listings and these have been added. Most important of these is Mary Cochrane Rogers' book, *A Battle Fought on Snow Shoes.*

[2] Those listed as On Saint Francis Raid are identified in Marge Bruchac's *Reading Abenaki Traditions* as well as other sources.

[3] Captain William Stark while traveling came across a Frenchman abusing a wolf-dog. Stark thrashed the Frenchman for abusing the animal and came away with the dog who was happy to have a new master. Stark placed him on his company roster as a sergeant drawing pay and rations for that rank. It became a very loyal dog.

[4] McLynn, *1759 The Year Britain Became Master of the World,* 339.

Index

Bold index page numbers in italics indicate pages with photographs or maps.

"

"Declaration of the thirteen united States of America," 226

7

75th Ranger Regiment, 275

A

Abenaki, 11, 12, 20, 26, 27, 28, 29, 64, 66, 85, 91, 93, 95, 96, 98, 102, 103, 105, 106, 107, 109, 110, 112, 113, 114, 115, 116, 118, 119, 121, 122, 123, 125, 128, 143, 284, 286, 287, 289, 297, 303, 308, 369, 370
Abercromby, James, 66, 69, 75, 76, *77*, 78, 283
Adams, John, 203, 205, 206, 376
Afghanistan, 275, 276, 277
Ainsse, Joseph-Louis, 194, 283
Alabama, 158, 306
Albany, 51, 55, 65, 67, 74, 80, 82, 87, 93, 101, 136, 137, 138, 141, 142, 219, 304
Alexander, William, See Lord Stirling
Algonquin, 30
Allegheny, 34, 37, 157, 304, 306
Allegheny River, 34
America, 9, 16, 17, 43, 64, 73, 110, 134, 138, 139, 151, 161, 164, 165, 166, 170, 183, 193, 198, 200, 204, 206, 207, 208, 209, 214, 220, 225, 228, 230, 236, 245, 264, 265, 266, 282, 283, 285, 287, 289, 291, 293, 295, 299, 308, 311, 313, 314, 315, 316
American Colonies, 246
Amherst, Jeffrey, 78, *79*, 85, 89, 91, 92, 93, 94, 98, 100, 104, 107, 108, 109, 121, 122, 128, 134, 135, 136, 139, 140, 143, 145, 148, 150, 158, 160, 161, 163, 164, 165, 166, 167, 168, 264, 265, 283, 292, 306
anti-Patriot, 223
Atecouando, Jerome, 284
Atlantic, 16, 17, 91, 129, 147, 166, 172, 173, 308
Attakullakulla, 159, 161, 284, 295

386

Avery, Elias, 108, 113, 114, 117, 284

B

Baker, Robert, 57, 59, 61
Bald Mountain, 72
Ballard, Samuel, 114
Barnes, Daniel, 13, 27, 28, 109, 127, 215, 284, 324, 343
BarringtonWilliam, 196, 284
Bartlett, Josiah, 222, 228, 229
Battle of Bennington, 203, 215, 298, 315
Battle of Bunker Hill, 214, 284, 296
Battle of Carillon, 78
Battle of Jumonville Glen, 4, 36, 288, 298, 304, 305, 311
Battle of Long Island, *232*, 255
Battle of Oswego, 52, 311
Battle of Princeton, 315
Battle of Trenton, 5, 255, 260, 291, 296, 314
Battle of White Plains, 5, 249, 255, 314
Battle on Snowshoes, 4, 70, 285, 286, 291, 292, 295, 298, 300, 312
Battles of Lexington and Concord, 203, 204, 314
Belestre, Francois-Marie Picote de, 147, 285
Blanchard, Joseph, 45, 52, 285
Boston, 45, 55, 65, 74, 80, 81, 82, 88, 91, 135, 142, 150, 155, 169, 194, 197, 203, 205, 209, 212, 214, 216, 218, 220, 233, 235, 238, 289, 307, 314
Bouquet, Henry, 151, 155, 156, 166, 285, 294
Bourlamaque, Francois Charles de., 85, 102, 104, 112, 119, 285
Braddock, Edward, 4, *46*, 47, *48*, 49, 50, 51, 64, 88, 93, 112, 144, 145, 151, 155, 156, 259, 285, 289, 298, 311
Bradley, Benjamin,113, 114, 115, 117, 126, 127
Bradstreet, John, 285
Brewer, David, 94, 300
Brewer, Moses, 285
Brigham, Jonathan, 215
British, 4, 9, 10, 12, 15, 16, 17, 20, 23, 34, 35, 37, 38, 41, 42, 46, 48, 49, 51, 52, 54, 55, 64, 66, 68, 69, 73, 75, 76, 77, 80, 81, 82, 84, 85, 89, 93, 95, 96, 98, 99, 100, 101, 102, 123, 125, 128, 129, 130, 131, 132, 133, 134, 135, 136, 137, 138, 139, 142, 143, 144, 145, 146, 147, 148, 152, 154, 155, 156, 157, 159, 160, 161, 163, 164, 165, 166, 172, 173, 178, 180, 181, 189, 190, 195, 197, 202, 203, 204, 205, 206, 208, 209, 214,

215, 216, 217, 219, 220, 223, 224, 226, 229, 230, 231, 233, 234, 235, 236, 237, 238, 240, 242, 243, 244, 245, 246, 250, 251, 252, 253, 254, 255, 256, 257, 261, 262, 264, 265, 266, 270, 283, 284, 285, 286, 287, 288, 289, 290, 291, 292, 293, 294, 295, 297, 298, 300, 301, 303, 304, 305, 306, 307, 308, 312, 314, 315

British Colonies, *15*, 283
Brooklyn, 233, 234, 236, 238, 241
Brooklyn Heights, 234, 235, 236, 238
Brown, Thomas, 23, 24, 55, 62, 208, 285
Browne, Arthur, 149, 150, 286, 296, 312
Browne, Elizabeth, Rogers, Elizabeth Browne
Bulkeley, Charles, 286
Bull, William, 159, 160, 284
Bunker (Breed's) Hill, *216*, 238, 314
Burbank, Jonathan, 286
Burgoyne, John, 286, 376
Butterfield, Captain, 101, 286
Byrd, William, 286

C

Cabatnatuan POW Camp, 303
Cadwalader, John, 255
Cambodia, 274
Campbell, George, 101, 113, 115, 116, 118, 123, 126
Campbell, John, 182, 286, 293
Canada, 11, 16, 20, 27, 66, 67, 74, 95, 132, 134, 135, 143, 146, 148, 183, 198, 219, 227, 265, 298, 305, 311
Canadian militia, 143, 157
candelabra, 96
candlesticks, 27, 109, 127
Cargill, 113, 116, 120
Carillon, 4, 12, 52, 54, 64, 70, 75, 76, 77, 80, 85, 214, 283, 285, 289, 291, 293, 294, 303, 306, 312
Carleton, Guy, *193*, 194, 212, 217, 219, 287
Carver, Jonathan, 4, 66, *177*, 178, 182, 183, 184, *185*, 186, 187, 188, 190, 195, 199, 287, 300, 313
Catholic, 26, 28
Celoron, Pierre-Joseph, 4, 34, 35, 287
Chambly, 103, 140, 293
Chandler, Jane, 115, 287

Charleston, 159, 160, 161
Cherokee, 4, 128, 148, 150, 151, 153, 155, 158, 159, 160, 161, 284, 286, 292, 293, 294, 295, 312
Cherokee War, 4, 150, 151, 161, 286, 312
Chief Gill, 112, 116, 118, 119, 290, 297
Chief Hendrick, 51, 52, 291, 299
Chippewa, 184, 189
Chippewa River, 184
Church, Benjamin, 270, 283, 287
Civil War, 3, 270, 294
Claus, Daniel, 189
Clinton, Henry, 219, 220, 238, 250, 288
Columbia Heights, 234
Committee of Public Safety, 206, 208
Concord, 28, 124, 214, 300
Congress, 1, 19, 33, 36, 46, 48, 53, 63, 75, 79, 84, 90, 99, 126, 133, 169, 175, 177, 193, 201, 203, 211, 213, 216, 221, 225, 226, 227, 228, 229, 246, 259, 261, 290, 307, 314
Connecticut, 104, 109, 114, 115, 116, 117, 118, 120, 121, 124, 223, 239, 247, 254, 266, 305, 306
Connecticut River, 104, 109, 114, 115, 116, 117, 118, 120, 121, 124, 305, 306
Continental Army, 203, 208, 215, 222, 229, 230, 235, 259, 314
Continental Congress, 134, 203, 205, 206, 299
Continental Divide, 187
Continental Navy, 233
Continental soldier, 239
Contrecour, Claude-Pierre de., 37, 288
counterfeit, 4, *43*, 44, 45
counterfeiting, 11, 44, 223, 226, 290, 299, 311
court-martial, 121, 180, 193, 195, 197, 224, 283, 291, 296, 299, 313
Crown Point, 34, 47, 49, 51, 52, 54, 56, 61, 91, 93, 97, 98, 99, 100, 102, 103, 104, 105, 108, 109, 113, 118, 119, 120, 122, 123, 125, 136, 137, 138, 141, 142, 143, 145, 293, 301, 304, 306
Crown-Point, 67, 80, 101, 129, 137
Cunningham, William, 246
Custis, Martha Dandridge, 201, 202, 288

D

Dak To, 3, 271, 273, 274

Dalyell, James, 164, 165, 288
Darby, William O., 270, 288
Dartmouth College, 211, 301
debtors' prison, 198, 199, 202, 211, 266, 267, 304, 308, 314
Declaration of Independence, 228, 245
Delaware, 20, 166, 239, 249, 258, 259
Delaware River, 255, 259
Demere, Paul, 160
Detroit, 4, 34, 145, 146, 147, 148, 151, 163, 164, 169, 181, 184, 285, 288, 295, 304
Diamond Island, 100
Dieskau, Marechal-de-Camp Jean-Armand, Baron de., 51, 52, 288
Dinwiddie, Robert, 35, 37, 38, 41, 144, 154, 288, 299
Dobbs, Arthur, 288
Duchess of Gordon, 219, 225
Duke Jacob, 115
Dumas, Jean Daniel, 112, 116, 117, 156, 289
Dunbar, James William, 101, 113, 116, 117, 124

E

East River, 234, 235, 236, 237, 238, 239, 244
Eastman, Amos, 29, 30
Eggleston, John Connor, 7, 15, 97, 111, 232
Eggleston, Margaret Rogers, 7
Eggleston, Michael A., 1, 2, 3, 7, 13, 282, 379, **403**
England, 21, 28, 46, 55, 139, 163, 181, 182, 183, 197, 198, 203, 207, 229, 233, 254, 261, 289, 290, 303, 307
English, 16, 17, 34, 35, 60, 66, 67, 80, 84, 85, 86, 92, 107, 109, 119, 122, 129, 141, 148, 154, 160, 166, 187, 192, 207, 239, 243, 252, 253, 261
Europe, 17, 133, 138, 162, 173, 176, 311
Evans, John, 113, 117, 124, 127, 289
Ewing, James, 255

F

Farrington, Jacob, 113, 118, 127, 140, 141
Forbes Expedition, 144
Forbes, John, 144, 151, 152, 155, 156, 157, 158, 159, 289
Fort Anne, 4, 82, 296, 304, 312
Fort Benning, 271, 304
Fort Brewerton, 136, 304

Fort Cumberland, 49, 50, 304
Fort Detroit, 163, 165, 188, 192, 288, 290, 304, 312
Fort Duquesne, 37, 47, 51, 144, 151, 156, 157, 158, 289, 294, 304, 306
Fort Edward, 51, 54, 55, 64, 65, 68, 69, 70, 78, 82, 304
Fort George, 94, 305
Fort Loudoun, 160, 305
Fort Michilimackinac, 174, *176*, 178, 179, 182, 184, 187, 188, 189, 190, 192, 194, 197, 198, 305
Fort Necessity, 155, 305
Fort Niagara, 305
Fort Ontario, 165, 305
Fort Oswego, 47, 52, 306
Fort Pitt, 145, 147, 151, 306
Fort Prince George, 159, 161, 306
Fort Prince William, 159
Fort St. Frederic, 47, 306
Fort Toulouse, 158, 306
Fort Wentworth, 117, 306
Fort William Henry, 4, 52, 54, 56, 60, 61, 64, 65, 66, 69, 80, 85, 88, 94, 178, 294, 300, 306, 311
France, 16, 17, 20, 23, 29, 34, 42, 45, 46, 66, 112, 122, 125, 138, 142, 143, 158, 161, 180, 181, 195, 204, 264, 287, 291, 294, 306, 311
Franklin, Benjamin, 134, 176, 199, 208, 289
Freemason, 9, 12, 52, 226, 289
Freemasonry, 307
French, 9, 12, 16, 17, 18, 20, 21, 23, 26, 28, 32, 34, 35, 37, 38, 39, 40, 41, 42, 43, 46, 49, 50, 51, 52, 54, 55, 56, 57, 58, 61, 62, 64, 65, 66, 70, 71, 72, 74, 75, 76, 78, 80, 81, 82, 84, 85, 86, 88, 89, 91, 93, 95, 96, 98, 99, 100, 102, 103, 104, 105, 106, 109, 110, 112, 113, 118, 122, 123, 125, 128, 130, 132, 133, 135, 137, 138, 139, 140, 141, 142, 143, 144, 145, 146, 148, 154, 156, 157, 158, 159, 162, 163, 164, 165, 178, 180, 181, 183, 184, 186, 187, 189, 190, 191, 192, 194, 195, 202, 203, 212, 214, 216, 217, 226, 233, 249, 264, 282, 283, 284, 285, 288, 289, 290, 291, 292, 293, 294, 295, 297, 298, 300, 301, 303, 304, 305, 306, 307, 308, 309, 311, 312
French and Indian War, 9, 12, 17, 20, 21, 23, 32, 78, 162, 164, 202, 203, 226, 249, 270, 284, 285, 291, 292, 293, 295, 297, 303, 305, 306, 308, 311, 312
French Canadians, 128
French, Christopher, 262

G

Gage, Thomas, 11, 49, 116, 135, 151, 162, 165, 168, ***169***, 178, 179, 180, 181, 182, 190, 192, 194, 196, 197, 205, 206, 209, 214, 289, 291, 292, 313

George III, 172, 174, ***175***, 183, 230, 289

Georgia, 16, 159, 271, 295, 304, 306

Germain, George, 214, 229

Gill, Joseph-Louis "Chief", 112, 127, 289, 290, 297

Gilman, Carty, 44, 45, 290

Gladwin, Henry, 180, 290

Gorham, John, 270, 290

Gould, Charles, 197

Governor's Island, 244

Grand Portage, 186, 187

Grant, James, 160, 161

Great Britain, 16, 17, 23, 29, 42, 44, 47, 64, 132, 133, 136, 138, 158, 161, 162, 163, 172, 173, 175, 181, 186, 187, 188, 189, 192, 197, 199, 203, 204, 206, 209, 210, 226, 228, 230, 233, 262, 266, 283, 284, 289, 293, 295, 305, 306, 307, 311, 315

Great Lakes, 16, 46, 145, 172, 178, 306

Great Meadows, 38, 39

Green Bay, 183, 191

Greene, Nathaniel, 223, 255, 259, 260

Griffith Bay, 140

Gulf of Mexico, 147

H

Hale, Nathan, 245, 246, 247, ***248***, 290, 314

Halifax, 66, 80, 150, 197, 225, 233

Hancock, John, 223

Haslet, John, 249

Haviland, William, 69, 70, 73, 135, 143, 291

Hazen, Moses, 136, 290

Hendrick, Chief, 51, 299

Henry, Patrick, 135

Hessians, 238, 251, 255, 256, 258, 259, 260, 261, 291, 307

Hewes, Joseph, 225, 227

Hickey, Thomas, 223, 224

Hill 875, 274

Ho Chi Minh, 274
Hoit, Stephen, 113, 114, 126, 291
Holland Pond, 115
Holmes, Robert, 140, 142
Honeyman, John, 256, 257, 291
Hopkins, Joseph, 100, 180, 181, 191, 194, 195, 196, 291
House of Burgesses, 202, 259
Howard, William, 188
Howe, George Augustus, *75*, 76, 80, 214, 291
Howe, Richard, 233
Howe, William, *213*, 214, 220, 224, 229, 233, 235, 236, 238, 246, 249, 250, 261, 262, 289, 291, 314
Hudson Bay, 147
Hudson River, 51, 54, *68*, 233, 234, 305, 307, 308
Huron, 20, 176, 305, 307

I

Illinois, 16, 157, 164, 183, 190
Indian, 9, 12, 16, 17, 18, 20, 21, 23, 28, 29, 30, 32, 34, 35, 38, 41, 43, 47, 51, 55, 56, 57, 59, 61, 62, 64, 65, 66, 67, 78, 82, 83, 85, 86, 87, 88, 89, 91, 92, 93, 95, 96, 100, 103, 106, 108, 109, 115, 118, 124, 128, 129, 130, 132, 142, 143, 145, 146, 151, 154, 155, 157, 162, 163, 164, 165, 169, 178, 183, 185, 186, 188, 190, 198, 202, 203, 204, 207, 208, 212, 217, 226, 243, 249, 270, 284, 285, 290, 291, 292, 293, 294, 295, 296, 297, 298, 303, 304, 305, 306, 307, 308, 311, 312
Innes, Alexander, 262
Intolerable Acts, 197, 202, 307
Ireland, 20, 28, 208
Iroquois, 20, 35, 84
Isle aux Noix, 100, 119
Isle La Mote, 141

J

Jameson, James, 141, 142
Jamica, 159
Jefferson, Thomas, 10, 226
Jenkins Party, 113, 118, 119, 124
Jesuit, 95, 204, 297

Johnson, Noah, 93, 136, 142
Johnson, Samuel, 227
Johnson, William, *19*, 20, 35, 47, 51, 52, 65, 66, 98, 165, 178, 179, 180, 181, 182, 188, 189, 190, 191, 192, 195, 196, 198, 288, 291, 292, 299, 306
Jumonville, Joseph Coulon DeVillers de, 38, 40, 41, 292,

K

K9 Program, 275, 277
Kennedy, Quinton, 89, 90, 91, 92, 93, 128, 287, 290, 292
Kennedy, Samuel, 55, 59
Ketchum, Isaac, 223
King George's War, 17, 23, 270, 290, 311
King Philip's War, 270
King William's War, 17
King's Bay, 140
Kirkwood, Robert, 110, 124, 125

L

Lake Champlain, 47, 54, 56, 61, 91, 98, 99, 100, 102, 118, 119, 135, 137, 139, 140, 303, 304, 306
Lake Chaplain, 123
Lake Erie, 34, 37, 47, 145, 146
Lake George, 4, 51, 52, 54, 55, 64, 70, 76, 93, 178, 288, 291, 292, 299, 301, 307, 311
Lake Itasca, 183
Lake Memphremagog, 112, 113, 115, 116
Lake Michigan, 176, 183, 305
Lake of the Woods, 186
Lake Onieda, 136
Lake Ontario, 34, 305
Lake Superior, 184, 186, 187, 191
Lamoille River, 119
Langdon, John, 222, 227
Langis, Jean-Baptist Levault de."Langy," 71, 119, 137, 138, 292
Langlade, Charles-Michel Moute de., 292
Langy, see Langis
Laos, 274
Levis, Francois-Gaston, Duc de, 103, 132, 140, 142, 292
Lewis and Clark, 187

Light Infantry, 91, 116, 140, 141
Lignery, Francois-Marie le Marchand de., 157, 292
Loescher, Burt Garfield, 114
London, 10, 17, 41, 131, 134, 164, 169, 170, 176, 178, 179, 180, 182, 187, 193, 197, 198, 199, 202, 204, 205, 206, 207, 208, 211, 214, 246, 264, 266, 281, 282, 294, 308, 313, 314, 315, 316
Long Island, 4, 223, 229, 234, 235, 236, 237, 238, 239, 240, 245, 247, 249, 283, 298, 314
Long Range Reconnaissance Patrols, 271, see also LLRP
Longueuil, Charles Le Moyne de., 293
Lord Stirling, 220, *221,* 283, 291, 249, 299
Lord Cornwallis, 261
Lord Dartmouth, 204, 214, 230
Loudoun, Lord, 25, 64 66, 160, 286, 289, 293, 317
Louis the XV, 125, *126*
Louisbourg, 64, 66, 80, 81, 89, 139, 283, 291
Louisiana, 162, 300
Lounsberry, William, 239
Loyalist, 223, 231, 233, 264, 281, 307, 309
LRRP, 271, 273, 274, 275, 307
Lusignan, Paul-Louis Dazemard de., 54, 293
Lyttelton, William, 158, 159, 293

M

Mackenzie, Frederick, 246, 247
Madonna, 27, 126
Manhattan, 224, 233, 235, 237, 249, 251
Mante, Thomas, 123, 371
Marie-Jeanne (Gill), 118, 290
Marin, Joseph, 82, 85, 293
Marines, 112
Marion, Francis, 161, 162, 293
Martin, Joseph Plumb, 167, 239, 245, 251, 255, 293, 378
Maryland, 21, 47, 181, 228, 239, 242, 304
Mason, George, 202
Massachusetts, 10, 18, 28, 45, 49, 88, 95, 177, 203, 205, 284, 298
Matthews, David, 223
McGuire rig ropes, 275
McMullen, Andrew, 104, 105
Merrill, Frank, 271, 276, 293

Merrill's Marauders, 271, 293
Methuen, 28
Michilimackinac, 146, 148, 176, 179, 182, 183, 184, 186, 187, 188, 189, 190, 192, 195, 198, 296, 313
militia, 28, 43, 64, 87, 101, 159, 177, 178, 234, 235, 255, 257, 261, 270, 305
Millan, John, 294
Minneapolis, 183
Missisquoi Bay, 92, 98, 102, 105, 112, 118, 119, 122, 140, 142
Mississippi River, 16, 147, 158, 172, 183, 184, 186, 187, 191
Mohawk, 20, 43, 51, 52, 98, 100, 101, 142, 179, 291, 299
Mohigan, 66, 294, 307
Monckton, Robert, 93, 145, 146, 147, 294
moneymaker, 43
Monongahela, 37, 39, 49, 112, 289, 293, 304, 306, 311
Monro, George, 64, 86, 294
Monroe, James, 65, 261
Montcalm, Louis-Joseph de, Marquis de., 52, *53*, 64, 65, 74, 75, 77, 86, 87, 98, 103, 178, 285, 292, 294
Montgomery, Archibald, 101, 294
Montreal, 4, 34, 51, 61, 62, 92, 95, 98, 103, 122, 128, 131, 135, 138, 139, 143, 145, 146, 190, 192, 193, 195, 197, 212, 217, 264, 292, 300, 312, 313
Moose River, 117, 118
Moran, Irvin "Bugs", 7, 271, *272*, 275
Mosby, John, 270, 294, 295
Mount Vernon, 202, 279
Multi-Purpose Canine, 275, 307
Murray, James, *131*, 132, 135, 139, 140, 143, 295

N

Napier, Surgeon-General, 141, 142
Native American, 11, 18, 43, 167, 211, 309
New France, 15, 16, 17, 28, 29, 34, 35, 54, 95, 132, 146, 162, 291, 292, 300
New Hampshire, 11, 17, 28, 43, 44, 45, 66, 88, 94, 95, 150, 161, 208, 222, 227, 228, 229, 264, 285, 286, 296, 299, 301, 305, 306
New Orleans, 16, 158, 191
New World, 4, 16, 20, 23, 28, 47, 132, 138, 139, 147, 148, 162, 181, 283, 298

New York, 12, 17, 18, 20, 41, 52, 67, 87, 95, 101, 135, 137, 148, 157, 165, 169, 173, 176, 196, 208, 209, 210, 211, 219, 220, 223, 224, 225, 226, 227, 228, 229, 233, 235, 236, 237, 238, 239, 244, 245, 246, 249, 253, 255, 261, 265, 266, 283, 290, 294, 300, 303, 304, 305, 306, 308, 313, 314, 315
New York City, 169, 173, 208, 211, 219, 220, 223, 225, 226, 229, 233, 234, 235, 237, 238, 239, 246, 247, 249, 266, 308, 313, 314, 315
Niagara, 47, 67, 137, 164, 305
North America, 9, 17, 80, 123, 135, 138, 145, 155, 161, 163, 172, 173, 174, 179, 187, 217, 219, 237, 283, 285, 286, 287, 288, 289, 294, 303, 304, 312, 314
North Vietnamese, 271, 273, 308
Northwest Passage, 170, 172, 173, 174, 176, 177, 178, 182, 183, 187, 188, 195, 199, 205, 206, 209, 214, 220, 228, 287, 288, 299, 300, 301, 308, 313
Nulhegan River, 117
Number Four, 104, 107, 110, 116, 121, 122, 123, 136, 305
Nut Island, 143
NVA, 273, 274, 308

O

Oconostota, 295
Odanak, 95, 127
Ogden, Amos, 107, 109, 295
Ohio, 20, 34, 35, 36, 37, 46, 144, 151, 157, 158, 164, 165, 202, 285, 287, 288, 299, 306, 311
Ohio Valley, 20, 46, 144, 165, 287, 311
Ojibwas, 20
Onondaga, 20
Oregon, 187
Ottawa, 20, 145, 147, 184, 295, 312
Otter River, 100

P

Pacific, 172, 173, 178, 184, 186, 270, 308
Paris, 17, 161
Parliament, 23, 172, 173, 203, 205, 211, 301, 307, 308
Patriot, 1, 10, 203, 205, 207, 208, 214, 218, 220, 222, 229, 245, 256, 261, 266, 280, 298, 308
Pennsylvania, 21, 37, 157, 158, 206, 220, 239, 255, 261, 265, 304, 306,

307, 311
Pherrins River, 117
Philadelphia, 49, 145, 148, 158, 205, 207, 208, 209, 210, 211, 222, 225, 226, 227, 228, 229, 230, 266
Phillips, William, 70, 72, 113, 119, 295
Pitt, William, *133*, 134, 139, 145, 158, 166, 285, 295, 304
Pittsburgh, 17, 37, 145, 304, 306, 311
Pointeau Fer, 140
Ponteach, 146, 164, 165, 166, 295
Pontiac, 4, *146*, 162, 163, 164, 165, 166, 285, 288, 290, 295, 296, 306, 312, 313
Portsmouth, 150, 161, 169, 206, 208, 212, 222, 286, 296, 301
Potawatomi, 20
Potter, Nathaniel, 191, 192, 194, 195, 196, 295
Prairie du Chien, 186
Presque Isle, 146, 157
prisoners, 30, 54, 55, 56, 58, 59, 60, 61, 62, 66, 67, 69, 72, 88, 91, 96, 108, 109, 110, 112, 113, 117, 118, 123, 124, 129, 138, 156, 206, 235, 271, 303, 318
Puckett, Ralph, 271, 296
Puritan, 28
Putnam, Israel, 71, 82, 83, *84*, 162, 205, 223, 239, 245, 296

Q

Quebec, 64, 66, 80, 89, 91, 92, 95, 98, 99, 102, 103, 127, 128, 131, 132, 135, 136, 138, 139, 140, 142, 143, 190, 204, 214, 265, 287, 291, 292, 294, 295, 301, 312
Queen Anne's War, 17, 270
Queen Marie Leszcynska, 126
Queen's American Rangers, 230, 238, 249, 261, 262, 297, 314

R

Rall, Johann, *250*, 251, 256, 260, 296
ranger:
  Rogers' Rangers, 11, 12, 25, 27, 28, 52, 54, 68, 69, 82, 91, 93, 94, 98, 100, 101, 102, 103, 104, 105, 106, 107, 108, 109, 110, 113, 114, 116, 117, 118, 119, 120, 123, 136, 137, 138, 139, 140, 142, 143, 145, 146, 147, 148, 150, 161, 164, 207, 214, 323
  Queen's American Rangers, 229, 249, 262, 264, 270, 271, 275, 289, 290, 298, 315, 317

Rhode Island, 134, 229
Roberts, Benjamin, 189, 190, 191, 192, 195, 296
Roche, John, 264, 297
Rogers, Arthur, 197, 212, 222, 296
Rogers, Elizabeth "Betsy" Browne, *149*, 150, 169, 178, 182, 194, 196, 205, 212, 222, 264, 281, 282, Elizabeth (Browne Rogers), 23, 149, 176, 194, 286, 296, 312, 315, 404
Rogers, James, Jr., 211, 264, 265, 297
Rogers, James, Sr., 28, 297
Rogers, Richard, 297
Rogers, Robert:
  French and Indian War, 1, 4, 5, 7, 9, 10, 11, 12, 13, 21, 25, 27, 28, 29, 31, 32, *33*, 43, 44, 45, 46, 47, 51, 52, 54, 55, 56, 57, 66, 67, 68, 69, 70, 71, 72, 73, 74, 76, 80, 82, 83, 91, 92, 93, 94, 98, 99, 100, 101, 102, 103, 104, 105, 106, 107, 108, 109, 110, 112, 113, 114, 115, 116, 117, 118
  War of Independence and after, 120, 121, 122, 123, 124, 125, 127, 128, 129, 132, 136, 137, 138, 139, 140, 141, 142, 145, 146, 147, 148, 150, 151, 152, 155, 158, 160, 161, 162, 163, 164, 165, 168, 169, 170, 172, 174, 176, 177, 178, 179, 180, 181, 182, 183, 184, 186, 187, 188, 189, 190, 191, 192, 193, 194, 195, 196, 197, 198, 199, 202, 203, 204, 205, 206, 207, 208, 209, 210, 211, 212, 214, 216, 217, 218, 219, 220, 221, 222, 225, 226, 227, 228, 229, 230, 231, 238, 239, 240, 245, 246, 249, 250, 262, 264, 265, 266, 267, 270, 271, 281, 282, 283, 284, 285, 286, 287, 288, 289, 290, 291, 292, 293, 294, 295, 296, 297, 298, 299, 300, 301, 306, 308, 311, 312, 313, 314, 315, 316, 317, 322
Rogers' Island, 4, 68, 69, 286, 308, 311
Roubaud, Father Pierre-Joseph-Antoine, 26, 27, 85, 86, 103, 112, 122, 123, 126, 128, 129, 204, 297
Royal Navy, 233, 236
Ruby Ring, 126
Rules of the King's Bench, 282, 308

S

Sabbatis, 297
Sachem, 308
Saint Francis, 4, 11, 13, 26, 27, 29, 30, 85, 89, 91, 92, 93, 94, 95, **97**, 98, 99, 102, 104, 105, 106, 107, 108, 109, 112, 113, 114, 117, 118, 119, 120, 122, 123, 124, 125, 127, 128, 130, 132, 137, 145, 204, 211, 283, 284, 285, 286, 287, 289, 290, 291, 292, 295, 297, 299, 300, 301, 306, 312

Saint Francis River, 95, 105
Saint Francis Village, 102, 105, 290
Saint Lawrence, 64, 80, 92, 95, 112, 113, 136, 138, 143, 145
Saint Mary-Newington, *281*
Samadagwis, 106, 109, 110, 297
Schuler, Philip, 219
Scotland, 28
Seven Years' War, 23, 73, 133, 143, 148, 162, 283, 289, 143, 172, 284, 289, 311, 312
Shawnees, 20
Shepherd, John, 249, 297
Shirley, William, 49, 50, *153*, 155, 209, 298
Silverheels, 38, 298
Simcoe, John Graves, 262, *263*, 298
Six Nations, 20
South Carolina, 41, 148, 150, 158, 159, 160, 161, 284, 293, 294
Spain, 16, 162, 264
Spanish, 17, 23, 186
Spiesmaker, Frederick, 192, 194, 195
Spikeman, Thomas, 55, 57, 58, 59, 298
spy, 190, 204, 217, 230, 245, 247, 256, 290, 291
St. Anthony, 183, 186
St. Francis, 92, 108, 127
St. Francois, 67, 88, 123, 129
St. John's, 140, 212, 217
St. Joseph river, 183
St. Peter, 143
St. Pierre, 185, 186
Stamp Act, 172, 181, 197, 202, 308
Stark, Caleb, 10, 216, 217, 298
Stark, John, 10, 29, 30, *31*, 54, 73, 94, 139, 162, 203, 214, 215, 216, 217, 298, 315, 331, 336
Stark, William, 264, 299
Staten Island, 223, 229, 234, 235, 238, 314
Stevens, Samuel, 104, 116, 121, 299
Stevenstown, 115
Stockbridge, 91, 94, 100, 102, 103, 109, 115, 118, 290
Straits of Mackinac, 176, 305
Sullivan, John, *218*, 219, 255, 259, 260, 299
Sullivan, Owen, 43, 44, 299

T

The 100 Toes Expedition, 136, 312
The French and Indian War, 17, 23, 32
Ticonderoga, 12, 54, 55, 56, 59, 61, 71, 80, 83, 85, 136, 137, 138, 285, 303, 306, 312
Tory, 220, 223, 224, 245, 256, 257, 266, 397, 309
Townsend Acts, 202
Townshend, Charles, 170, *171*, 172, 176, 182, 187, 197, 299, 313
traitor, 203
treason, 188, 191, 194, 205, 295, 296, 313, 314
Treaty of Hubertusburg, 161
Treaty of Paris, 312
Trent, William, 37, 300, 306
Trenton, 255, 256, 258, 259, 260, 261
Trois-Rivieres, 112
Troupes de la Marine, 288, 292, 309
Tryon, William, *210*, 211, 214, 219, 221, 223, 224, 225, 226, 227, 230, 299
Turner, George, 108, 113, 116, 117, 300
Tute, James, 178, 182, 183, 184, 186, 195, 300

U

United States, 3, 16, 202, 237, 261, 287, 289, 299, 309
Upper Ammonoosuc River, 117, 306

V

Vaudreuil, Francois-Pierre de Rigaud, de., 62, *63*, 103, 143, 147, 300
Venango, 157
Vermont, 12, 18, 27, 95, 115, 116, 120, 127, 211, 284, 290, 306
Virginia, 13, 17, 21, 34, 35, 37, 38, 41, 134, 135, 144, 151, 153, 154, 155, 158, 160, 202, 203, 204, 207, 230, 282, 286, 288, 294, 299, 305, 314

W

Waite, Joseph, 113, 120, 136, 300
Walker, Timothy, 281, 282, 300
War of Independence, 4, 9, 12, 13, 21, 31, 49, 84, 143, 156, 161, 168, 172, 201, 202, 203, 239, 270, 283, 284, 286, 287, 290, 291, 293, 296, 297, 298, 299, 300
War of Spanish Succession, 17

War of the Austrian Succession, 17, 20, 283
War of the League of Augsburg, 17
War on Terror, 275, 309
Washington, George:
  French and Indian War, 1, 9, 10, 11, 12, 17, 21, 35, 36, 37, 38, 40, 41, 42, 43, 47, 48, 49, 50, 51, 134, 143, 144, 148, 151, 152, 154, 155, 156, 157, 158, 162, 168, 176,
  War of Independence and after, 201, 202, 203, 204, 205, 207, 209, 211, 212, 214, 217, 218, 219, 220, 223, 224, 225, 226, 227, 229, 230, 233, 234, 235, 236, 237, 238, 239, 245, 247, 249, 250, 251, 255, 256, 257, *258*, *259*, 260, 261, 262, 266, *279*, 280, 283, 288, 290, 291, 292, 294, 296, 298, 300, 304, 305, 308, 312, 314, 315
Washington, Martha, *201*, 202, 280, 288
Webb, Daniel, 64, 65, 66, 301
Wentworth, Benning, 301
West Indies, 229
West Point, 341
West Virginia, 202
Wheelock, Eleazar, 211, 212, 217, 218, 219, 300
Whipple, William, 222, 227, 228
White Devil, 130
White Plains, 242, 249, 250, 251, 252, 254, 255
Whitworth, Richard, 206, 209, 301
Wigwam Martinique, 140, 142
Williams, Ephrain, 51, 301
Williams, Samuel, 100, 101, 108, 301
Williamsburg, 35, 37, 38, 204, 314
Wolfe, James, 68, 89, *90*, 91, 92, 98, *99*, 139, 287, 291, 292, 294, 295, 301
World War II, 270, 271, 275, 288, 293, 303

X

Xavier (Gill), 119

Michael A. Eggleston is an author who has published books and articles about America's wars including several about the war in Vietnam where he served two tours of duty in the 1960s and seventies. He was born and raised in Minnesota and is a 1961 graduate of the U. S. Military Academy (USMA) at West Point. Eggleston has thirty year's service in the U.S. Army and twenty years' experience in industry retiring as a Senior Director. He is a member of the Sons of the American Revolution, the Association of Graduates, USMA, and the Minnesota Historical Society. Mr. Eggleston and his wife of 45 years, the former Margaret Rogers reside in Nokesville, Virginia. The Egglestons have four children and seven grandchildren who also reside in Virginia. The Egglestons enjoy running, volunteer work, history and are dedicated fans of DC United and the Washington Redskins.

Eggleston can be contacted at maeggleston@comcast.net (June 2017).

Made in the USA
Columbia, SC
02 February 2022